TOEFL MAP®

MAP

New TOEFL® Edition

Reading

Basic

DARAKWON

TOEFL® MAP
New TOEFL® Edition

Reading Basic

Publisher Chung Kyudo
Editors Cho Sangik, Zong Ziin
Authors Michael A. Putlack, Stephen Poirier, Allen C. Jacobs, Maximilian Tolochko
Proofreader Talib Din
Designers Park Narae, Lee Seunghyun

First published in June 2022
By Darakwon, Inc.
Darakwon Bldg., 211, Munbal-ro, Paju-si, Gyeonggi-do 10881
Republic of Korea
Tel: 82-2-736-2031 (Ext. 250)
Fax: 82-2-732-2037

ISBN 978-89-277-8026-7 14740
     978-89-277-8025-0 14740 (set)

www.darakwon.co.kr

Photo Credits
Shutterstock.com

Components Main Book / Answers and Explanations
10 9 8 7 6 5 4   24 25 26 27 28

Introduction

Studying for the TOEFL® iBT is no easy task and is not one that is to be undertaken lightly. It requires a great deal of effort as well as dedication on the part of the student. It is our hope that, by using *TOEFL® Map Reading Basic* as either a textbook or a study guide, the task of studying for the TOEFL® iBT will become somewhat easier for the student and less of a burden.

Students who wish to excel on the TOEFL® iBT must attain a solid grasp of the four important skills in the English language: reading, listening, speaking, and writing. The Darakwon *TOEFL® Map* series covers all four of these skills in separate books. There are also three different levels in all four topics. This book, *TOEFL® Map Reading Basic*, covers the reading aspect of the test at the basic level. Students who want to read passages, learn vocabulary terms, and study topics that appear on the TOEFL® iBT will have their wishes granted by using this book.

TOEFL® Map Reading Basic has been designed for use both in a classroom setting and as a study guide for individual learners. For this reason, it offers a comprehensive overview of the TOEFL® iBT Reading section. In Part A, the different types of questions that are found on the TOEFL® iBT Reading section are explained, and hints on how to answer these questions properly are also provided. There are also several practice exercises for each type of question. In Part B, learners have the opportunity to build their background knowledge of the topics that appear on the TOEFL® iBT by studying the reading passages of varying lengths that are found in each chapter. Each passage is followed by the types of questions that appear on the TOEFL® iBT, and each chapter also has a vocabulary section, which enables learners to test their knowledge of vocabulary that is specific to the particular topic covered in each chapter. Finally, in Part C, students can take several TOEFL® iBT practice tests. These are long passages that have the same numbers and types of questions that appear on actual TOEFL® iBT Reading section passages. Combined, all of these should be able to help learners prepare themselves to take and, more importantly, to excel on the TOEFL® iBT.

TOEFL® Map Reading Basic has a great amount of information and should prove to be invaluable as a study guide for learners who are preparing for the TOEFL® iBT. However, while this book is comprehensive, it is up to each person to do the actual work. In order for *TOEFL® Map Reading Basic* to be of any use, the individual learner must dedicate him or herself to studying the information found within its pages. While we have strived to make this book as user friendly and as full of crucial information as possible, ultimately, it is up to each person to make the best of the material in the book. We wish you luck in your study of both English and the TOEFL® iBT, and we hope that you are able to use *TOEFL® Map Reading Basic* to improve your abilities in both of them.

Michael A. Putlack
Stephen Poirier
Allen C. Jacobs
Maximilian Tolochko

TABLE OF CONTENTS

Part C | Experiencing the TOEFL iBT Actual Tests

How Is This Book Different?

When searching for the ideal book to use to study for the TOEFL® iBT, it is often difficult to differentiate between the numerous books available on a bookstore's shelves. However, *TOEFL® Map Reading Basic* differs from many other TOEFL® iBT books and study guides in several important ways.

Many TOEFL® iBT books arrange the material according to the types of questions on the test. This often results in learners reading one passage on astronomy, followed by a passage on history, followed by a passage on economics, and so on. Simply put, there is little cohesion except for the questions. However, *TOEFL® Map Reading Basic* is arranged by subject. This book has eight chapters, all of which cover subjects that appear on the TOEFL® iBT. For instance, there are chapters on history, life sciences, and physical sciences, among others. By arranging the chapters according to subjects, learners can read passages related to one another all throughout each chapter. This enables them to build upon their knowledge as they progress through each chapter. Additionally, since many vocabulary terms are used in certain subjects, learners can more easily recognize these specialized terms, understand how they are used, and retain the knowledge of what these terms mean. Finally, by arranging the chapters according to subjects, learners can cover and become familiar with every TOEFL® iBT question type in each chapter rather than just focus on a single type of question.

TOEFL® Map Reading Basic, unlike many other TOEFL® iBT books and study guides, does not have any translations into foreign languages within its pages. All too often, learners rely on translations in their native languages. They use these translations to help them get through the material. However, the actual TOEFL® iBT has no translations, so neither does this book. This will better prepare learners to take the test by encouraging them to learn difficult terms and expressions through context, just as native speakers of English do when they encounter unfamiliar terms and expressions. Additionally, learners will find that their fluency in English will improve more rapidly when they use *TOEFL® Map Reading Basic* without relying on any translations.

Finally, the passages in *TOEFL® Map Reading Basic* are based on topics that have appeared on the actual TOEFL® iBT in the past. Therefore, learners can see what kinds of topics appear on the TOEFL® iBT. This will enable them to recognize the difficulty level, the style of TOEFL® iBT passages, and the difficulty of the vocabulary on the test. Second, learners can enhance their knowledge of topics that have appeared on the TOEFL® iBT. By knowing more about these topics when they take the actual test, test takers will be sure to improve their scores. Third, learners will also gain knowledge of the specialized vocabulary in particular topics, which will help them understand passages on the actual test. Finally, many topics appear multiple times on the TOEFL® iBT. Thus, students who study some of these topics may be pleasantly surprised to find the same topic when they take the actual TOEFL® iBT. That will no doubt help them improve their test scores.

How to Use This Book

TOEFL® Map Reading Basic is designed for use either as a textbook in a classroom in a TOEFL® iBT preparation course or as a study guide for individuals who are studying for the TOEFL® iBT on their own. *TOEFL® Map Reading Basic* has been divided into three sections: Part A, Part B, and Part C. All three sections offer information which is important to learners preparing for the TOEFL® iBT. Part A is divided into 10 sections, each of which explains one of the question types that appears on the TOEFL® iBT Reading section. Part B is divided into 8 chapters, each of which covers one of the subjects that appears on the TOEFL® iBT. Part C has 2 complete practice tests that resemble those which appear on the TOEFL® iBT.

Part A Understanding Reading Question Types

This section is designed to acquaint learners with each question type on the TOEFL® iBT Reading section. Therefore there are 10 sections in this chapter—one for each question type. Each section is divided into 5 parts. The first part offers a short explanation of the question type. The second part shows the ways in which questions of that particular type often appear on the test. The third part provides helpful hints on how to answer these questions correctly. The fourth part has one or two short passages followed by a question and an answer explanation. The fifth part has either two or four shorter practice passages followed by a question.

Part B Building Background Knowledge of TOEFL Topics

The purpose of this section is to introduce the various subjects that most frequently appear on the TOEFL® iBT. There are 8 chapters in Part B. Each chapter covers one subject and contains 10 Reading passages of various lengths as well as short passages and vocabulary words and exercises. Each chapter is divided into several parts.

Introduction

This is a short description of the subject of the chapter. The purpose of this section is to let learners know what fields of study people focus on in this subject.

Mastering Question Types

This section contains 3 Reading passages that are between 130 and 160 words in length. Following each passage, there are 3 or 4 Reading questions. Each question is identified by type. All 10 question types are covered in this section. In addition, there are four true-false questions about the passage for learners to answer after the questions.

Mastering the Subject

This section contains 3 Reading passages that are between 250 and 300 words in length. Following each passage, there are 4 Reading questions. These questions may be from any of the 10 types of Reading questions. In addition, there are four sentences with blanks for learners to fill in the correct answers after the questions.

TOEFL Practice Test

This section contains 1 Reading passage that is between 400 and 500 words in length. Each passage has 10 Reading questions of any type. The purpose of this section is to acquaint learners with the types of passages and questions they will encounter when they take the TOEFL® iBT.

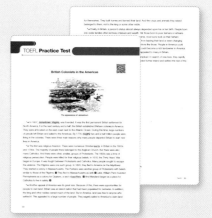

Star Performer Word Files and Vocabulary Review

This section contains around 40 vocabulary words that were used in the passages in each chapter. The words include nouns, verbs, adjectives, and adverbs. Definitions and sample sentences are provided for each word. There are also 12 questions that review the vocabulary words that learners cover in each chapter. The purpose of this section is to teach learners specific words that often appear in passages on certain subjects and to make sure that learners know the meanings of these words and how to use them properly.

Part C Experiencing the TOEFL Actual Tests

This section contains 6 long TOEFL® iBT Reading section passages and questions. The purpose of this section is to let learners experience long Reading passages and to see if they can apply the knowledge they have learned in the course of studying *TOEFL® Map Reading Basic*.

Part A

Understanding Reading Question Types

Vocabulary questions require the test taker to understand the meanings of words and phrases in the passage. A word or phrase in the text is highlighted. Then, the test taker must select the word or phrase with a similar meaning. Many times, highlighted words have several meanings. So the test taker must determine the correct meaning according to how the word is used in the passage. Recently, most passages have two Vocabulary questions.

Vocabulary questions often look like this:

▶ The word "X" in the passage is closest in meaning to

▶ In stating "X", the author means that

Tips for answering the questions:

■ Many words and phrases have multiple meanings. The most common meaning of a word is not always the correct answer.

■ Focus on how the word or phrase is used in the sentence.

■ All answer choices can be substituted for the highlighted word or phrase in the passage.

Examples of Vocabulary Questions

Amphibians are cold-blooded vertebrates. There are many kinds of amphibians. The most common are frogs, toads, and salamanders. Amphibians are similar to reptiles. But there are some differences between them.

Almost all amphibians are born in the water. At that time, they are water-breathing animals. They also lack limbs. During the first stage of their lives, they live entirely in the water. Then, they undergo a metamorphosis. They develop four legs. Their tail disappears. And they become able to breathe air. As adults, amphibians live on land most of the time. But they are capable of living in the water.

Q The word "metamorphosis" in the passage is closest in meaning to

ⓐ transmission

ⓑ change

ⓒ version

ⓓ style

⊘ Answer Explanation

Choice Ⓑ has the closest meaning to the highlighted word. A metamorphosis is a kind of change. In addition, the rest of the paragraph describes what kinds of changes amphibians experience. Choices Ⓐ, Ⓒ, and Ⓓ are all incorrect.

Edgar Allen Poe lived a relatively short life. He was born in 1809 and died in 1849. But during his life, he was a highly influential writer. Even today, many writers consider Poe to be one of their greatest influences.

Poe's most renowned work is *The Raven*. But he was not just a poet. Poe is considered the father of mystery writing. *The Purloined Letter* is one of his most well-known detective stories. He also wrote about the supernatural. *The Masque of the Red Death*, *The Black Cat*, and *The Fall of the House of Usher* are all noted for their mysterious aspects.

Q The word "renowned" in the passage is closest in meaning to

Ⓐ published

Ⓑ notorious

Ⓒ remembered

Ⓓ famous

⊘ Answer Explanation

Choice Ⓓ has the closest meaning to the highlighted word. Something that is renowned is famous. The rest of the paragraph also focuses on Poe's other famous works. Similar words such as "well-known" and "noted" are used. These provide hints as to the meaning of "renowned." Something "notorious" is well-known, but that word has a negative meaning. So Choice Ⓑ is incorrect. Choices Ⓐ and Ⓒ are also incorrect.

Exercises with Vocabulary Questions

Exercise 1

A flood occurs when the level of a body of water rises too high. Then, water spills into new areas. Heavy rains and melting snow and ice often cause floods. Floods can cause great amounts of damage. They may quickly erode an area. So valuable topsoil and other land get carried away.

Q In stating that valuable topsoil and other land "get carried away," the author means that topsoil and land

- Ⓐ become cleaned
- Ⓑ are deposited
- Ⓒ are avoided
- Ⓓ get removed

Exercise 2

Some animals live deep beneath the ocean. The sun's light cannot reach down that far. So the ocean bottom is extremely dark. As a result, some animals have their own light sources. They use something called bioluminescence. They may create light, or parts of them may glow. Most use their light to see or to hunt with.

Q The word "extremely" in the passage is closest in meaning to

- Ⓐ fairly
- Ⓑ exactly
- Ⓒ highly
- Ⓓ partially

A city-state includes a city and the land around it. In ancient Greece, there were many powerful city-states. Athens, Sparta, and Thebes were among the greatest. Large numbers of people lived in the cities themselves. But the surrounding land was also crucial. There, the food that fed everyone in the region was grown.

Q The word "surrounding" in the passage is closest in meaning to

- Ⓐ fertile
- Ⓑ nearby
- Ⓒ hostile
- Ⓓ extensive

When animals or plants die, their remains may be preserved. These are called fossils. There are all kinds of fossils. Some are the bones of animals. Others are merely imprints of plants or animals on stone. In rare cases, entire animals are fossilized. This happens in cold areas such as the Arctic.

Q The word "imprints" in the passage is closest in meaning to

- Ⓐ pictures
- Ⓑ visions
- Ⓒ portraits
- Ⓓ traces

Reference questions require the test taker to understand the relationships between certain words and what they refer to in the passage. A word in the text is highlighted. It is usually a pronoun such as *he*, *she*, *it*, or *they*. It might also be a word like *this*, *that*, *these*, or *those*. Then, the test taker must select the word or phrase the highlighted word refers to. Reference questions do not appear very often anymore. Many times, a passage may have no Reference questions.

Reference questions often look like this:

▶ The word "X" in the passage refers to

Tips for answering the questions:

■ The case and the number of the pronoun and the word it refers to must be the same. Singular pronouns refer to singular words. Plural pronouns refer to plural words.

■ Substitute the highlighted word with each answer choice. Doing that will help you determine which answer choice is correct.

■ The answer choices are always the same words and phrases that appear in the passage. They appear in the same order that they were used in the passage.

Examples of Reference Questions

Many animals live in the same regions their entire lives. But others often move from place to place. This is called migration. Animals often migrate in certain seasons. For instance, many birds migrate. In late fall, numerous species of birds begin to fly south. They are heading for warmer lands. This lets them experience warmer weather. There is also more food in warmer areas. When spring comes, the birds fly back north. After they arrive, they often build nests and lay eggs. They repeat this activity on a yearly basis. Most scientists believe animal migration is an instinctual activity.

Q The word "They" in the passage refers to

    Ⓐ The same regions

    Ⓑ Animals

    Ⓒ Certain seasons

    Ⓓ Many birds

⊘ Answer Explanation

Choice Ⓓ is what *They* refers to. The sentence with the highlighted word mentions "heading for warmer lands." The only possible answers are "animals" and "many birds." However, the sentence before the one with the highlighted word focuses on birds flying south. So Choice Ⓓ is correct. Choices Ⓐ and Ⓒ are incorrect because neither regions nor seasons can move to warmer lands.

Constantinople was founded in 330. It was built by Constantine the Great. The city was the capital of the Byzantine Empire. It became the most magnificent city in the Western world. It was also the West's largest city for many years. Hagia Sophia and other outstanding works of architecture were built in Constantinople. The city was often attacked by invaders. But its enormous walls always defeated them. However, in 1453, the Ottoman Turks managed to defeat the Byzantine Empire. They entered the city and destroyed much of it. After that, its name was changed to Istanbul. Today, it is the largest city in Turkey.

Q The word "its" in the passage refers to

Ⓐ the Western world

Ⓑ Hagia Sophia

Ⓒ Constantinople

Ⓓ the Byzantine Empire

⊘ Answer Explanation

Choice Ⓒ is what *its* refers to. The previous sentence mentions "the city was often attacked by invaders." The sentence with the highlighted word notes that "its enormous walls always defeated them." Here, *its* refers to "the city." But that is not an answer choice. The only city listed in the answer choices is "Constantinople." So Choice Ⓒ is correct. Choices Ⓐ, Ⓑ, and Ⓓ are incorrect because they are not cities.

Exercises with Reference Questions

Exercise 1

The desert is a harsh environment. A large number of plants and animals cannot survive in it. But some do. They have to adapt to the conditions in the desert. For example, many animals become nocturnal. They sleep during the heat of the day. At night, it is cooler. So they become more active.

Q The word "it" in the passage refers to

Ⓐ the desert

Ⓑ a harsh environment

Ⓒ a large number

Ⓓ plants and animals

Exercise 2

In order to raise funds, governments levy taxes on their citizens. There are all kinds that people must pay. For example, some common ones are sales taxes and income taxes. But many people must also pay property taxes on the lands and buildings they own. There are almost always taxes on imports and exports as well.

Q The word "ones" in the passage refers to

Ⓐ funds

Ⓑ governments

Ⓒ taxes

Ⓓ citizens

Exercise 3

One of the greatest epic poems in Western literature is the *Aeneid*. It was written by Virgil, a Roman. The *Aeneid* tells the story of Aeneas. It describes his escape from the city of Troy after the Greeks defeated it. Aeneas and his followers eventually went to Italy. There, his descendants founded Rome.

Q The word "it" in the passage refers to

Ⓐ Western literature

Ⓑ the *Aeneid*

Ⓒ the story of Aeneas

Ⓓ the city of Troy

Exercise 4

In the past few decades, many American parents have stopped sending their children to schools. Instead, they prefer to homeschool their children. The children stay home. There, they study with their parents or a private tutor. This gives parents more control over their children's education. These children often get excellent educations.

Q The word "they" in the passage refers to

Ⓐ the past few decades

Ⓑ many American parents

Ⓒ their children

Ⓓ schools

Factual Information questions require the test taker to understand the facts in a passage. These questions ask about details, definitions, and explanations. The questions often ask about a specific paragraph. The test taker needs to focus on the details in the passage to answer these questions. Nowadays, most passages have two Factual questions.

Factual Information questions often look like this:

▶ According to the paragraph, which of the following is true of X?

▶ The author's description of X mentions which of the following?

▶ According to the paragraph, X occurred because . . .

▶ According to the paragraph, why did X do Y?

▶ Select the TWO answer choices from paragraph 1 that identify X. *To receive credit, you must select TWO answers.*

Tips for answering the questions:

▪ Focus on the facts in the passage.

▪ Some answer choices have information that is partially correct. However, if one word in an answer choice is wrong, do not choose that answer choice.

▪ Answer choices sometimes have information that was not mentioned in the passage. These answer choices are incorrect.

Examples of Factual Information Questions

³➜ One way that people mine is by doing strip-mining. This technique is useful when a mineral is near the surface. Basically, the top of the land gets stripped away. Bulldozers, scrapers, and other types of equipment are used. The desired material is removed. Then, the earth is replaced. This is an effective form of mining. It causes severe damage to the land though. As a result, companies that do strip-mining have to repair the land. For instance, they must plant trees in the ground. And they must take other steps to make sure that valuable topsoil does not get eroded.

Q According to paragraph 3, companies use strip-mining when

Ⓐ it is the most inexpensive form of mining Ⓑ repairing the land is simple to do

Ⓒ some material is close to the surface Ⓓ they do not have complex equipment

⊘ Answer Explanation

Choice Ⓒ is correct. The passage reads, "This technique is useful when a mineral is near the surface." That explains why some companies use strip-mining. Choice Ⓐ is incorrect because nothing is mentioned about money. Choice Ⓑ is not mentioned in the passage either. And Choice Ⓓ is incorrect because the complexity of the equipment is not mentioned.

[3]→ Rote learning involves repetition. A student memorizes various facts with this method. Students who use rote learning can often recall a large amount of information. Rote learning is common in some subjects. These include both math and science. Students use rote methods to memorize formulas or data. But there are a lot of critics of this style. Some claim that students do not understand what they learn. Thus many educators try to avoid using only rote methods with their students. Instead, they combine rote learning with other types of teaching methods. This way, they can educate their students more effectively.

Q In paragraph 3, the author's description of rote learning mentions which of the following?

Ⓐ How educated students become by doing it

Ⓑ Why teachers believe it is the best way to learn

Ⓒ Why math and science teachers often use it

Ⓓ What information students must memorize

⊘ Answer Explanation

Choice Ⓓ is correct. According to the passage, "A student memorizes various facts with this method," and, "Students use rote methods to memorize formulas or data." So rote learning makes students memorize facts, formulas, and data. Choice Ⓐ is incorrect because it is not mentioned in the passage. Choice Ⓑ is incorrect because the passage mentions that many educators dislike rote learning. And Choice Ⓒ is incorrect because there is nothing mentioned in the passage about why math and science teachers often use rote learning methods.

Exercises with Factual Information Questions

Exercise 1

[4]→ One of the most famous jazz musicians was Louis Armstrong. He began his career in New Orleans. But he soon formed his own band. Together, they toured the country. Many people know about Armstrong for his trumpet playing. But his voice is recognizable even to casual fans of jazz. He was outstanding at improvising as well.

Q According to paragraph 4, Louis Armstrong is famous because

- Ⓐ he played the trumpet well
- Ⓑ he helped create jazz music
- Ⓒ he was excellent at improvising
- Ⓓ he had a great singing voice

Exercise 2

[1]→ The Internet has changed society in many ways. Yet not all of them are positive. Some people have reduced their human contact because of the Internet. These people rarely socialize in person. Instead, they prefer to meet and speak with others online. Psychologists warn that this can cause harm to people.

Q According to paragraph 1, why do some people avoid socializing in person?

- Ⓐ They are afraid to use the Internet.
- Ⓑ They are shy about speaking with others.
- Ⓒ They live far away from others.
- Ⓓ They like to socialize online.

5→ Thousands of years ago, the ships people built were unsafe. They often sank. And they could not sail in deep water. Most sailors preferred to stay in sight of land at all times. So ships were built for rivers or lakes. Few ships were seaworthy enough to sail on the sea or ocean.

Q According to paragraph 5, ships in the past were built for rivers or lakes because

- Ⓐ humans were afraid of the sea
- Ⓑ people only lived next to rivers
- Ⓒ sailors wanted to be able to see land
- Ⓓ sailing in shallow water was simple

2→ Notre-Dame de Paris took almost two centuries to complete. Construction began in 1163. But it was not finished until the fourteenth century. It was built in the Gothic style. One feature of the cathedral is its many statues. There are numerous gargoyles all over it. There are all sorts of statues depicting other figures as well.

Q According to paragraph 2, which of the following is true of Notre-Dame de Paris?

- Ⓐ It has a lot of different statues.
- Ⓑ Construction on it began in the 1300s.
- Ⓒ Gargoyles are its only decorations.
- Ⓓ It was built two hundred years ago.

04 Negative Factual Information

Negative Factual Information questions require the test taker to understand the facts in a passage. These questions ask about details, definitions, and explanations. But they require the test taker to identify incorrect information. Three answer choices contain correct information. The test taker must avoid them and choose the answer choice with the incorrect information.

Negative Factual Information questions often look like this:

▶ According to the passage, which of the following is NOT true of X?

▶ The author's description of X mentions all of the following EXCEPT:

▶ In paragraph 2, all of the following questions are answered EXCEPT:

Tips for answering the questions:

■ Focus on the facts in the passage.

■ The information in the answer choices is often found in a single paragraph. The question will identify the paragraph, so focus only on that paragraph to find the answer.

■ The correct answer is often the opposite of information that appears in the passage. It may also be a correct statement but may not refer to the topic of the question.

Examples of Negative Factual Information Questions

2 ➙ One of the biggest advantages of trains is economic. Trains are the most efficient form of land transportation. They can move large amounts of goods long distances in a short amount of time. This makes trains more efficient than trucks, vans, and cars. In the United States, most major cities are connected by a railroad network. So products can easily be sent from one city to another. This is especially important for people in cities that are not near rivers or waterways. For these people, using trains is the cheapest and fastest way to transport goods.

Q In paragraph 2, the author's description of trains mentions all of the following EXCEPT:

Ⓐ the relative price of transporting goods with them

Ⓑ their efficiency compared to cars

Ⓒ their ability to move goods faster than planes

Ⓓ their connecting of cities in the United States

Answer Explanation

Choice Ⓒ is the only statement that is NOT mentioned. In the passage, the author does not mention anything about planes. It may be a true statement, but it is not included in the passage. So this is the answer choice the test taker should choose. Choices Ⓐ, Ⓑ, and Ⓓ are all mentioned in the paragraph, so they should not be chosen.

³➜ Humans have been utilizing ceramics for thousands of years. One reason for this is that they have a number of uses. Humans most commonly store food, water, or other items in ceramics. That is likely the original reason why people began making ceramics. People also eat and drink with ceramics. They put the food on plates and in bowls. Then, they eat from the plates and bowls. People use cups to drink water, wine, or other beverages from as well. Ceramics also have an artistic function. For centuries, people have decorated their ceramics. Some individuals have displayed them like works of art.

Q According to paragraph 3, which of the following is NOT true of ceramics?

Ⓐ They harm people who drink with them.
Ⓑ They can be displayed like works of art.
Ⓒ Some of them are used to store food in.
Ⓓ People use plates and bowls to eat with.

Answer Explanation

Choice Ⓐ is the only statement that is NOT true. According to the passage, people drink beverages from ceramics. So it is not true that they harm people. Choices Ⓑ, Ⓒ, and Ⓓ are all correct statements, so they should not be chosen.

Exercises with Negative Factual Information Questions

Exercise 1

³→ The northwestern part of Holland is a coastal area. Much of this region lies below sea level. In fact, a large percentage of the land has been reclaimed from the ocean. There is an extensive series of dikes in the region. These prevent sea water from flooding the land.

Q According to paragraph 3, which of the following is NOT true of Holland?

    Ⓐ Some areas in Holland are below sea level.

    Ⓑ There are few dikes in northwestern Holland.

    Ⓒ Parts of Holland are next to the ocean.

    Ⓓ Dikes are used in Holland to stop floods.

Exercise 2

²→ There are many species of squirrels. One of the most unique is the flying squirrel. This animal is native to North America, Europe, and Asia. It cannot actually fly. But it can glide for long distances. Some squirrels can glide up to ninety meters. This allows them to evade predators trying to catch them.

Q In paragraph 2, all of the following questions are answered EXCEPT:

    Ⓐ Where does the flying squirrel come from?

    Ⓑ How are flying squirrels able to glide in the air?

    Ⓒ How do flying squirrels use their gliding ability?

    Ⓓ What is the greatest distance some flying squirrels can glide?

Exercise 3

²→ These days, alternative energy has become more common. It includes solar, wind, and geothermal energy. They are all renewable sources of energy. So unlike fossil fuels, they will never be exhausted. They are fairly clean sources of energy as well. They do not pollute the air like burning coal, oil, and gas does.

Q According to paragraph 2, which of the following is NOT true of alternative energy?

Ⓐ It is cleaner than coal, oil, and gas.

Ⓑ It is more common nowadays.

Ⓒ It can cause some air pollution.

Ⓓ It is a renewable source of energy.

Exercise 4

⁴→ Earthquakes vary in intensity. Every day, there are large numbers of them all around the world. But most are minor. Only sensitive machines can even detect them. More powerful earthquakes are rare. Still, every year, there are some devastating earthquakes. These can kill thousands of people. And they can destroy buildings, bridges, and roads.

Q In paragraph 4, the author's description of earthquakes mentions all of the following EXCEPT:

Ⓐ the methods scientists use to predict them

Ⓑ the number of people that some of them kill

Ⓒ their power in comparison to one another

Ⓓ the fact that most of them are not very strong

05 | Sentence Simplification

Sentence Simplification questions require the test taker to simplify a sentence in the passage. A sentence in the passage is highlighted. The test taker must choose the sentence that best restates the highlighted one. The test taker must make sure that every main point is included in the simplified sentence. When they appear, there is only one Sentence Simplification question in a passage.

Sentence Simplification questions often look like this:

▶ Which of the sentences below best expresses the essential information in the highlighted sentence in the passage? *Incorrect* answer choices change the meaning in important ways or leave out essential information.

Tips for answering the questions:

■ A highlighted sentence often has two or more clauses. Focus on the main point or idea of each clause.

■ The answer choice you select must cover all of the important information in the highlighted sentence.

■ The correct answer has no information that disagrees with the main sentence, and it does not omit important information either. It also does not add any new information that is not in the highlighted sentence.

Example of a Sentence Simplification Question

In 492 B.C., King Darius I of Persia ordered an invasion of Greece. He was acting mostly against the Greek city-states Athens and Eretria. They had supported some cities in Ionia that had rebelled against Persia. Darius was upset and wanted to punish the Greeks. Darius was also interested in extending the rule of Persia into Europe, so he hoped that his war against the Greeks would be the first of many victories. At first, the Persian invasion was successful. But both Athens and Sparta refused to surrender to the Persians.

In 490, Darius ordered a second invasion of Greece to subdue the Athenians and Spartans. The Persians invaded Greece by sea. First, they captured the island of Naxos. Then, they sailed to some more islands. They successfully captured all of them. The Persians landed at Eretria, which they also defeated. Next, the Persians went to Marathon. At Marathon, there was an Athenian army. The Persian army was much larger. But the Greek hoplites, as their soldiers were called, were well-trained heavy infantry. They used excellent tactics, too. The Persian army was defeated, and the Persians ended their invasion of Greece. Soon afterward, Darius died, and his son Xerxes I became the king. Under Xerxes, the Persians did not invade Greece again until 480 B.C.

Q Which of the sentences below best expresses the essential information in the highlighted sentence in the passage? *Incorrect* answer choices change the meaning in important ways or leave out essential information.

- (A) Darius was convinced that he would be able to defeat the Greeks in many battles.
- (B) There was a lot of land in Europe that Darius was interested in ruling.
- (C) The Greeks defeated Darius, so he could not move his Persian armies into Europe.
- (D) Darius thought he could defeat the Greeks and capture land in Europe for Persia.

⊘ Answer Explanation

Choice (D) best restates the important information in the highlighted sentence. There are two main ideas in the sentence: 1) Darius wanted to rule land in Europe, and 2) Darius believed he could defeat the Greeks in battle. Choice (D) includes both pieces of information. Choice (A) is incorrect because it only contains one of the main ideas. Choice (B) is incorrect for the same reason. And Choice (C) is incorrect because the highlighted sentence does not mention that the Greeks defeated Darius.

Exercises with Sentence Simplification Questions

Patents are used to give inventors the rights to their own creations. With a patent, an inventor may profit from the work that was made. The inventor can do this in a number of ways. Some inventors merely sell the rights to their inventions to a person, government, or company. If that happens, then the inventor receives a one-time payment for the product. The buyer then becomes the sole owner of the invention. But many other inventors choose to license their products to companies, which allows them to maintain ownership of their creations. In cases like this, both the inventor and the manufacturer profit. The inventor receives a certain percentage of the sale price of the product. This is called a royalty. The percentage depends on what the inventor and the manufacturer negotiate. Then, the maker of the invention may keep the remainder.

Q Which of the sentences below best expresses the essential information in the highlighted sentence in the passage? *Incorrect* answer choices change the meaning in important ways or leave out essential information.

Ⓐ It can be very profitable for an inventor to retain ownership of an item.

Ⓑ By licensing their inventions, inventors can still own their products.

Ⓒ Most inventors prefer to license their products in order to make money.

Ⓓ Some inventors are not allowed to be the owners of the products they make.

Green plants have a unique way of making their own energy. The method is called photosynthesis. It is possible due to chloroplasts. They are found in the green parts of plants—usually their leaves—and contain chlorophyll. Thanks to chlorophyll, plants can convert the sun's light into food. In addition to sunlight, plants need two things to undergo photosynthesis. They require water and carbon dioxide. They get water either by collecting falling rain or by absorbing it from the ground. And they get carbon dioxide from the air. What happens next is that plants undergo a process in which the chlorophyll transforms water and carbon dioxide into glucose, a form of sugar, and oxygen. The oxygen is a byproduct. It is released into the air. Humans and other animals breathe it. But plants use the glucose they make as energy for themselves. This gives plants all the energy that they need to survive.

Q Which of the sentences below best expresses the essential information in the highlighted sentence in the passage? *Incorrect* answer choices change the meaning in important ways or leave out essential information.

A Chlorophyll starts a reaction that results in water and carbon dioxide turning into glucose and oxygen.

B Unless plants have enough chlorophyll, they will be unable to create enough glucose and oxygen to use.

C Carbon dioxide and water can transform glucose and oxygen into chlorophyll, which plants use.

D Almost all plants use chlorophyll to undergo photosynthesis in order to produce glucose for themselves.

Inference

Inference questions require the test taker to understand arguments the author makes. The test taker must think about the information in the passage and then come to a conclusion about it. The answers to these questions are always implied. So they do not appear in the passage. The test taker must therefore infer what the author means.

Inference questions often look like this:

▶ Which of the following can be inferred about X?

▶ The author of the passage implies that X . . .

▶ Which of the following can be inferred from paragraph 1 about X?

Tips for answering the questions:

■ Many times, the author hints at secondary meanings. Learn how to read between the lines.

■ Many passages have cause-effect relationships. When the author describes an event, idea, or phenomenon, think about what some of their effects may be.

■ The correct answer never contradicts the main point of the passage. Do not select answer choices that disagree with the main idea of the passage.

Examples of Inference Questions

[3] → Sometimes underwater volcanoes erupt. They spew lava far beneath the ocean. The lava often cools off quickly in the water. Over time, the volcano becomes bigger. After enough eruptions, the volcano breaks the surface of the water. This creates an island. In the Pacific Ocean, many islands were formed by volcanic eruptions. The Hawaiian Islands are examples of them. There are hundreds of islands that were formed because of volcanoes. At first, a volcanic island that forms is empty of plants and animals. But over time, both often arrive on them. Today, many volcanic islands around the world are rich in life.

Q In paragraph 3, the author implies that volcanic islands

   Ⓐ can form after a single eruption

   Ⓑ do not always have life on them

   Ⓒ are only found near Hawaii

   Ⓓ can become larger than most islands

⊘ Answer Explanation

Choice Ⓑ is implied about volcanic islands. The author writes, "At first, a volcanic island that forms is empty of plants and animals. But over time, both often arrive on them." By writing "both often arrive on them," the author implies that some islands are empty of life. Choices Ⓐ, Ⓒ, and Ⓓ are not hinted at in the passage. So they are incorrect.

²➜ The Industrial Revolution completely changed the way people made goods. Previously, items were made by hand. This was a slow and difficult process. But the Industrial Revolution introduced new machines. With them, people could make manufactured goods very quickly. It was also fairly simple to make new products. Most of the early advances in the Industrial Revolution were in textiles. Thanks to these advances, clothes became rather cheap. This also increased the need for cotton, which people used to make many clothes. Factory owners were not the only people who benefitted. Many farmers also became rich during this time as well.

Q Which of the following can be inferred from paragraph 2 about the Industrial Revolution?

Ⓐ It took place more than 300 years in the past.
Ⓑ It first occurred in England and moved elsewhere later.
Ⓒ The changes in it caused some problems for people.
Ⓓ A large number of people made money during it.

⊘ Answer Explanation

Choice Ⓓ can be inferred about the Industrial Revolution. The author notes that factory owners and farmers both made money. So it can be inferred that many people became rich. Choices Ⓐ, Ⓑ, and Ⓒ are all factual statements. However, they are not hinted at in the passage. So they are incorrect.

Exercises with Inference Questions

Exercise 1

[2]→ Early motion pictures had no sound at all. These were known as silent movies. To make the audience understand what was happening, performers had to overact. They used exaggerated motions. When movies began to add sound, most silent movie actors could not make the transition to this new form.

Q In paragraph 2, which of the following can be inferred about movies with sound?

Ⓐ They use a smaller number of actors than silent movies.

Ⓑ They require different acting styles from silent movies.

Ⓒ They take a long time to produce because they are complicated.

Ⓓ They make much more money than silent movies did.

Exercise 2

[3]→ Camels have either one or two humps. They are native to Africa and Asia and thrive in desert conditions. They can go without water for several days. People once thought that they store water in their humps. However, camels' humps contain fat. They use this fat to provide sustenance when food and water are in short supply.

Q In paragraph 3, the author implies that camels' humps

Ⓐ are useful to people riding on the camels

Ⓑ help camels survive in the desert

Ⓒ are somewhat annoying to camels

Ⓓ may disappear if camels use the fat in them

⁴➜ Black holes are among the most mysterious bodies in the universe. It is impossible to see them. But scientists are positive that they exist. Black holes have strong gravity. Nothing—not even light—can escape a black hole's gravity. Some astronomers believe that every galaxy has an enormous black hole at its center. This helps stabilize the entire galaxy.

Q Which of the following can be inferred from paragraph 4 about black holes?

(A) Very little is known about them.

(B) They can move rather quickly.

(C) Some might be located near Earth.

(D) They are larger than the sun.

³➜ Sandro Botticelli was a brilliant Renaissance artist. He was from the city of Florence. During his life, he did work in the Sistine Chapel. He also painted the famous *The Birth of Venus*. He made other paintings with mythological themes as well. Other paintings of his focused on religion. Today, he is recognized as a master painter from that period.

Q In paragraph 3, the author implies that *The Birth of Venus*

(A) focuses on a religious topic

(B) is in the Sistine Chapel

(C) was Botticelli's first work

(D) has a mythological theme

Rhetorical Purpose questions require the test taker to understand why something is in the passage. The test taker must recognize the function of the material in the passage. The meaning of the information is not important. The correct answer can be found either in an entire paragraph or an individual sentence.

Rhetorical Purpose questions often look like this:

▶ The author discusses "X" in paragraph 2 in order to . . .

▶ Why does the author mention "X"?

▶ The author uses "X" as an example of . . .

Tips for answering the questions:

▪ Find the part of the passage that has the topic being asked about. Think about how that topic relates to the entire passage.

▪ Words such as *definition*, *example*, *illustrate*, *explain*, *contrast*, *compare*, *refute*, *note*, *criticize*, or *function* are often important.

▪ The question is usually not about the entire topic. So just focus on the paragraph or section that mentions the topic of the question.

Examples of Rhetorical Purpose Questions

⁴➔ Another important canal was the Erie Canal. It stretched almost 600 kilometers across the state of New York. It went from Buffalo to Albany. Buffalo was located on Lake Erie. Albany was on the Hudson River, which flowed down to New York City. The Erie Canal was built between 1817 and 1825. It was an enormous project at that time. Before it was built, the longest canal in the United States was fewer than 45 kilometers long. Most people doubted it could be built. But the canal was successfully completed. It helped connect the Great Lakes with the Atlantic Ocean.

Q In paragraph 4, why does the author mention "the Hudson River"?

   Ⓐ To name one end of the Erie Canal

   Ⓑ To describe an important river in New York

   Ⓒ To note how long it is

   Ⓓ To explain its connection with New York City

⊘ Answer Explanation

Choice Ⓐ is the reason why the author mentions the Hudson River. The author mentions that the Erie Canal went from Buffalo to Albany. Buffalo was located by Lake Erie. And Albany was on the Hudson River. So the Hudson River was one end of the Erie Canal. Choice Ⓑ is incorrect because the author mentions nothing about how important the Hudson River was. Choice Ⓒ is not mentioned in the passage. And Choice Ⓓ is mentioned in the passage, but it is not the reason why the author writes about the Hudson River.

[3]→ Prey animals have many defenses to protect themselves from predators. Some defenses are rather unique. Turtles have hard shells. They can retract their head and legs when predators come. This offers them protection. Some squid can shoot dark ink when predators are near. This makes the water difficult to see in while the squid quickly swims away. The porcupine has sharp quills that can hurt a predator attempting to eat it. And skunks have a very unusual defense mechanism. They can spray animals with a bad-smelling odor. Predators quickly learn to avoid skunks anytime they see them.

Q The author discusses "defenses" in paragraph 3 in order to

Ⓐ compare squid with turtles

Ⓑ describe a few unusual defense mechanisms

Ⓒ prove that porcupines' defenses are not effective

Ⓓ show how some animals protect themselves

⊘ Answer Explanation

Choice Ⓓ explains why the author describes defenses. In the entire paragraph, the author writes about some specific animal defenses. So the author is showing how certain animals protect themselves. Choice Ⓐ is incorrect because the author does not directly compare squid with turtles. Choice Ⓑ is incorrect because it suggests the author's focus is on unusual defense mechanisms. And Choice Ⓒ is incorrect because the author writes nothing about how effective porcupines' defenses are.

Exercises with Rhetorical Purpose Questions

Exercise 1

[2]→ Charles Darwin was a supporter of gradualism. This is a type of evolution. However, it does not involve sudden changes. Instead, it states that species make gradual changes over several generations. Darwin came to believe in gradualism because of his trip to the Galapagos Islands. While there, he saw evidence of slow changes rather than fast ones.

Q In paragraph 2, why does the author mention "the Galapagos Islands"?

Ⓐ To indicate that Charles Darwin visited them

Ⓑ To show how they affected Charles Darwin's thoughts on gradualism

Ⓒ To point out that many animals evolved on those islands

Ⓓ To declare that the theory of evolution was first proved there

Exercise 2

[2]→ Lunar eclipses are much more common than solar eclipses. A lunar eclipse happens when the moon passes through Earth's shadow. There are both total eclipses and partial eclipses. During a total lunar eclipse, the moon appears to be red in color. On average, lunar eclipses take place around two to four times a year.

Q The author discusses "Lunar eclipses" in paragraph 2 in order to

Ⓐ compare them with solar eclipses

Ⓑ explain when the next one will occur

Ⓒ mention how long they usually last

Ⓓ provide some information about them

²→ Many caves with paintings on their walls have been found in Europe. The oldest have been found at Chauvet in France. They are more than 32,000 years old. Other paintings in Spanish caves date back to the Ice Age. Both art historians and archaeologists are interested in the art that primitive people drew.

Q In paragraph 2, the author uses "Chauvet" as an example of

- Ⓐ a cave that is located in France
- Ⓑ a cave that formed thousands of years ago
- Ⓒ a cave with the oldest paintings on its walls
- Ⓓ a cave many art historians have studied

³→ The best way to counter viruses is by using vaccinations. These make the body immune to certain diseases. There are vaccines for a number of deadly viruses. These include polio, cholera, and typhoid. Some vaccinations last for a very short time. Others last for several years or even for a person's lifetime.

Q In paragraph 3, why does the author mention "polio, cholera, and typhoid"?

- Ⓐ To state that there are vaccinations for them
- Ⓑ To name the three deadliest viruses
- Ⓒ To claim that the vaccinations for them last a short time
- Ⓓ To explain how they can harm some people

Insert Text questions require the test taker to determine where a new sentence can be placed in the passage. The test taker should consider grammar, logic, connecting words, and flow. Insert Text questions are always the second-to-last question asked. Nowadays, there is almost always one Insert Text question for each passage.

Insert Text questions often look like this:

▶ Look at the four squares [■] that indicate where the following sentence could be added to the passage.

[You will see a sentence in bold.]

Where would the sentence best fit?

Tips for answering the questions:

▪ There will be four black squares in the passage. Put the new sentence in each black square and then read it. This can help you find the correct place for the sentence.

▪ Connecting words such as *therefore*, *similarly*, *in contrast*, *for example*, *for instance*, *finally*, *meanwhile*, *on the other hand*, and *as a result* are often used in the new sentence. Use them to help find the correct place for the sentence.

▪ Make sure that the place you choose for the new sentence is logical so that the sentence fits.

Example of an Insert Text Question

During the 1800s in Europe, there was renewed interest in folklore. Two German brothers played an important role in this. They were Jacob and Wilhelm Grimm. The two brothers were fascinated by folklore and fairy tales. They spoke with villagers in towns all around the country. From them, the Grimm brothers learned many of the oral stories the villagers passed on from one person to another. Then, they recorded their stories.

In 1812, they published *Tales of Children and the Home*. This was their first collection of fairy tales. There were 86 stories in that book. Two years later, they published another book of fairy tales. It had 70 stories. Throughout their lives, they published several editions of fairy tales. The brothers continued adding stories until the final edition. **1** It contained 211 stories. **2** Among these fairy tales were some of the best-known stories in the world. **3** They included *Cinderella*, *Snow White*, *Sleeping Beauty*, and *Rapunzel*. **4** They also published some works that included hundreds of old German legends. The Grimm brothers' works were instantly popular. People in Europe and other places eagerly read their stories. And scholars began to record the folktales of many cultures as a result of their work. This has helped preserve many stories from the past.

Q Look at the four squares [■] that indicate where the following sentence could be added to the passage.

In addition, *Hansel and Gretel* and *Rumpelstiltskin* were included in the work.

Where would the sentence best fit?

Click on a square [■] to add the sentence to the passage.

⊘ Answer Explanation

The sentence best fits after the fourth square. The sentence before the fourth square reads, "They included *Cinderella*, *Snow White*, *Sleeping Beauty*, and *Rapunzel*." The new sentence mentions the titles of two more works. This connects the two sentences. The connecting phrase "in addition" is also used. This provides a hint as to where the new sentence should go. The other three squares are inappropriate places for the new sentence. The passage would not flow well or make sense if the new sentence were added next to them.

Exercises with Insert Text Questions

Exercise 1

When the Industrial Revolution began, people moved to big urban centers. Both their jobs and homes were located there. In the 1900s, this changed. Large numbers of people still worked in big cities. But they no longer lived in them. Instead, they preferred to dwell in the suburbs.

Suburbs are small cities that are located around larger ones. They are mostly residential in nature. There are few—if any—factories in them. In the United States, suburbs have both houses and apartments. And the majority of people living in them are families with children. Many parents prefer that their children grow up in the suburbs. They are generally safer than big cities. **1** The public school systems are better as well. **2** The air is cleaner, and housing prices are much lower than they are in urban centers. **3** When all of these factors are considered together, it is easy to see why people prefer the suburbs to urban centers. **4**

Q Look at the four squares [■] that indicate where the following sentence could be added to the passage.

For example, crime rates are much lower in suburban areas.

Where would the sentence best fit?

Click on a square [■] to add the sentence to the passage.

One common feature in parts of the American Southwest and Mexico is the saguaro cactus. These distinct cacti grow in harsh desert conditions. They are noted primarily for their unique appearance. They have one large stem that may grow to be more than fifteen meters high. They also have other stems that look like arms. The arms rise straight toward the sky. These arms, however, do not appear until a cactus is around seventy-five years old. **1** The cactus itself may live for up to 200 years. **2** In spring, white and yellow flowers bloom on the cactus. **3** In June, a dark red fruit ripens. **4** The fruit is valued by some Native American tribes. It is consumed by animals as well. The saguaro cactus provides homes for many species of birds. Owls, woodpeckers, and other birds often make nests in holes in the cacti.

Q Look at the four squares [■] that indicate where the following sentence could be added to the passage.

In most cases, saguaro cacti die after being uprooted by the wind or rain.

Where would the sentence best fit?

Click on a square [■] to add the sentence to the passage.

09 Prose Summary

Prose Summary questions require the test taker to recognize the main idea of the passage and then to choose sentences that focus on it. These questions include one sentence that summarizes the entire passage. There are six sentences that contain information from the passage. The test taker must choose the three sentences that most closely relate to the summary statement. These are the last question in a reading passage but do not always appear. A Fill in a Table question may appear instead. However, Prose Summary questions are much more common than Fill in a Table questions.

Prose Summary questions often look like this:

▶ **Directions**: An introductory sentence for a brief summary of the passage is provided below. Complete the summary by selecting the THREE answer choices that express the most important ideas of the passage. Some sentences do not belong because they express ideas that are not presented in the passage or are minor ideas in the passage. **This question is worth 2 points**.

Tips for answering the questions:

▪ The introductory sentence always includes the main themes or ideas of the passage.

▪ Correct answer choices refer to the main themes or ideas.

▪ Incorrect answer choices refer to minor themes or ideas. Some answer choices have correct information that is not mentioned in the passage. These choices are also incorrect.

Example of a Prose Summary Question

The discovery of agriculture changed people's lives in many ways. The first major way was that people began to live in permanent settlements. They no longer had to live as hunter-gatherers. So they did not have to follow animals to get their food. Instead, they could stay in the same place year after year. This allowed people to have some stability in their lives.

Another feature was that people's diets improved. Previously, people merely ate whatever food they caught or found. In some seasons, there was plenty to eat. At other times, there was little to eat. By growing their own food, people could ensure that they had a constant source of food all year long.

The most important feature of agriculture was that it let humans develop civilization. As hunter-gatherers, most of the work that humans did involved finding food for the day. Usually, the men hunted while the women gathered. Thanks to farming, fewer people were needed to collect food.

Some people could instead focus on different things. Thus they learned new skills. They discovered how to shape metal. They constructed buildings. They made towns and cities. And they created civilizations. This was all thanks to the discovery of how to farm the land.

Q *Directions*: An introductory sentence for a brief summary of the passage is provided below. Complete the summary by selecting the THREE answer choices that express the most important ideas of the passage. Some sentences do not belong because they express ideas that are not presented in the passage or are minor ideas in the passage. *This question is worth 2 points*.

Drag your answer choices to the spaces where they belong.
To remove an answer choice, click on it. To review the passage, click on **View Text**.

Human lives changed very much after people learned about agriculture.

-
-
-

Answer Choices

1 People who farmed gained a constant source of food.

2 Some primitive people stopped farming to work with metal.

3 The earliest humans were all hunter-gatherers.

4 Farming enabled groups of people to build societies.

5 Agriculture was first discovered by humans thousands of years ago.

6 By farming, humans were able to stop wandering after animals.

⊙ Answer Explanation

Choices 1, 4, and 6 are all correct. Choice 1 is stressed in paragraph 2. Choice 4 is the main topic of paragraph 3. And Choice 6 is the main topic of paragraph 1. They are all ways in which human lives changed when people learned about agriculture. Choice 2 is a correct statement, but it is a minor point. The same is true of Choice 3. And Choice 5 is a correct statement, but it is not mentioned in the passage. So it is incorrect.

Exercises with Prose Summary Questions

During the Middle Ages, people in many countries relied on feudalism as their system of government. In a feudal system, every person from the king to the lowest individual had various roles to fulfill. The king was the head of the government. He owned the land in the kingdom. Beneath the king were nobles. These included dukes, earls, and barons. They were the king's vassals. In return for their loyalty, the king gave land to the nobles. The nobles owed the king tax money and had to provide soldiers when the king went to war. The nobles parceled out land to the people beneath them. These people were knights and other men. The lowest people were the serfs. They had no land of their own. They farmed the land and got to keep some crops for themselves. But they owed a large amount of the crops to their noble. The serfs were also tied to the land. So they could not move anywhere without their lord's permission.

Q *Directions*: An introductory sentence for a brief summary of the passage is provided below. Complete the summary by selecting the THREE answer choices that express the most important ideas of the passage. Some sentences do not belong because they express ideas that are not presented in the passage or are minor ideas in the passage. *This question is worth 2 points*.

Drag your answer choices to the spaces where they belong.
To remove an answer choice, click on it. To review the passage, click on **View Text**.

In the system of feudalism, every person had various responsibilities to others.

-
-
-

Answer Choices

1. Dukes, earls, and barons were all nobles in the Middle Ages.

2. The lowest people in the feudal system were the serfs.

3. Most of the places that used feudalism were in Northern Europe.

4. Nobles had to support the king with money and soldiers.

5. Serfs worked on the land and provided crops for their lords.

6. The king gave land to the nobles if they were loyal to him.

Mammals are different from reptiles in a number of ways. The major difference is that mammals are warm-blooded animals. This means that mammals are able to regulate their body temperatures. Unlike reptiles, they do not rely on the sun to heat their bodies. But mammals must have a constant supply of energy to keep themselves warm. So they need to eat on a continual basis. This is much different from reptiles, which do not need to eat regularly. Mammals also generally give birth to live young. There are some exceptions, such as the platypus and the echidna, which lay eggs. And female mammals nurse their young since most of them are born helpless and need nourishment to survive. Mammals, even those that live in the water, also have hair on their bodies. This is quite different from reptiles, which have no hair at all.

Q *Directions*: An introductory sentence for a brief summary of the passage is provided below. Complete the summary by selecting the THREE answer choices that express the most important ideas of the passage. Some sentences do not belong because they express ideas that are not presented in the passage or are minor ideas in the passage. *This question is worth 2 points*.

Drag your answer choices to the spaces where they belong.
To remove an answer choice, click on it. To review the passage, click on **View Text**.

Mammals and reptiles have many differences.

-
-
-

Answer Choices

1 Snakes and lizards are the most common reptiles people know.

2 Mammals need food to warm themselves, but reptiles use the sun.

3 The platypus and the echidna are two unusual mammals.

4 Mammals have hair on their bodies while reptiles do not.

5 Most mammal babies look like their parents when they are born.

6 Reptiles eat food much less often than mammals do.

10 Fill in a Table

Fill in a Table questions require the test taker to understand all of the information in the passage. These questions ask about a theme or main point in the passage. They have several sentences or phrases as answer choices. The test taker must match them with the correct theme or main point. This is the last question in a reading passage but does not always appear. A Prose Summary question may appear instead. In fact, Fill in a Table questions are much less common than Prose Summary questions.

Fill in a Table questions often look like this:

▶ **Directions**: Select the appropriate phrases from the answer choices and match them to the type of X to which they relate. TWO of the answer choices will NOT be used. *This question is worth 3 [4] points*.

Tips for answering the questions:

▪ Recognize the main points or themes of the passage.

▪ Cause-effect passages and compare-contrast passages frequently have Fill in a Table questions.

▪ These questions always have two incorrect answer choices. Do not select them.

Example of a Fill in a Table Question

Venus and Mars

    The two planets closest to Earth are Venus and Mars. In many ways, they are similar to each other. Yet the two planets also have several distinct differences.

    First, both Venus and Mars are terrestrial planets. There are four of those. The other two are Mercury and Earth. So Venus and Mars have similar compositions. They are rocky planets with solid surfaces. They also have dense inner cores. Their cores are mostly iron and nickel. Both planets have atmospheres. In their atmospheres, there are clouds, carbon dioxide, and traces of other gases. Finally, neither planet is known to contain any life.

    While they have several similarities, they have even more differences. First, Venus is closer to the sun than Mars. And Venus is larger than Mars. In fact, Venus is called Earth's sister planet because it is almost as big as Earth. Mars, however, is considerably smaller than Venus and Earth. It is slightly more than half the size of Earth. On the other hand, Mars has two moons orbiting it while Venus has none. And Mars takes about three times as long to orbit the sun as Venus. Since Mars is farther away from the sun, its temperature is colder than that of Venus.

Q *Directions*: Select the appropriate phrases from the answer choices and match them to the planet to which they relate. TWO of the answer choices will NOT be used. ***This question is worth 3 points***.

> Drag your answer choices to the spaces where they belong.
> To remove an answer choice, click on it. To review the passage, click on **View Text**.

Answer Choices	PLANET
1 Takes longer to orbit the sun	**Venus**
2 Has a temperature similar to Mercury's	•
3 Has as many moons as Earth	•
4 Is closer to the sun	**Mars**
5 Has two moons that go around it	•
6 Has colder temperatures	•
7 Is about the same size as Earth	•

⊘ **Answer Explanation**

Choices 4 and 7 refer to Venus. Venus is closer to the sun than Mars. And Venus is around the same size as Earth, so it is called Earth's sister planet. Choices 1, 5, and 6 refer to Mars. Mars has an orbit three times longer than that of Venus. Mars also has two moons orbiting it. And the temperature on Mars is colder than on Venus. Choices 2 and 3 are incorrect.

Exercises with Fill in a Table Questions

The Effects of Dams

Many rivers have dams. Sometimes one river has several dams in different places. Dams have both advantages and disadvantages.

One of the most important things dams do is control the flow of water in a river. Rivers often flood during the rainy season. In addition, in spring, melting snow can cause rivers to flood. But dams can prevent floods. Many dams also create hydroelectric power. This can supply thousands of homes and businesses with electricity. A lake always forms behind a dam. People use these lakes for recreational purposes. They go fishing, boating, and swimming in the lakes.

Yet dams greatly change the environment. When a lake forms, it displaces both the people and the animals living on the land behind the dam. Some species of fish and other water creatures have their habitats disturbed as well. And dams prevent valuable silt from going downriver. This makes the land beyond the dams much less fertile.

Q *Directions*: Select the appropriate phrases from the answer choices and match them to the aspect of dams to which they relate. TWO of the answer choices will NOT be used. ***This question is worth 3 points***.

Drag your answer choices to the spaces where they belong.
To remove an answer choice, click on it. To review the passage, click on **View Text**.

Answer Choices	DAMS
1 Cost a lot of money to build	**Advantage**
2 Give people places to go fishing and boating	•
3 Force people to move elsewhere	•
4 Stop floods from occurring	•
5 Can provide electricity for people	**Disadvantage**
6 Prevent silt from moving down the river	•
7 Are difficult to maintain and repair	•

The Boston Tea Party

On December 16, 1773, some American colonists disguised themselves as Mohawk Indians. At night, they boarded some ships that belonged to the East India Tea Company. They threw all of the boxes of tea that were on board into Boston Harbor. This event was the Boston Tea Party.

The colonists were protesting the Tea Act. This was a law passed by the British Parliament. It was a tax on tea. Previously, the British had fought an expensive war against France. Some battles had been in America. The British wanted the American colonists to help pay for the war. The colonists did not want to pay the taxes. The Americans also had no representatives in Parliament. They thought that was unfair.

After the Boston Tea Party, Britain was very angry. Several new laws were passed. Britain wanted to punish all of Boston for the Tea Party. Relations between the Americans and the British got worse. Two years later, the American Revolution began.

Q *Directions*: Select the appropriate sentences from the answer choices and match them to the cause and effect of the Boston Tea Party to which they relate. TWO of the answer choices will NOT be used. *This question is worth 3 points*.

Drag your answer choices to the spaces where they belong.
To remove an answer choice, click on it. To review the passage, click on **View Text**.

Answer Choices	BOSTON TEA PARTY
① There were no Americans in Parliament.	**Cause**
② America fought a war against Britain.	•
③ The French had some American colonies.	•
④ France and Britain fought battles in America.	•
⑤ Britain tried to punish the people of Boston.	**Effect**
⑥ The East India Tea Company had ships with tea.	•
⑦ The Tea Act was passed.	•

Part B

Building Background Knowledge of TOEFL Topics

Chapter 01 History

History is the study of the past. There are many areas of history. Historians may study political, military, economic, social, women's, and cultural history. In all cases, historians try to understand what happened in the past and why it happened. They do this by examining the facts about the past that are available to them. Then, they try to interpret the facts to explain why certain historical events occurred.

Mastering **the Question Types** A

☑ Vocabulary   □ Fill in a Table   □ Factual Information   □ Negative Factual Information   ☑ Prose Summary

□ Insert Text   □ Reference   ☑ Rhetorical Purpose   □ Sentence Simplification   □ Inference

Palaces

¹➡ Palaces are large buildings. In the past, they were the homes of kings, queens, and high-ranking nobles. Palaces were common years ago. They were built for two main reasons: protection and **prestige**.

In ancient times, palaces had walls around them. Soldiers with weapons **manned** the walls. They protected palaces and their occupants. Enemies often attacked palaces. In many cases, the soldiers and the walls kept the palaces safe.

More modern palaces lack walls. They were built for prestige purposes. They show off the wealth of the rulers. The Palace of Versailles in France is one such palace. It is one of the most opulent palaces in the world. In Russia, the rulers copied the French style. They built many extensive palaces in the St. Petersburg area. Today, most palaces are no longer the homes of rulers. They are museums, art galleries, or seats of government.

• **Glossary** •

prestige: status; stature; standing
man: to guard; to protect; to defend

1 In paragraph 1, why does the author mention "kings, queens, and high-ranking nobles"?

    Ⓐ To describe some members of the nobility

    Ⓑ To name some people who lived in castles

    Ⓒ To explain who ordered the construction of castles

    Ⓓ To show how many people could live in a castle

2 The word "opulent" in the passage is closest in meaning to

    Ⓐ magnificent

    Ⓑ expensive

    Ⓒ unique

    Ⓓ well-defended

3 *Directions:* An introductory sentence for a brief summary of the passage is provided below. Complete the summary by selecting the THREE answer choices that express the most important ideas of the passage. Some sentences do not belong because they express ideas that are not presented in the passage or are minor ideas in the passage. ***This question is worth 2 points.***

People in the past built palaces to protect themselves and to add to their prestige.

> -
> -
> -

Answer Choices

① The tsar of Russia had a great palace constructed in St. Petersburg.	④ The Palace of Versailles is a large palace located in France.
② Kings and queens often lived in palaces that they had built.	⑤ Palaces had big walls around them to keep out enemies.
③ Some palaces were built to show how rich their owners were.	⑥ The soldiers that guarded castles kept their occupants safe.

✒ Checking Reading Accuracy   Mark the following statements T (true) or F (false).

    T   **F**

1 ☐ / ☐   Kings, queens, and nobles often lived in palaces.

2 ☐ / ☐   Ancient palaces rarely had walls around them.

3 ☐ / ☐   The Palace of Versailles showed the wealth of the French king.

4 ☐ / ☐   There is a large palace in St. Petersburg in Germany.

Mastering **the Question Types** B

☐ Vocabulary   ☑ Fill in a Table   ☐ Factual Information   ☑ Negative Factual Information   ☐ Prose Summary
☐ Insert Text   ☐ Reference   ☐ Rhetorical Purpose   ☐ Sentence Simplification   ☑ Inference

Spanish and French Colonies in the Americas

1→ Christopher Columbus found the <u>New World</u> in 1492. After that, many other explorers from Europe went across the Atlantic Ocean. Spain and France sent many of them. Both of them also started colonies in the Americas. But their colonies were not very similar to each other.

2→ The Spanish went to Central and South America. But the French settled in North America. For instance, they had some colonies in Canada. They also had some islands in the Caribbean Sea. The Spanish went to get rich. They searched for gold, silver, and other valuables. They wanted to convert the natives to Christianity, too. The French, on the other hand, wanted animal furs. They also did a lot of exploring.

Their actions toward the natives were quite different. The Spanish treated them very poorly. They killed many natives. They <u>enslaved</u> the natives as well. The French got along with them better though. They often tried to learn the natives' languages and customs.

• **Glossary** •

New World: North and South America
enslave: to make a person a slave

1 In paragraph 1, the author implies that Christopher Columbus

    Ⓐ sailed to the New World on a French ship

    Ⓑ started some colonies in the Americas

    Ⓒ worked for the Spanish and the French at times

    Ⓓ was the first European to visit the Americas

2 In paragraph 2, all of the following questions are answered EXCEPT:

    Ⓐ How much gold and silver did the Spanish find in the New World?

    Ⓑ Which part of the New World did the French have colonies in?

    Ⓒ What were the French interested in doing in the Americas?

    Ⓓ Why did the Spanish start their own colonies in the Americas?

3 *Directions*: Select the appropriate sentences from the answer choices and match them to the country to which they relate. TWO of the answer choices will NOT be used. ***This question is worth 3 points***.

Answer Choices	COUNTRY
① Had friendly relationships with the natives	**Spain**
② Taught the natives many things	•
③ Wanted to become wealthy	•
④ Tried to learn about the natives' religions	•
⑤ Had colonies in South America	**France**
⑥ Made slaves of many natives	•
⑦ Were interested in animal furs	•

✐ **Checking Reading Accuracy**   Mark the following statements T (true) or F (false).

    T   **F**

1 ☐ / ☐ Christopher Columbus sailed to the New World in 1492.

2 ☐ / ☐ The Spanish and the French had colonies in the same areas.

3 ☐ / ☐ The Spanish wanted the natives to learn about Christianity.

4 ☐ / ☐ The French learned about the customs of the natives

Mastering **the Question Types**

☐ Vocabulary   ☐ Fill in a Table   ☑ Factual Information   ☐ Negative Factual Information   ☐ Prose Summary
☑ Insert Text   ☑ Reference   ☐ Rhetorical Purpose   ☑ Sentence Simplification   ☐ Inference

The Nara Period in Japan

The Nara Period in Japan lasted from 710 to 794. For much of this time, the Japanese emperors lived in the city of Nara. It was a golden age for Japan. Many people learned to write then. Poets wrote many great poems, and other writers made outstanding works of literature during the Nara Period.

The Chinese were a major influence on Japan then. For instance, the Japanese wrote with Chinese characters. They copied Chinese fashions and architecture. And Buddhism came to Japan from China around that time.

³→ ❶ Yet it was not a perfect era. ❷ There was a lot of political **intrigue**. ❸ Many people tried to **sway** the emperors. ❹ This was particularly true of some families. The Fujiwara family was one. A few Fujiwara daughters married emperors. So their children became quite powerful. In fact, the Fujiwara family influenced Japan for more than 300 years after the Nara Period ended.

• **Glossary** •

intrigue: secret plots or plans, often those which concern politics or government
sway: to influence; to affect in some manner

1 Which of the sentences below best expresses the essential information in the highlighted sentence in the passage? *Incorrect* answer choices change the meaning in important ways or leave out essential information.

    Ⓐ The Nara Period was a time when there were many writers.

    Ⓑ The Japanese began writing poems during the Nara Period.

    Ⓒ In the Nara Period, there were some good works of literature.

    Ⓓ There was much great writing during the Nara Period.

2 The word "They" in the passage refers to

    Ⓐ The Chinese

    Ⓑ The Japanese

    Ⓒ Chinese characters

    Ⓓ Chinese fashions and architecture

3 According to paragraph 3, which of the following is true of the Fujiwara family?

    Ⓐ It produced many emperors of Japan.

    Ⓑ Its daughters sometimes ruled Japan.

    Ⓒ It was a very influential family in Japan.

    Ⓓ It lasted for around 300 years.

4 Look at the four squares [■] that indicate where the following sentence could be added to the passage.

Some of them were quite successful and achieved their goals.

Where would the sentence best fit?

✍ Checking Reading Accuracy Mark the following statements T (true) or F (false).

	T	F	
1	☐ / ☐		The Nara Period was a golden age in Japan.
2	☐ / ☐		The Chinese tried to invade Japan during the Nara Period.
3	☐ / ☐		The Fujiwara family was very powerful in Japan.
4	☐ / ☐		Most Japanese emperors came from the Fujiwara family.

The Maintaining of Control in the Roman Empire

¹→ Almost from its founding, Rome began to expand. At its greatest point, the Roman Empire was enormous. It controlled land in most of Europe and parts of the Middle East and North Africa. Millions of people lived within its borders. Yet most of them had been conquered in battle. So the emperors often worried about their loyalty to Rome. To keep these people from rebelling, the Romans used two primary methods.

²→ First, they stationed troops all over the empire. The number of soldiers in a region depended on its danger level. The Roman Empire was divided into three main areas. First was the homeland on the Italian peninsula. This area was the most secure. Thus the least number of troops were there. Second were the senatorial provinces such as Spain. They had long been a part of Rome. The people were used to Roman rule. They rarely caused problems. So few soldiers were in those areas, too.

³→ The third region included the imperial provinces. These were on the empire's borders. The emperor directly ruled them. Many soldiers, known as legionaries, were posted in the imperial provinces in units called legions. A single legion could control a large area. Some legions were in Britain. Others were along the Rhine and Danube rivers and in the Middle East. They controlled the local **populace**.

⁴→ But the Romans did not rely only on force to maintain unity. They also offered citizenship to people in the provinces. This gave people many rights and privileges. At first, local leaders were made citizens. Over time, others became citizens, too. This helped the people feel that they were Romans. This system proved to be effective. The Pax Romana, or "Roman Peace," was a result of these policies. For decades, Rome was united and suffered few internal problems.

• **Glossary** •

loyalty: trustworthiness; faithfulness
populace: a population; the people living in a certain area

1   According to paragraph 1, which of the following is true of the Roman Empire?

    (A) It was not defeated in battle for several hundred years.

    (B) Many of its people had been conquered in wars.

    (C) The strongest part of the empire was in Europe.

    (D) Its rulers were rarely concerned with the people's loyalty.

2   Which of the following can be inferred from paragraphs 2 and 3 about Roman provinces?

    (A) Roman senators were required to live in senatorial provinces.

    (B) The most people lived in provinces in the Italian homeland.

    (C) Imperial provinces were more dangerous than senatorial ones.

    (D) Britain was the largest of all the imperial provinces.

3   In paragraph 4, why does the author mention "The Pax Romana"?

    (A) To provide the original Latin and its English translation

    (B) To show the success of the Roman policy of granting citizenship

    (C) To explain why some of Rome's provinces occasionally rebelled

    (D) To note that it lasted for a relatively short time in history

4   *Directions*: Select the appropriate phrases from the answer choices and match them to the part of the Roman Empire to which they relate. TWO of the answer choices will NOT be used. *This question is worth 3 points*.

Answer Choices	**PART OF THE ROMAN EMPIRE**
① Had people who were used to Roman rule	**The Italian Peninsula Homeland**
② Gave citizenship to all of the people in the region	•
③ Had large numbers of legionaries in them	•
④ Comprised the most secure area	**The Senatorial Provinces**
⑤ Had been part of the empire for a long time	•
⑥ Included the region of Spain	•
⑦ Helped achieve the Pax Romana	•
⑧ Had the fewest troops in the empire	**The Imperial Provinces**
⑨ Were under the direct control of the emperor	•
	•

Reading Comprehension   Complete the following sentences. Use the words in the box.

a. known as legions	b. the Middle East	c. the danger level	d. the *Pax Romana*

1 The Roman Empire included land in Europe, ＿＿＿＿＿＿＿＿＿ , and North Africa.

2 ＿＿＿＿＿＿＿＿＿ of a region determined the number of soldiers stationed in it.

3 Roman soldiers were organized into groups that were ＿＿＿＿＿＿＿＿＿ .

4 ＿＿＿＿＿＿＿＿＿ was a period of peace when Rome had few internal problems.

Brazilian Independence

Portuguese explorers first landed in Brazil in 1500. They quickly made it a colony. They developed an economy based on sugar **plantations** and gold mines. To work in both places, the Portuguese imported slaves from Africa. By the 1800s, the descendants of those slaves had come to think of themselves as Brazilians. Yet Brazil was still a colony of Portugal. In the early 1800s, a series of events occurred. In the end, they led to Brazil gaining its independence.

In Europe in 1807, a French army of Napoleon's invaded Portugal. **1** The Portuguese royal family promptly fled to Brazil. **2** There, King John VI declared that Brazil and Portugal were a joint empire. **3** This made Brazil the equal of Portugal. **4** This pleased the Brazilians. A few years later, in 1815, Napoleon was defeated. In 1821, the king returned home. He left his son Dom Pedro behind to rule Brazil. A little later, the king announced that Brazil had returned to colony status. Many Brazilians were upset. They refused to accept that. So they **rebelled**.

³➡ Dom Pedro was ordered home. He refused and remained in Brazil. He became the leader of the rebellion. Brazilian rebels fought the Portuguese. The revolution lasted for almost four years. It was a difficult time. But the Brazilians received some vital aid from Thomas Cochrane. He was a former British naval officer. Cochrane had a small fleet of nine ships. They were enough to let the rebels emerge victorious. Despite losing, Portugal wanted to continue to fight. But the British pressured the king to end the war. In August 1825, the rebellion ended. Brazil, Portugal, and Britain signed a treaty. Brazil became a free country. And Dom Pedro was named the first emperor of Brazil.

• **Glossary** •

plantation: a large farm on which various cash crops are grown
rebel: to revolt; to fight against one's leaders

1 The word "vital" in the passage is closest in meaning to

    (A) critical   (B) individual

    (C) well-timed   (D) military

2 Which of the following can be inferred from paragraph 3 about Dom Pedro?

    (A) He never met anyone from his family after the rebellion.

    (B) He considered himself Brazilian instead of Portuguese.

    (C) He was well trained in how to lead military operations.

    (D) He reigned as the emperor of Brazil for more than a decade.

3 Look at the four squares [■] that indicate where the following sentence could be added to the passage.

The king was convinced that escaping was a better option than fighting.

Where would the sentence best fit?

4 *Directions*: An introductory sentence for a brief summary of the passage is provided below. Complete the summary by selecting the THREE answer choices that express the most important ideas of the passage. Some sentences do not belong because they express ideas that are not presented in the passage or are minor ideas in the passage. *This question is worth 2 points*.

Brazil remained a colony of Portugal until a rebellion led by Dom Pedro helped the country gain its independence.

-
-
-

Answer Choices

1️⃣ The Brazilians were aided by some foreigners in their rebellion.

2️⃣ When the revolution ended, Dom Pedro became the emperor of Brazil.

3️⃣ Dom Pedro was the son of the king of Portugal, John VI.

4️⃣ Many of the slaves that lived in Portugal were imported from Africa.

5️⃣ Brazil was a Portuguese colony for more than 300 years.

6️⃣ King John VI first went to Brazil to avoid Napoleon's armies.

✒ Reading Comprehension Complete the following sentences. Use the words in the box.

a. some naval forces	b. gold mines	c. fled the country	d. became the leader

1 The Portuguese established sugar plantations and ＿＿＿＿＿＿＿ in Brazil.

2 When one of Napoleon's armies invaded, the Portuguese king ＿＿＿＿＿＿＿ .

3 Dom Pedro ＿＿＿＿＿＿＿ of the rebelling Brazilian forces.

4 Thomas Cochrane provided ＿＿＿＿＿＿＿ to help the Brazilians.

Ancient Sumer

One of the world's first civilizations was founded in Sumer. It was located in an ancient land known as Mesopotamia. It arose between the Tigris and Euphrates rivers. Sumer lasted from around 5300 B.C. to 1700 B.C. During this time, its people built one of the great ancient civilizations.

The people of Sumer were among the first humans to **dwell** in permanent settlements. They stopped being hunter-gatherers. They did this because they had learned about agriculture. The Sumerians were able to farm the land. In fact, the Sumerians developed advanced farming methods, such as irrigation, which enabled them to grow enough food to last all year round. As a result, the Sumerian population grew. Over time, more settlements were built. These eventually became small city-states.

³➡ The Sumerians also had their own religion. They worshiped many gods from temples they built in their city-states. There was a priestly class that controlled all religious activities. But the Sumerians were led by kings, so they constructed palaces as well. Yet both the kings and priests needed support. This led to the formation of a **bureaucracy**. By around 3000 B.C., the Sumerians had their own writing system. This was cuneiform. It utilized wedge-shaped symbols. The Sumerians mainly used it to write down their history and to record trades for goods.

⁴➡ Over time, the Sumerian civilization began to decline. Historians believe that the changing climate may have caused this. The land in southern Sumer became salty. Farmers' crops then failed. People began to move north to seek better lands. Outsiders also invaded Sumerian lands around 1900 B.C. This further weakened them. By 1700 B.C., the Babylonians had become the rulers of Mesopotamia. The Sumerians disappeared, leaving nothing but their legacy.

• Glossary •

dwell: to live in
bureaucracy: a civil service; an administration

1 Which of the sentences below best expresses the essential information in the highlighted sentence in the passage? *Incorrect* answer choices change the meaning in important ways or leave out essential information.

- Ⓐ Sumerian farmers were able to grow their food during every season of the year.
- Ⓑ Thanks to irrigation methods, the Sumerians learned how to farm the land.
- Ⓒ Sumerian farmers learned how to grow enough food to support people all year long.
- Ⓓ Because they were able to farm the land, the Sumerians discovered irrigation methods.

2 According to paragraph 3, the Sumerians developed a bureaucracy because

- Ⓐ priests and kings competed against each other
- Ⓑ the ruling class needed to have support
- Ⓒ they needed to invent a writing system
- Ⓓ it helped them trade with other countries

3 In paragraph 3, the author implies that the Sumerians' religion

- Ⓐ was more powerful than the king
- Ⓑ was led by the king
- Ⓒ was important to them
- Ⓓ was not practiced by everyone

4 In paragraph 4, the author's description of the decline of Sumerian civilization mentions all of the following EXCEPT:

- Ⓐ why farmers' crops did not grow well
- Ⓑ what caused the civilization to become weaker
- Ⓒ when outsiders began to invade the region
- Ⓓ how cold temperatures caused problems

✎ Reading Comprehension Complete the following sentences. Use the words in the box.

a. the Sumerian bureaucracy	b. became city-states	c. the Babylonians	d. was founded

1 Sumerian civilization _____ sometime around 5300 B.C.

2 Many Sumerian cities grew in size until they _____.

3 _____ was created to support both kings and priests.

4 Around 1700 B.C., _____ took total control of Sumerian land.

British Colonists in the Americas

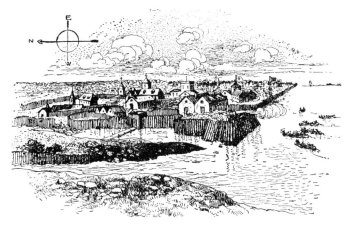

The appearance of Jamestown

¹➙ In 1607, Jamestown, Virginia, was founded. It was the first permanent British settlement in North America. For the next century and a half, the British established thirteen colonies in America. They were all located on the east coast next to the Atlantic Ocean. During this time, large numbers of people left Britain and sailed to the Americas. By 1776, roughly two and a half million people were living in the colonies. There were three main reasons why many people departed Britain to start new lives in America.

²➙ The first was religious freedom. There were numerous Christian **sects** in Britain in the 1600s and 1700s. The majority of people there belonged to the Anglican Church. But there were also many Catholics. And there were other, smaller, groups of Protestants. The 1600s was a time of religious persecution. People were killed for their religious beliefs. In 1618, the Thirty Years' War began in Europe. It was fought between Protestants and Catholics. Many people sought to escape the violence. The Pilgrims were one such group. In 1620, they fled to America on the *Mayflower*. They started a colony in Massachusetts. The Puritans were another group of Protestants with beliefs similar to those of the Pilgrims. **1** They fled to Massachusetts as well. **2** Later, William Penn founded Pennsylvania as a colony for Quakers, a sect of **pacifists**. **3** And Maryland began as a place for Catholics to live in safety. **4**

³➙ Another appeal of America was its great size. Because of this, there were opportunities for people to own land. Britain was an island nation that had been populated for centuries. In addition, the king and other nobles owned much of the land. But in America, land was free to anyone who settled it. This appealed to a large number of people. They eagerly sailed to America to claim land

for themselves. They built homes and farmed their land. And the crops and animals they raised belonged to them, not to the king or some other noble.

[4] Finally, in Britain, a person's status almost always depended upon his or her birth. People born into noble families often led lives of leisure and wealth. Yet those born to poor farmers or artisans could expect lives of hard work for little reward. At that time, most sons took on their fathers' professions. Laws and customs usually banned people from leaving their land or even changing jobs. But in the American colonies, there were no restrictions like those. People in America could become anything they wanted. A poor farmer in Britain could become a rich landowner in America. Thus the prospect of improving one's personal welfare appealed to many in Britain.

For these reasons, people came to America by the shipload. In search of new lives, they rapidly filled up the east coast. As more people came, they headed further inland and settled the rest of the country.

• **Glossary** •

sect: a group, often religious in nature, that has its own set of beliefs
pacifist: a person who believes in peace and refuses to fight

1   In paragraph 1, why does the author mention "Jamestown, Virginia"?

     Ⓐ To compare it with the Pilgrim colony in Massachusetts

     Ⓑ To show how it led to the success of the American colonies

     Ⓒ To depict it as the most successful of all British colonies

     Ⓓ To name the first permanent British settlement in America

2   The word "roughly" in the passage is closest in meaning to

     Ⓐ surely

     Ⓑ independently

     Ⓒ coincidentally

     Ⓓ approximately

3   According to paragraph 1, which of the following is true of the British colonies in North America?

     Ⓐ They were all founded in the 1600s.

     Ⓑ There were only a dozen of them.

     Ⓒ They were located next to water.

     Ⓓ They became free from Britain in 1776.

4   In paragraph 2, all of the following questions are answered EXCEPT:

     Ⓐ What types of people lived in Pennsylvania and Maryland?

     Ⓑ Why did many people leave Britain and sail to the Americas?

     Ⓒ Who was the winner of the Thirty Years' War when it ended?

     Ⓓ What was the name of the ship that the Pilgrims sailed on?

5   According to paragraph 3, many people left Britain for America because

     Ⓐ the British nobles had taken their land

     Ⓑ they felt oppressed by the king of Britain

     Ⓒ they disliked living in an island nation

     Ⓓ they wanted to possess their own land

6   In paragraph 3, the author of the passage implies that many people in Britain

     Ⓐ were unhappy with the distribution of land

     Ⓑ were members of the nobility

     Ⓒ thought Britain offered many opportunities

     Ⓓ did not enjoy farming

7 The word "prospect" in the passage is closest in meaning to

(A) hope

(B) guarantee

(C) occupation

(D) ability

8 According to paragraph 4, in Britain, people in noble families

(A) typically had access to a lot of money

(B) had to work hard to keep their positions

(C) were uninterested in becoming tradesmen

(D) had little contact with regular individuals

9 Look at the four squares [■] that indicate where the following sentence could be added to the passage.

However, people of other religious beliefs were also welcome there.

Where would the sentence best fit?

Click on a square [■] to add the sentence to the passage.

10 *Directions*: An introductory sentence for a brief summary of the passage is provided below. Complete the summary by selecting the THREE answer choices that express the most important ideas of the passage. Some sentences do not belong because they express ideas that are not presented in the passage or are minor ideas in the passage. *This question is worth 2 points*.

Drag your answer choices to the spaces where they belong.
To remove an answer choice, click on it. To review the passage, click on **View Text**.

Many people left Britain to settle in the American colonies for three primary reasons.

-
-
-

Answer Choices

1 People could improve their lives by moving to the American colonies.

2 Many Protestants left Europe and moved to various places in America.

3 The king and his nobles were the owners of most of the land in Britain.

4 There were chances for people to own land if they moved to America.

5 People had the freedom to practice their own religion in America.

6 The American people wanted to gain their freedom from British rule.

★ Star Performer Word Files

- **appeal** (v) to be attractive to
  Which field of history **appeals** the most to you?

- **artisan** (n) a skilled worker, such as a blacksmith or baker
  It takes years for an **artisan** to learn some skills.

- **border** (n) a line that separates one country from another
  There are soldiers on both sides of the **border**.

- **colony** (n) a land that is ruled by another country
  The people in the **colony** live far from their homeland.

- **construct** (v) to build; to make; to erect
  How long will it take to **construct** the temple?

- **conquer** (v) to defeat; to take over
  The general's soldiers **conquered** the enemy.

- **convert** (v) to change from one thing to another
  Many people in the New World **converted** to Christianity.

- **copy** (v) to imitate; to do the same thing as another person
  Do not **copy** me; try doing something original.

- **defeat** (v) to win against someone, often in a game or war
  We hope to **defeat** the other team this Saturday.

- **enemy** (n) a person who is opposed to another
  The **enemy** forces are planning to invade the country.

- **enormous** (adj) huge; very large
  He borrowed an **enormous** amount of money from the bank.

- **expand** (v) to increase in size; to become bigger
  The empire **expanded** by conquering more land.

- **flee** (v) to run away from; to escape from
  The prisoners **fled** from jail as they tried to escape.

- **fleet** (n) a group of ships
  There are more than twenty ships in that **fleet**.

- **freedom** (n) independence
  The people rebelled because they wanted more **freedom**.

- **hunter-gatherer** (n) a person who hunts animals and gathers food to eat
  All early humans were **hunter-gatherers** since they could not farm the land.

- **inland** (adj) relating to the interior of a place; away from the ocean or sea
  They will move to the **inland** part of the country.

- **influence** (v) to control; to have an effect on
  You cannot **influence** my decision about that matter.

- **invade** (v) to attack; to assault
  The enemy **invaded** but was defeated by the defenders.

- **irrigation** (n) a method of watering crops in fields
  Thanks to **irrigation**, it is possible to farm a lot of land.

- **legionary** (n) a soldier in the Roman Empire

  The **legionaries** patrolled the province and kept the peace.

- **maintain** (v) to keep

  Please **maintain** order despite the bad situation.

- **native** (n) a person born in a certain area

  The **natives** of this country have many unique traditions.

- **occupant** (n) a person who lives in a certain place

  That house across the street has four **occupants**.

- **peninsula** (n) a piece of land that has water on three sides

  Korea and Italy are both **peninsulas**.

- **perfect** (adj) ideal; having no faults or problems

  This paper is **perfect** and has absolutely no mistakes.

- **persecution** (n) mistreatment; punishment

  Persecution for their beliefs made the group leave the country.

- **rebel** (n) a person fighting in a revolution

  The government could not capture all of the **rebels**.

- **record** (v) to write down; to keep a record of

  Please **record** everything that I say at the meeting.

- **refuse** (v) to turn down; to reject

  You should not **refuse** this offer.

- **revolution** (n) a rebellion, often against a government

  The **revolution** lasted for almost ten years.

- **rule** (v) to manage or run a city, state, or country as the leader

  The king **rules** well because he listens to his people.

- **ruler** (n) a leader

  Who was the **ruler** of that country twenty years ago?

- **sect** (n) a division; a faction

  There are many **sects** that have their own religious beliefs.

- **station** (v) to position; to assign a person to work in a certain place

  Hundreds of soldiers were **stationed** at a fort on the border.

- **storm** (v) to attack; to assault

  The angry citizens **stormed** the government office.

- **treat** (v) to act in a certain way toward someone

  He always **treats** his sister very nicely.

- **troop** (n) a soldier

  How many **troops** are guarding the camp?

- **upset** (adj) angry; displeased; unhappy

  The workers were **upset** to hear the company was closing.

- **weaken** (v) to cause to lose strength; to make weak

  Joe's strength **weakened** as he got older.

❗ Choose the word or phrase closest in meaning to the highlighted part of the sentence.

1   Another appeal of America was its great size.
   Ⓐ attraction
   Ⓑ option
   Ⓒ decision
   Ⓓ feature

2   They often tried to learn the natives' languages and customs.
   Ⓐ ideas
   Ⓑ habits
   Ⓒ sayings
   Ⓓ appearances

3   This gave people many rights and privileges.
   Ⓐ wealth
   Ⓑ attempts
   Ⓒ votes
   Ⓓ advantages

4   This area was the most secure.
   Ⓐ safe
   Ⓑ responsible
   Ⓒ violent
   Ⓓ loud

5   The Sumerians disappeared, leaving nothing but their legacy.
   Ⓐ immigrated
   Ⓑ improved
   Ⓒ moved
   Ⓓ vanished

6   He became the leader of the rebellion.
   Ⓐ army
   Ⓑ revolution
   Ⓒ colony
   Ⓓ government

7   They eagerly sailed to America to claim land for themselves.
   Ⓐ swiftly
   Ⓑ willingly
   Ⓒ apparently
   Ⓓ slowly

8   There were three main reasons why many people departed Britain to start new lives in America.
   Ⓐ returned to
   Ⓑ considered
   Ⓒ left
   Ⓓ sought

9   They were enough to let the rebels emerge victorious.
   Ⓐ pleased
   Ⓑ stronger
   Ⓒ successful
   Ⓓ concerned

10 They built many extensive palaces in the St. Petersburg area.
   Ⓐ rich
   Ⓑ well-protected
   Ⓒ large
   Ⓓ expensive

11 This was particularly true of some families.
   Ⓐ rarely
   Ⓑ especially
   Ⓒ always
   Ⓓ somewhat

12 In addition, the king and other nobles owned much of the land.
   Ⓐ traded
   Ⓑ farmed
   Ⓒ rented
   Ⓓ possessed

Part B

Chapter 02 The Arts

The arts focus on creating works that are pleasing to the eye and ear. Some fields in the arts are visual art, music, literature, and architecture. Each of these fields has many genres within it. For instance, art includes painting, drawing, etching, sculpting, and photography. There are also countless genres of music in both instrumental and choral works. Many artists are creative individuals. Yet they often look to the past for inspiration from previous artists.

Mastering **the Question Types** A

☑ Vocabulary   ☐ Fill in a Table   ☐ Factual Information   ☐ Negative Factual Information   ☑ Prose Summary
☐ Insert Text   ☐ Reference   ☑ Rhetorical Purpose   ☐ Sentence Simplification   ☐ Inference

Stage Blocking

[1] → During a stage performance, the actors stand in certain places and move in certain ways. They plan all of their moves before the performance begins. This is called stage blocking. It is used for plays, operas, musicals, and ballets. It is an **integral** part of anything that is performed on a stage.

Usually, the director and the performers make the plan together. They decide where each person should stand or move. Stage blocking takes several factors into account. First, the **audience** should be able to see the actors' faces. Second, the audience needs to be able to hear the actors' voices. Third, the actors' positions must allow for the proper dramatic effect. For example, a performer's back should not be toward the audience. Doing that would make it difficult for the audience to hear the lines or to see the actor's facial expressions and gestures.

• **Glossary** •

integral: important; critical
audience: the people who watch a performance

1 In paragraph 1, why does the author mention "plays, operas, musicals, and ballets"?

    Ⓐ To explain that they all take place on a stage

    Ⓑ To stress that they are performances with audiences

    Ⓒ To note some performances that use stage blocking

    Ⓓ To describe the types of performances they are

2 The word "gestures" in the passage is closest in meaning to

    Ⓐ motions

    Ⓑ dialogue

    Ⓒ emotions

    Ⓓ acting

3 *Directions*: An introductory sentence for a brief summary of the passage is provided below. Complete the summary by selecting the THREE answer choices that express the most important ideas of the passage. Some sentences do not belong because they express ideas that are not presented in the passage or are minor ideas in the passage. ***This question is worth 2 points***.

Stage blocking is an important aspect of any stage performance.

-
-
-

Answer Choices

① Actors have been doing stage blocking for many centuries.

② Stage blocking determines where on stage the actors will stand.

③ Plays, musicals, operas, and ballets are all performed on stage.

④ All staged performances have both a director and performers.

⑤ The performers must let the audience see their facial expressions.

⑥ Being able to hear the actors' voices is one part of stage blocking.

✔ Checking Reading Accuracy **Mark the following statements T (true) or F (false).**

    T   **F**

1 ☐ / ☐ Stage blocking describes where the actors stand on stage.

2 ☐ / ☐ The director usually determines the stage blocking all alone.

3 ☐ / ☐ Seeing the actors' faces is important for the audience.

4 ☐ / ☐ A performer's back should not be toward the audience.

☐ Vocabulary   ☑ Fill in a Table   ☐ Factual Information   ☑ Negative Factual Information   ☐ Prose Summary
☐ Insert Text   ☐ Reference   ☐ Rhetorical Purpose   ☐ Sentence Simplification   ☑ Inference

Early Movie Projectors

Nowadays, people watch movies on DVD, the Internet, smartphones, and television. But the early days of movies were different. Then, films were shown on movie projectors. The first movie projectors were made in the 1890s. They were box-like **devices**. They showed a short **film strip**. It was usually less than a minute long. The viewer had to look through a lens to see the film.

²→ There were several problems with these machines. First, the films were very short. Second, they were small, so only one person could view the film strip at a time. Third, they often developed mechanical problems and broke down. To show films to more people, inventors created better projectors. These could show longer movies on bigger screens. That way, a larger paying audience could watch the films. This became the main way that people watched movies until the videocassette recorder was invented in the 1970s.

• **Glossary** •

device: a mechanical object or item
film strip: a piece of film that can be shown on a projector

1 Which of the following can be inferred from paragraph 2 about early movie projectors?

    (A) They were only used in the United States.

    (B) They could not show films to large audiences.

    (C) They were difficult to manufacture.

    (D) They utilized the most advanced technology.

2 According to paragraph 2, which of the following is NOT true of early movie projectors?

    (A) They let people watch movies on videotape.

    (B) They sometimes needed to be repaired.

    (C) They were first used in the 1890s.

    (D) They showed films that were very short.

3 *Directions*: Select the appropriate sentences from the answer choices and match them to the problem or solution to early movie projectors to which they relate. TWO of the answer choices will NOT be used. *This question is worth 3 points*.

Answer Choices	**EARLY MOVIE PROJECTORS**
① The projectors often broke down.	**Problem**
② People are able to watch movies on the Internet.	•
③ The videocassette recorder was invented in the 1970s.	•
④ Projectors became able to show movies on screens.	•
⑤ Only one person could watch a film at one time.	**Solution**
⑥ Better projectors were made by inventors.	•
⑦ The projectors could only show short films.	•

✐ **Checking Reading Accuracy** Mark the following statements T (true) or F (false).

    T   **F**

1 ☐ / ☐ The first films were shown on videotapes.

2 ☐ / ☐ Early film strips were often about ten minutes long.

3 ☐ / ☐ Early movie projectors frequently broke down.

4 ☐ / ☐ In the 1970s, the videocassette recorder was invented.

Mastering **the Question Types** C

☐ Vocabulary   ☐ Fill in a Table   ☑ Factual Information   ☐ Negative Factual Information   ☐ Prose Summary
☑ Insert Text   ☑ Reference   ☐ Rhetorical Purpose   ☑ Sentence Simplification   ☐ Inference

Ancient Egyptian Art

Ancient Egyptian society lasted for more than 3,000 years. The Egyptians were known for being impressive builders and also created a great amount of art. They mostly made paintings and statues. Many paintings decorated the **tombs** of pharaohs. Statues were put in tombs as well as in temples and other buildings.

For 3,000 years, Egyptian art changed little. Artists always preferred the colors black, red, green, gold, and blue. **1** They also painted figures in a similar manner. **2** For example, people's faces, waists, arms, and legs were painted in **profile**. **3** Yet the eyes and the shoulders were painted with a frontal view. **4**

³➡ Very much Egyptian art from the past has survived to the present day. This is due to the hot, dry climate in Egypt. Thanks to these works of art, experts today know much about ancient Egyptian culture. They know what Egyptians once looked like. They also know what clothes people wore then.

• **Glossary** •

tomb: a grave; a place in the ground where a person is buried
profile: the outline of a part of a body when viewed from the side

1 Which of the sentences below best expresses the essential information in the highlighted sentence in the passage? *Incorrect* answer choices change the meaning in important ways or leave out essential information.

- Ⓐ The greatest builders and artists in ancient times were the Egyptians.
- Ⓑ Most people know the Egyptians for the buildings and art they made.
- Ⓒ The Egyptians were great builders and made a lot of art.
- Ⓓ The art of the Egyptians was even better than their impressive buildings.

2 The word "They" in the passage refers to

- Ⓐ these works of art
- Ⓑ experts
- Ⓒ Egyptians
- Ⓓ clothes people wore

3 According to paragraph 3, there is a lot of ancient Egyptian art today because

- Ⓐ the Egyptians buried it in tombs
- Ⓑ the climate of Egypt preserved it
- Ⓒ the Egyptians used long-lasting paint
- Ⓓ the materials used were of high quality

4 Look at the four squares [■] that indicate where the following sentence could be added to the passage.

The resulting images from these two styles make Egyptian art easy even for casual observers to identify.

Where would the sentence best fit?

⫝ Checking Reading Accuracy Mark the following statements T (true) or F (false).

	T	F	
1	☐ / ☐		The ancient Egyptians had a culture that lasted for three millennium.
2	☐ / ☐		There were many changes in Egyptian art over the years.
3	☐ / ☐		The Egyptians painted people's entire bodies in profile.
4	☐ / ☐		People have learned about ancient Egypt thanks to its art.

Charles Ives

[1]→ Charles Ives was a great American **composer**. He wrote more than 100 pieces of music. Sadly, his work was largely unknown during his lifetime. Ives was born in 1874 and died in 1954. His father was a band leader and taught his son about music. Ives never made a living from his music. Instead, he entered the insurance business, which was quite profitable for him. In his spare time, he composed music at home. In the 1930s, he abruptly stopped writing music. He felt there was no more that he could do.

[2]→ Most of Ives's music was original. His sources were music he heard in churches and town squares that he combined with classical European styles. Ives used complex arrangements in his compositions. This made them difficult for musicians to play. That was one reason why he was fairly unknown during his life. Another reason is that he was never fully satisfied with his music. So he often changed the pieces. This has made it hard to date each of his musical works. Ives rarely performed in public. Nor did he like the radio or recorded music. He did, however, record some of his works before his death. This helped preserve his **legacy**.

In the last few years of his life, Ives started to gain popularity. Several famous conductors led orchestras that played his music at live concerts or on the radio. After he died, his fame increased even more. By the end of the 1900s, he was regarded as an original composer. His works have influenced a number of modern forms of music. Today, Charles Ives is recognized around the world as one of the greatest American composers.

• **Glossary** •

composer: a person who writes music
legacy: an inheritance; something handed down from one person to another

1 In paragraph 1, the author implies that Charles Ives

- (A) became a wealthy man
- (B) was happily married
- (C) could play no musical instruments
- (D) studied music at school

2 The word "them" in the passage refers to

- (A) churches
- (B) town squares
- (C) classical European styles
- (D) his compositions

3 According to paragraph 2, which of the following is NOT true about Charles Ives's musical compositions?

- (A) They could be hard to perform at times.
- (B) Some of his works of music were rewritten.
- (C) None was ever recorded by Charles Ives.
- (D) Some were influenced by European music.

4 *Directions*: An introductory sentence for a brief summary of the passage is provided below. Complete the summary by selecting the THREE answer choices that express the most important ideas of the passage. Some sentences do not belong because they express ideas that are not presented in the passage or are minor ideas in the passage. *This question is worth 2 points*.

Charles Ives was an original American composer who was mostly unknown during his life.

- •
- •
- •

Answer Choices

1. Ives seldom performed his own music, so few people knew about him.
2. Ives's father taught him how to compose pieces of music.
3. Nowadays, many people are aware of the music that Ives composed.
4. During his life, Ives wrote more than 100 works of music.
5. Ives used church music and European styles to create his own music.
6. Ives's music was difficult to play, which made him less popular with musicians.

Reading Comprehension Complete the following sentences. Use the words in the box.

a. complex arrangements	b. became more popular	c. in his spare time	d. changed his music

1 Charles Ives was not a professional but wrote music _____ .

2 Ives used _____ that were sometimes hard to play.

3 Ives often _____ because he was never fully pleased with it.

4 After he died, more people learned about Ives, so he _____ .

Portraits

A portrait is a work of art that shows a person's face, head, and upper body. In the past, the rich and famous often had their portraits painted. People would commission artists to paint their pictures. Another type of portrait is the self-portrait. This involves artists painting pictures of themselves. Artists have used different methods to make portraits as art styles change. Before photography, portraits were the only way to capture people's images.

²→ A portrait almost always shows its subject in a flattering way. The artist attempts to create an exact likeness of the person. Most painted portraits show the person with a **neutral** expression. So the person does not often smile. In some cases though, an individual may have a slight smile. The *Mona Lisa*, Leonardo da Vinci's masterpiece, is one such painting. Most portraits show a person from a slight side view rather than a full, frontal view. The portrait may be of the head, the head and the shoulders, or the entire upper body. Some portraits show the person sitting or standing in a dramatic pose, but that is **atypical**.

The painting of portraits began in ancient times. They were made of dead people for their funerals. Few of these portraits have survived to the present day. During the Renaissance, portrait painting became more common. Then, artists tried to perfect the human image in the portraits they made. Centuries later, the camera led to a new style of portraits. Despite the fact that cameras were new technology, taking a photograph was cheaper than hiring an artist to paint a person's portrait. So the subjects of many photographs in the 1800s looked like they were sitting to have their portraits made. Today, painted portraits are still done. But photographic portraits are far more usual.

• Glossary •
neutral: indefinite
atypical: unusual; not normal

1 The word "flattering" in the passage is closest in meaning to

(A) individual

(B) accurate

(C) random

(D) pleasing

2 In paragraph 2, the author uses "The *Mona Lisa*" as an example of

(A) a great work by Leonardo da Vinci

(B) the most famous portrait in the world

(C) a picture showing someone from the front

(D) a portrait in which the person is smiling

3 Which of the sentences below best expresses the essential information in the highlighted sentence in the passage? *Incorrect* answer choices change the meaning in important ways or leave out essential information.

(A) While cameras were new, having a portrait painted still cost more than taking a picture.

(B) Since cameras were brand new, they were cheaper to use, so people stopped hiring artists.

(C) Because people did not hire artists, new camera technology made it cheap to take pictures.

(D) Although cameras were new, it still cost less to paint a portrait than to take a picture.

4 *Directions*: Select the appropriate phrases from the answer choices and match them to the feature of portraits to which they relate. TWO of the answer choices will NOT be used. *This question is worth 3 points*.

Answer Choices	PORTRAITS
1 May be taken by a photographer	**How They Look**
2 Show the head, the face, and the upper body of a person	•
	•
3 Were made for funerals after people died	•
4 Can become very famous, such as the *Mona Lisa*	**How They Are Made**
5 Can be painted by an artist	•
6 May be a picture of the actual artist	•
7 Often show a person with a neutral expression	

Reading Comprehension Complete the following sentences. Use the words in the box.

a. the Renaissance	b. a neutral expression	c. a self-portrait	d. is smiling

1 _____ is a painting that an artist makes of himself.

2 The person in a portrait often has _____ on his face.

3 The *Mona Lisa* is an example of a portrait in which the person _____ .

4 Portrait painting became common during _____ .

Mastering **the Subject** C

Neoclassical Art

¹→ Neoclassical Art was common from the middle of the 1700s to the early 1800s. It was based on the artistic ideas of ancient Greece and Rome. The Neoclassical style was used for paintings, sculptures, architecture, dramatic performances, and music. It became popular during the 1740s. This was when the ancient Roman towns of Pompeii and Herculaneum were discovered. In the first century A.D., an eruption of the volcano Mt. Vesuvius buried both towns under a layer of ash. When the towns were <u>unearthed</u>, they were mostly intact. This included their paintings, sculptures, and architecture. Images of them rapidly spread across Europe. This led to the creation of Neoclassical Art.

²→ It also arose as a reaction to Rococo and Baroque Art. Both were seen as too <u>elaborate</u>. Neoclassical artists tried to be more "pure" in form. They believed they were expressing the purity of Rome. At that time, people thought the Romans had been heroic, stoic, and self-sacrificing. The Romans had thought that the empire was more important than the individual. Neoclassical artists therefore tried to paint people and events in heroic ways.

³→ The movement began in England and France. It reached its height from 1790 to 1815. This was the time of the French Revolution and the Napoleonic Wars. One of the greatest artists of the period was Jacque-Louis David. His works always featured heroic subjects. His most famous painting is *Napoleon Bonaparte Crossing the Alps*. It shows Napoleon seated on a white horse. He also painted many scenes from Greek and Roman history. Those works, such as *The Death of Socrates*, show the value of self-sacrifice and loyalty. **1** Neoclassical Art lasted through the late 1800s. **2** The more lavish Romanticism became more influential than it though. **3** Romanticism, ironically, began as a reaction against the simple, pure style of Neoclassical Art. **4**

• **Glossary** •

unearth: to dig up from underground, often on purpose
elaborate: ornate; fancy; complex

1 According to paragraph 1, Neoclassical Art gained popularity because

    (A) the volcano Mt. Vesuvius erupted in Italy

    (B) people all over Europe began to study art

    (C) two ancient Roman towns were discovered

    (D) Greece and Rome became more powerful

2 The author discusses "Rococo and Baroque Art" in paragraph 2 in order to

    (A) explain why Neoclassical Art began

    (B) describe the style of art that they used

    (C) mention when they were popular styles

    (D) discuss the influence of Rome on them

3 In paragraph 3, the author's description of Jacque-Louis David mentions which of the following?

    (A) His position working for Napoleon

    (B) His fame as a Neoclassical artist

    (C) His founding of Neoclassical Art

    (D) The skills that he learned in Rome

4 Look at the four squares [■] that indicate where the following sentence could be added to the passage.

But it steadily lost influence all throughout the century.

Where would the sentence best fit?

✎ Reading Comprehension   Complete the following sentences. Use the words in the box.

a. Rococo and Baroque	b. Jacque-Louis David	c. by the ideas	d. Neoclassical artists

1 Neoclassical Art was influenced _____ of ancient Greece and Rome.

2 _____ were the two styles that came before Neoclassical Art.

3 _____ thought highly of Rome and the people who lived in it.

4 One of the greatest of all Neoclassical artists was _____ .

The Influence of Humanism on Art and Music

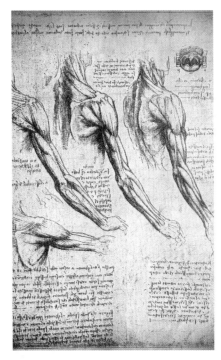

An anatomical drawing made by Leonardo da Vinci (1492)

1➜ Humanism is an intellectual movement that began in Italy in the 1300s. Its central idea was that God made the universe but that people had to develop and maintain it. To do this, they required a better understanding of the world. They believed that the study of history, grammar, poetry, philosophy, and rhetoric was necessary. Humanists looked to the ancient world of Greece and Rome for their ideas. They thought that these societies represented the peak of human achievements. Over time, humanism spread throughout Europe. It had a great impact on people. One of its biggest effects was making Europe a more **secular** land.

2➜ After the fall of Rome in the fifth century, the Middle Ages began. Many aspects of life in Europe declined. These included art and music. During the Middle Ages, artists and musicians were seen as merely workers. They worked for the Church and rich nobles. Artists created art for churches while musicians made music for church services. A few rich nobles also paid some artists and musicians to work for them. But humanism changed the situation for artists and musicians. Humanist ideas helped initiate the Renaissance in the fourteenth century. During that period, the Church became less important. Instead, people began to focus more on secular interests.

³→ The Renaissance was a crucial time for artists. **1** They rediscovered old ways of painting. **2** They developed more depth in their works. **3** They also learned how to draw people that were <u>anatomically</u> correct. **4** These improvements came about due to their study of ancient Greek and Roman art forms. Artists such as Leonardo da Vinci, Michelangelo, Raphael, and Botticelli were among this new school of artists. They created a new form of art that continues to be admired to this day.

⁴→ Renaissance artists were also helped by humanism. Some humanist ideas led to the growth of the merchant class. Previously, the Church had taught that making money was not always a good thing. But the humanists disagreed. They considered making money to be a positive feature. So during the Renaissance, many merchants became wealthy. Some of them were interested in acquiring works of art for themselves. They hired struggling artists. This gave many artists a guaranteed source of income. The artists were then able to focus more on developing their work. This improved the overall quality of their art.

⁵→ Music, on the other hand, was not influenced by humanism as quickly as was art. Through the Renaissance, most music was still made for the Church. This trend continued even after that period came to an end. But in the 1600s and 1700s, music slowly became more secular. There were many popular composers during this time. Johann Sebastian Bach was one of them. Bach wrote many religious pieces. Yet much of his music was of a secular nature. The same was true of many other famous composers of this period.

• **Glossary** •

secular: worldly in nature; not related to the church
anatomically: pertaining to the human body

1 According to paragraph 1, which of the following is true of humanism?

- (A) It was a movement that was religious in nature.
- (B) It started in ancient Greece and Rome.
- (C) It made people try to understand the world more.
- (D) It took place only in fourteenth-century Italy.

2 The word "initiate" in the passage is closest in meaning to

- (A) dominate
- (B) start
- (C) influence
- (D) change

3 Which of the following can be inferred from paragraph 2 about artists in the Middle Ages?

- (A) Their status was low.
- (B) They were religious.
- (C) They had advanced skills.
- (D) There were large numbers of them.

4 According to paragraph 2, which of the following is NOT true of the Middle Ages?

- (A) They took place before the Renaissance.
- (B) Many artists worked for the Church during that time.
- (C) Art and music experienced a renewal during them.
- (D) That period started after the fall of Rome.

5 According to paragraph 3, which of the following is true of the Renaissance?

- (A) Artists began to paint humans for the first time.
- (B) A lot of artists started going to schools to learn to paint.
- (C) Most art imitated paintings from ancient Greece and Rome.
- (D) Artists learned about painting methods from the past.

6 According to paragraph 4, humanism helped Renaissance artists because

- (A) artists could paint all types of paintings then
- (B) newly wealthy merchants hired many artists
- (C) it helped them sell their paintings for more money
- (D) the Church began to employ more of them

7 In paragraph 5, the author uses "Johann Sebastian Bach" as an example of

    Ⓐ a musician who lived during the Renaissance

    Ⓑ a popular composer after the Renaissance

    Ⓒ the first composer to write secular music

    Ⓓ the most famous composer of the Renaissance

8 According to paragraph 5, humanism affected music less than art during the Renaissance because

    Ⓐ most music was made for the Church

    Ⓑ few people were interested in music

    Ⓒ there were not many talented composers

    Ⓓ many musical instruments had not been invented yet

9 Look at the four squares [■] that indicate where the following sentence could be added to the passage.

The ability to do this made their works look more three dimensional.

Where would the sentence best fit?

> Click on a square [■] to add the sentence to the passage.

10 *Directions*: An introductory sentence for a brief summary of the passage is provided below. Complete the summary by selecting the THREE answer choices that express the most important ideas of the passage. Some sentences do not belong because they express ideas that are not presented in the passage or are minor ideas in the passage. *This question is worth 2 points.*

> Drag your answer choices to the spaces where they belong.
> To remove an answer choice, click on it. To review the passage, click on **View Text**.

Humanism during and after the Renaissance made Europe more secular, which influenced both art and music.

-
-
-

Answer Choices

① In the Middle Ages, almost all artists and musicians worked for the Church.

② Humanists studied many different fields in order to understand the world better.

③ Music became more secular in the 1600s and 1700s thanks to many popular composers.

④ Renaissance artists learned many new techniques by studying art from the past.

⑤ Some artists had steady incomes because wealthy merchants hired them to paint.

⑥ Johann Sebastian Bach was a composer who made both religious and secular music.

★ **Star Performer** Word Files

- **abruptly** (adv) suddenly

  He **abruptly** stood up and left the room.

- **admire** (v) to like very much

  Many people **admire** the work of Monet.

- **ballet** (n) a stage performance in which the performers dance to music

  They will see a **ballet** this Friday night.

- **break down** (v) to stop working

  Jane's car seems to **break down** a lot these days.

- **commission** (v) to hire a person to do a certain task

  Mary **commissioned** the artist to make a painting for her.

- **complex** (adj) complicated

  This is a **complex** system that is difficult to understand.

- **composition** (n) something that has been made, such as a piece of music

  He wrote that **composition** in only two hours.

- **date** (v) to determine when something was made or existed

  Experts **date** that work of art back to the Renaissance.

- **decorate** (v) to furnish something with ornaments to make it look better

  They will **decorate** the Christmas tree with many ornaments.

- **director** (n) a person who manages an artistic performance

  The **director** will show the actors what to do.

- **expression** (n) a look upon an individual's face

  Tim had a surprised **expression** on his face.

- **facial** (adj) relating to the face

  The comedian's **facial** expressions are always funny.

- **factor** (n) a feature; an aspect

  There are several **factors** that you need to know about.

- **fame** (n) renown; popularity

  Sue's **fame** grew because of her role in the movie.

- **funeral** (n) a ceremony held in honor of a dead person

  Hundreds of people attended the mayor's **funeral**.

- **heroic** (adj) brave; like a hero

  The firefighter behaved in a **heroic** manner.

- **intact** (adj) in one piece

  Even though Dave dropped the vase, it remained **intact**.

- **intellectual** (adj) academic; relating to the mind

  He likes to make **intellectual** arguments with his friends.

- **lens** (n) a glasslike object that can make small objects appear larger or more clearly

  The **lens** in the telescope is very powerful.

- **likeness** (n) an image; a replica

  The painter created an exact **likeness** of Nancy.

- **masterpiece** (n) a great creative work

  Sam's **masterpiece** took four years to complete.

- **musical** (n) a performance which includes singing and dancing as part of the story

  The actors in the **musical** put on a wonderful show.

- **opera** (n) a stage performance in which the performers often sing

  Mozart wrote a few very famous **operas**.

- **orchestra** (n) a group of musicians that play together

  The **orchestra** will perform this Saturday night.

- **original** (adj) creative

  She has many **original** ideas, so her stories are fun to read.

- **performer** (n) an actor or actress

  Some **performers** earn millions of dollars for each movie.

- **pharaoh** (n) a king of ancient Egypt

  Tutankhamen is one of the most famous **pharaohs** of ancient Egypt.

- **preserve** (v) to save

  We must **preserve** the works of writers from the past.

- **profitable** (adj) beneficial; gainful; money-making

  Some movies are **profitable** while others lose money.

- **proper** (adj) correct; right

  What is the **proper** way to pronounce this word?

- **regard** (v) to consider; to believe to be true

  People **regard** Peter as one of the best musicians in the city.

- **slight** (adj) minor; small

  You need to make a **slight** change in your acting style.

- **stage** (n) a raised platform upon which actors may perform

  There are several props on the **stage** right now.

- **statue** (n) a three-dimensional work of art often made of stone, wood, or metal

  This museum has many famous **statues**.

- **subject** (n) a focal point

  Who is the **subject** of that painting?

- **survive** (v) to remain in existence or use

  Many stories from ancient times have **survived** until now.

- **temple** (n) a building in which a god or gods are worshiped

  The priests in the **temple** prayed to their gods.

- **unknown** (adj) anonymous; unheard of

  Although Lisa is an **unknown** artist, she makes wonderful ceramics.

- **view** (v) to look at; to see; to observe

  I am going to the museum to **view** the exhibits.

- **waist** (n) the part of the body between the hips and the torso

  He lost weight, so now his **waist** is much smaller.

Vocabulary **Review**

❗ Choose the word or phrase closest in meaning to the highlighted part of the sentence.

1   Instead, people began to focus more on secular interests.
   Ⓐ resemble
   Ⓑ concentrate
   Ⓒ listen
   Ⓓ ignore

2   Some humanist ideas led to the growth of the merchant class.
   Ⓐ traveler
   Ⓑ trader
   Ⓒ manufacturer
   Ⓓ interpreter

3   To show films to more people, inventors created better projectors.
   Ⓐ producers
   Ⓑ manufacturers
   Ⓒ employers
   Ⓓ originators

4   Previously, the Church had taught that making money was not always a good thing.
   Ⓐ Before
   Ⓑ After
   Ⓒ Since
   Ⓓ Somewhat

5   The Egyptians were known for being impressive builders and also created a great amount of art.
   Ⓐ advanced
   Ⓑ stylish
   Ⓒ remarkable
   Ⓓ creative

6   Another reason is that he was never fully satisfied with his music.
   Ⓐ completely
   Ⓑ eventually
   Ⓒ gradually
   Ⓓ finally

7   Before photography, portraits were the only way to capture people's images.
   Ⓐ pictures
   Ⓑ thoughts
   Ⓒ writings
   Ⓓ expressions

8   Some portraits show the person sitting or standing in a dramatic pose, but that is atypical.
   Ⓐ playful
   Ⓑ staged
   Ⓒ thoughtful
   Ⓓ silly

9   They thought that these societies represented the peak of human achievements.
   Ⓐ appearance
   Ⓑ virtue
   Ⓒ growth
   Ⓓ height

10   Images of them rapidly spread across Europe.
   Ⓐ carefully
   Ⓑ faithfully
   Ⓒ swiftly
   Ⓓ ultimately

11   In his spare time, he composed music at home.
   Ⓐ free
   Ⓑ relaxed
   Ⓒ work
   Ⓓ previous

12   It also arose as a reaction to Rococo and Baroque Art.
   Ⓐ failed
   Ⓑ considered
   Ⓒ began
   Ⓓ avoided

Part B

Chapter 03   Archaeology and Anthropology

Archaeology and anthropology involve the study of prehistoric and ancient humans. Archaeologists research ruins, artifacts, and written texts from past civilizations. Anthropologists study how humans have developed over time. They examine human beliefs, cultures, and social and physical development. Both fields involve extensive research and fieldwork. But the lack of written records makes studying these fields somewhat difficult.

☐ Vocabulary   ☐ Fill in a Table   ☐ Factual Information   ☐ Negative Factual Information   ☑ Prose Summary
☐ Insert Text   ☐ Reference   ☑ Rhetorical Purpose   ☐ Sentence Simplification   ☐ Inference

Bronze Age Tools and Weapons

For most of human history, people made tools and weapons from stone. This period of time was the Stone Age. Gradually, humans learned how to make metal tools and weapons. One of the first metals people worked with was bronze, an **alloy** of copper and tin. When people started using it, their civilization entered the Bronze Age.

²→ Cultures began the Bronze Age at different times. The oldest bronze tools discovered date to 3800 B.C. They were found in Iran. Many societies entered the Bronze Age around 3000 B.C. It generally lasted until around 1200 to 1000 B.C. During this **era**, bronze arrowheads, swords, spear points, and armor were common. Bronze tools included axes and knives.

Bronze had many advantages over stone and metals such as copper. It was stronger and lasted longer. It was easier to shape than stone. And bronze objects sharpened more easily than copper.

• **Glossary** •

alloy: a substance that is created by the combination of two or more metals
era: a unique period of time in history

1 In paragraph 2, why does the author mention "Iran"?

   Ⓐ To note that it entered the Bronze Age very late

   Ⓑ To state where some old bronze tools were found

   Ⓒ To claim that it had an advanced early society

   Ⓓ To argue that bronze was first created there

2 The word "shape" in the passage is closest in meaning to

   Ⓐ repair

   Ⓑ melt

   Ⓒ form

   Ⓓ combine

3 ***Directions***: An introductory sentence for a brief summary of the passage is provided below. Complete the summary by selecting the THREE answer choices that express the most important ideas of the passage. Some sentences do not belong because they express ideas that are not presented in the passage or are minor ideas in the passage. ***This question is worth 2 points***.

During the Bronze Age, humans learned how to make tools and weapons from bronze.

-
-
-

Answer Choices

① The Stone Age was the period that came prior to the Bronze Age.

② Bronze was more useful than stone and copper for several reasons.

③ The Bronze Age ended in many places around 1000 B.C.

④ The Bronze Age began in some societies only a few centuries ago.

⑤ The majority of societies entered the Bronze Age around 3000 B.C.

⑥ Bronze can be made from a combination of copper and tin.

Checking Reading Accuracy   Mark the following statements T (true) or F (false).

	T	F	
1	☐	/ ☐	People started to use metal tools during the Stone Age.
2	☐	/ ☐	The Bronze Age began at the same time in all societies.
3	☐	/ ☐	During the Bronze Age, people made bronze axes and knives.
4	☐	/ ☐	Bronze is stronger than copper and also lasts longer.

Ancient Rituals

A ritual is a ceremony that serves a special purpose. The people who conduct rituals follow specific <u>procedures</u>. Humans have practiced them since ancient times.

People had rituals for a number of reasons. Some were for worshiping gods. For instance, many tribes sacrificed animals to their gods. Sheep and oxen were some animals that were commonly used. Others, such as the Aztecs, a Central American tribe, performed human sacrifices.

³→ A large number of rituals related to farming. In spring, many societies held ceremonies that were done to ensure good farming conditions. Some were meant to make the soil fertile. Others were done to bring rain. In fall, farmers thought that some rituals would make their harvests <u>bountiful</u>.

⁴→ Ancient people had rituals for other events as well. These included marriages, births, and funerals. Warrior cultures also often held rituals both before and after the battles they fought.

• **Glossary** •

procedure: a method for doing something; a process
bountiful: abundant; plentiful

1   In paragraph 3, the author implies that many farmers

(A) failed to conduct the proper rituals

(B) blamed bad harvests on the lack of rituals

(C) believed that their rituals were effective

(D) performed the same rituals in both spring and fall

2   In paragraphs 3 and 4, the author's description of rituals mentions all of the following EXCEPT:

(A) what events they were held for

(B) how they were related to battles

(C) where they were often held

(D) why people sometimes held them

3   *Directions*: Select the appropriate phrases from the answer choices and match them to the type of ritual to which they relate. TWO of the answer choices will NOT be used. ***This question is worth 3 points.***

Answer Choices	TYPE OF RITUAL
① Involved sacrificing animals	**Worshiping Gods**
② Were conducted for marriages	•
③ Were performed to bring rain	•
④ Happened after battles ended	**Farming**
⑤ Were done by the Aztecs	•
⑥ Were meant to make the soil good	•
⑦ Took place during spring	•

🖋 **Checking Reading Accuracy**   Mark the following statements T (true) or F (false).

	T	**F**	
1	☐	/ ☐	Ancient people had rituals for many occasions.
2	☐	/ ☐	The Aztecs only conducted sacrifices of sheep and oxen.
3	☐	/ ☐	Farmers held rituals in fall to give them good harvests.
4	☐	/ ☐	Some cultures held rituals before battles began.

Mastering **the Question Types** C

☐ Vocabulary   ☐ Fill in a Table   ☑ Factual Information   ☐ Negative Factual Information   ☐ Prose Summary

☑ Insert Text   ☑ Reference   ☐ Rhetorical Purpose   ☑ Sentence Simplification   ☐ Inference

L'anse aux Meadows

¹➙ It was long believed that the Vikings had visited North America centuries before the Europeans sailed there in the 1490s. Yet nobody was able to prove it. Finally, in the 1960s, a Viking site was discovered. It was in Newfoundland, Canada. The name of the place was L'anse aux Meadows.

The **excavations** of the site revealed several buildings. Among them were traditional Viking **longhouses** and a workshop. Hundreds of artifacts were dug up, too. Some of them were nails, a loom, and a forge. The artifacts were made of iron, bone, stone, and bronze. They had a variety of uses. Based upon the artifacts they found, archaeologists believe that both men and women lived in the settlement.

❶ It has also been determined that the Vikings arrived there between the years 990 and 1050 A.D. ❷ They stayed for no more than ten years. ❸ It is believed that they were driven out by the natives. ❹

• **Glossary** •

excavation: an area such as an archaeological site that is being dug up

longhouse: a long, narrow building in which many people lived

1 According to paragraph 1, L'anse aux Meadows proved that

Ⓐ the Vikings reached Canada in the 1490s

Ⓑ the Vikings had a successful colony in Canada

Ⓒ the Europeans sailed to North America first

Ⓓ the Vikings had reached North America

2 The word "Some" in the passage refers to

Ⓐ The excavations

Ⓑ Several buildings

Ⓒ Traditional Viking longhouses and a workshop

Ⓓ Artifacts

3 Which of the sentences below best expresses the essential information in the highlighted sentence in the passage? *Incorrect* answer choices change the meaning in important ways or leave out essential information.

Ⓐ There were all kinds of artifacts that have been found by archaeologists.

Ⓑ The items found make experts believe men and women lived in the colony.

Ⓒ Some of the artifacts found were used by men while others were owned by women.

Ⓓ The settlement was known to have both men and women living in it.

4 Look at the four squares [■] that indicate where the following sentence could be added to the passage.

In fact, they may have only been there for as few as three years.

Where would the sentence best fit?

🖉 Checking Reading Accuracy **Mark the following statements T (true) or F (false).**

    T   **F**

1 ☐ / ☐   Nobody used to believe the Vikings reached North America before the 1490s.

2 ☐ / ☐   L'anse aux Meadows is located in Newfoundland, Canada.

3 ☐ / ☐   All of the buildings found at L'anse aue Meadows were Viking longhouses.

4 ☐ / ☐   The Vikings probably left the settlement because they were attacked by natives.

The Wheel

One of the most important inventions in history is the wheel. It was first made more than 5,000 years ago. Since then, people have used it for myriad reasons. Mostly, they have installed it in various machines. This has made both work and transportation easier for people over the centuries.

²➡ No one knows exactly which culture had the wheel first. The earliest proof of its existence comes from the Mesopotamian city of Ur. A tablet with a picture of a **potter's wheel** was found in its ruins. The tablet has been dated to around 3500 B.C. However, it seems that the wheel appeared in several cultures almost simultaneously. The majority were in the Near East and the Mediterranean region.

³➡ After it was created, the wheel was mostly utilized for two purposes. First, people used it to make pottery. The potter's wheel enabled **artisans** to make better ceramics. It let potters shape clay more easily. Thus, they produced a better quality of pottery. Even today, people who make ceramics use the potter's wheel.

The next major purpose of the wheel was for transportation. In ancient times, it was attached to both two- and four-wheeled vehicles. Most of these were simple carts. They were pulled by animals such as horses, mules, and oxen. Later, the chariot was invented. Then, the wheel became a valuable tool of war.

Despite having the wheel, many cultures avoided using it for transportation. The main reason was a lack of smooth surfaces. Ancient roads were typically poorly made. So most people walked or rode on animals. Animals could move smoothly over rough terrain. But wheeled vehicles could not. This made using carts impractical. It was not until Roman times that roads improved. From then on, wheeled vehicles became much more common.

• **Glossary** •

potter's wheel: a tool with a rotating disc that potters use to shape clay
artisan: a skilled worker

1 According to paragraph 2, which of the following is true of the wheel?

    Ⓐ It was definitely first used in Ur.

    Ⓑ Some think it was invented in Africa.

    Ⓒ It had been invented by 3500 B.C.

    Ⓓ The first wheel was made of stone.

2 In paragraph 3, why does the author mention "ceramics"?

    Ⓐ To indicate when ceramics were first made

    Ⓑ To point out the first culture to start making it

    Ⓒ To state an advantage of the potter's wheel

    Ⓓ To describe how it looked in ancient times

3 The word "terrain" in the passage is closest in meaning to

    Ⓐ nation   Ⓑ mountains

    Ⓒ streets   Ⓓ land

4 *Directions*: An introductory sentence for a brief summary of the passage is provided below. Complete the summary by selecting the THREE answer choices that express the most important ideas of the passage. Some sentences do not belong because they express ideas that are not presented in the passage or are minor ideas in the passage. *This question is worth 2 points.*

After inventing the wheel, people mostly used it for making pottery and for transportation.

<table>
<tr><td>•

•

• </td></tr>
</table>

Answer Choices

1 Early wheels were attached to carts with two and four wheels.

2 People rode on animals or walked before the wheel was invented.

3 When roads improved, people used the wheel more often.

4 An ancient picture of the wheel was found in the ruins of Ur.

5 The potter's wheel made the quality of pottery get better.

6 Artisans in the present use the potter's wheel to make ceramics.

Reading Comprehension Complete the following sentences. Use the words in the box.

a. work and transportation	b. the chariot	c. smooth surfaces	d. a tablet

1 Thanks to the wheel, _____ became easier for people.

2 _____ with a picture of a potter's wheel proved the wheel was known in 3500 B.C.

3 The wheel was used in war when _____ was invented.

4 The lack of _____ made using wheeled vehicles difficult.

Why Primitive Tribes Disappear

During the course of history, many tribes of primitive people have disappeared. On occasion, they left evidence of why they died out. Yet most of the time, they just vanished. There are three primary reasons why these tribes died. They are disease, defeat in war, and natural disasters.

2→ Diseases have killed countless people around the world. One of the most tragic incidents took place in the New World. In the 1500s, European explorers started to visit the Americas. But many Europeans carried deadly diseases with them. The Native Americans had no **natural immunity** to these illnesses. This made them get sick easily. As a result, some diseases infected millions of people. Most of them died. Entire tribes of people were sometimes wiped out.

Humans have long fought wars against one another. In many cases, when one group of people fought another, the winner simply killed all of the members of the losing tribe. But other groups acted in a different way. Some Native American tribes tried to capture the losers. The winners forced these captives to join their own tribes. So the losing tribes ceased to exist as unique cultures.

4→ Famines, droughts, earthquakes, volcanic eruptions, and tsunamis are all natural disasters. In modern times, they can kill large numbers of people. In ancient times, they were able to destroy some cultures. The Anasazi, a tribe in North America, may have died from a famine. It took place due to a long-lasting drought. In ancient Crete, the Minoan civilization may have ended when a tsunami hit it. The huge wave could have been caused by an erupting volcano. Other civilizations suffered similar fates. Most of the time, there were no written records of them. So those cultures vanished forever.

• **Glossary** •

natural immunity: the ability to resist disease or illness
famine: a time when there is little or no food available

1 The author discusses "European explorers" in paragraph 2 in order to

    Ⓐ explain why many Native Americans died of diseases

    Ⓑ claim that they intentionally killed the Native Americans

    Ⓒ criticize them for using too much violence

    Ⓓ give the date when they first arrived in the New World

2 Which of the sentences below best expresses the essential information in the highlighted sentence in the passage? *Incorrect* answer choices change the meaning in important ways or leave out essential information.

    Ⓐ There were often great battles between the winners and losers.

    Ⓑ It was hard for one tribe to kill all of the others in battle.

    Ⓒ By winning a battle, a tribe gained the right to kill the losers.

    Ⓓ The winners in battles usually killed all of the losers.

3 Which of the following can be inferred from paragraph 4 about Minoan civilization?

    Ⓐ It was advanced for its time.

    Ⓑ It was found in North America.

    Ⓒ It was located near the sea.

    Ⓓ It was based on a farming culture.

4 *Directions*: Select the appropriate sentences from the answer choices and match them to the reason why tribes disappeared to which they relate. TWO of the answer choices will NOT be used. *This question is worth 3 points*.

Answer Choices	REASON FOR DISAPPEARING
① It caused the Anasazi to die out.	**Disease**
② An earthquake could destroy a culture.	•
③ The Europeans killed many people thanks to this.	•
④ It killed entire tribes in North America.	**Natural Disaster**
⑤ The Minoans were wiped out by this.	•
⑥ Tribes battled one another and killed the losers.	•
⑦ Some tribes were forced to join others.	•

⌖ Reading Comprehension Complete the following sentences. Use the words in the box.

a. Native Americans	b. the New World	c. volcanoes and earthquakes	d. forced to join

1 European explorers brought diseases with them to _____ .

2 Millions of _____ died since they were not immune to diseases.

3 Sometimes, losing tribe members were _____ the winning tribe.

4 _____ sometimes destroyed ancient civilizations.

Eurasian Nomads

[1]→ Nomads are people who lack permanent homes. They travel very often. They do this to find food or places to graze their animals. Most nomads carry some sort of shelter with them. This may be something like a tent or a teepee. At one time, all humans were nomads. Gradually, most people began to settle in villages, towns, and cities. But there have been groups of nomads all throughout history. The most famous nomads lived on the vast plains of **Eurasia**. Tribes such as the Huns and the Mongols traveled on these grasslands for centuries.

Eurasia has the world's largest area of mostly flat grasslands. These are ideal for nomads with large herds of animals. For centuries, waves of nomads moved across these lands. They normally traveled from east to west. They went from China and Mongolia into Russia. Then, they ventured into either Europe or the **Middle East**. Most nomads traveled far distances because of their increasing numbers. They required more land for their animals to graze on. These nomads often came into conflict with people living in civilized areas in the West.

[3]→ One well-known tribe of nomads was the Mongols. They originated in Mongolia. They had few permanent settlements. Instead, they lived most of their lives on horseback. They hunted and tended large herds of animals. The Mongols were also fierce warriors. Genghis Khan was their most famous leader. In the thirteenth century, he led armies of Mongols across the Eurasian plains. He conquered land as far away as Europe. **1** And he created the world's largest empire. **2** Genghis Khan's empire did not last long after his death though. **3** The nomadic Mongols were ill suited to rule and administer such a large empire. **4**

• **Glossary** •

Eurasia: the land of Europe and Asia together
Middle East: the land from Libya to Afghanistan, including the countries Egypt, Turkey, and Saudi Arabia

1 According to paragraph 1, which of the following is NOT true of nomads?

    (A) Many nomads gave up wandering to live in cities.

    (B) There are no more people living nomadic lives today.

    (C) They may have animals that they take care of.

    (D) They usually live in some sort of portable shelter.

2 The word "ventured" in the passage is closest in meaning to

    (A) moved

    (B) attacked

    (C) fled

    (D) explored

3 According to paragraph 3, which of the following is true of the Mongols?

    (A) It took them thirteen centuries to conquer much of Asia.

    (B) They both hunted and farmed the land for their food.

    (C) Their leader Genghis Kahn founded an enormous empire.

    (D) They were defeated in battle by the Europeans.

4 Look at the four squares [■] that indicate where the following sentence could be added to the passage.

It stretched from the Pacific Ocean to Eastern Europe at one point.

Where would the sentence best fit?

✏ Reading Comprehension **Complete the following sentences. Use the words in the box.**

a. tents and tepees	b. traveled west	c. the grasslands	d. fierce nomads

1 A lot of nomads lived in shelters such as _____ .

2 _____ of Eurasia were popular lands for nomads in the past.

3 Many nomads _____ from China to Europe or the Middle East.

4 The Mongols were _____ who created a large empire.

Finding Historical Sites

The ruins of Troy

¹→ The study of past civilizations is the work of archaeologists. They examine the remains of buildings and artifacts from ancient cultures. But knowing where to search for dig sites is not simple. Many old settlements have disappeared. They have been swallowed by jungles or buried beneath deserts. Wars and natural disasters have destroyed many as well. When selecting places to dig, archaeologists rely upon three main methods. The first is to do research. They read historic records and stories from the past. ❶ The second method is accidental in nature. ❷ On occasion, farmers, construction workers, and others find ancient ruins while digging. ❸ The third involves guesswork. ❹ Archaeologists dig in an area where they believe a site is in the hope of finding something.

²→ A few ancient records describe where certain places were located. This is true of historical records. It is also true of various works of literature. This includes poems and stories. Archaeologists may use them to find lost sites. Arguably the most famous example of this involves the ancient city of Troy. According to the epic poem the *Iliad*, the Greeks attacked and destroyed Troy in a war that took place thousands of years ago. Most people believed that the story was only a myth. One man, Heinrich Schliemann, did not. He used the *Iliad* and Homer's other famous work, the *Odyssey*, as historical documents. Schliemann went to the place in Turkey where Homer said that Troy was. He began digging. He found the remains of several ancient cities. One of them was later determined to have been the historical Troy.

³→ Sometimes people who are digging may find sites by accident. This often happens in cities such as Rome, Athens, and Jerusalem. They are among the oldest cities in the world that are still inhabited. In ancient times, people frequently built new buildings on top of old sites. In the

present, builders may uncover them. When this happens, construction there ceases immediately. Archaeologists are brought to the site. They try to learn what they can from it. After they are done, construction may begin anew.

[4]→ In a lot of situations, archaeologists do not know precisely where a site is. But they may have a general idea as to its location. Some decide to dig to try to discover the lost site. First, they make a plot of the area. It can cover a small amount of space. Or it can cover a large area of land. Then, the archaeologists begin digging in sections of each plot. If they do not find anything, they go to another area. And they start to dig again. Many times, they search in vain for weeks or months. But if they are lucky, they discover the remains of a past civilization. It takes hard work and **perseverance**. But this method has resulted in some successes.

• **Glossary** •

epic poem: a long poem often written about a hero
perseverance: determination to continue what one is doing and not to quit

1   According to paragraph 1, many ancient sites have disappeared because

    (A) people decided to live somewhere else

    (B) various disasters destroyed them

    (C) no one remembers where they were

    (D) people are uninterested in finding them

2   Which of the sentences below best expresses the essential information in the highlighted sentence in the passage? *Incorrect* answer choices change the meaning in important ways or leave out essential information.

    (A) The Greeks conquered Troy thousands of years ago.

    (B) The Trojans and the Greek fought each other in a war.

    (C) One of the most famous epic poems is the *Iliad*.

    (D) The *Iliad* tells the story of the Greek defeat of Troy.

3   In paragraph 2, why does the author mention "Heinrich Schliemann"?

    (A) To describe his role in the finding of Troy

    (B) To accuse him of using poor archaeological methods

    (C) To note that he did not really discover ancient Troy

    (D) To compare his works with those of Homer's

4   In paragraph 2, the author's description of the *Iliad* mentions all of the following EXCEPT:

    (A) what the main focus of it is

    (B) what kind of work it is

    (C) what language it is written in

    (D) who the author is

5   In paragraph 3, the author implies that Rome, Athens, and Jerusalem

    (A) were the first cities that humans built

    (B) have strict laws concerning dig sites

    (C) were ancient centers of knowledge

    (D) contain the ruins of many ancient sites

6   According to paragraph 3, why does construction on a new building sometimes stop?

    (A) An ancient site is discovered in the same place.

    (B) Archaeologists do not want the new building to be made.

    (C) People believe the new building will harm an ancient site.

    (D) Construction workers are afraid of harming artifacts.

7   In stating that archaeologists "search in vain," the author means that archaeologists

    (A) find nothing

    (B) make important discoveries

    (C) discover valuable items

    (D) look for rare relics

8   According to paragraph 4, the plots that archaeologists make of an area

    (A) are always effective

    (B) can vary in their size

    (C) make digging much easier

    (D) let them find ruins quickly

9   Look at the four squares [■] that indicate where the following sentence could be added to the passage.

This good luck has resulted in many important archaeological discoveries.

Where would the sentence best fit?

Click on a square [■] to add the sentence to the passage.

10   *Directions*: Select the appropriate phrases from the answer choices and match them to the method for finding historical sites to which they relate. TWO of the answer choices will NOT be used. *This question is worth 3 points.*

Drag your answer choices to the spaces where they belong.
To remove an answer choice, click on it. To review the passage, click on **View Text**.

Answer Choices	**METHOD FOR FINDING HISTORICAL SITES**
1 May involve many months of hard work	**Using Ancient Records**
2 Can happen in cities that were inhabited long ago	•
3 Is the way in which Troy was discovered	•
4 Happens when archaeologists make plots on the land	•
5 Relies on research on works of literature	**Finding Sites by Accident**
6 Was the method utilized by Heinrich Schliemann	•
7 May be unearthed by construction workers	•

Star Performer Word Files

- **administer** (v) to run; to manage
  The governor has to **administer** the entire state.

- **accidental** (adj) by accident; not on purpose
  My mistake was **accidental**; I am sorry about that.

- **age** (n) a significant period of time
  We live in an **age** of great discoveries.

- **arrowhead** (n) the sharp point of an arrow
  I found an **arrowhead** while digging in my garden.

- **bronze** (n) an alloy made of copper and tin
  The helmet and the armor were made of **bronze**.

- **capture** (v) to seize; to take prisoner
  They will **capture** their enemies rather than kill them.

- **cart** (n) a wagon
  There are two horses pulling the farmer's **cart**.

- **cease** (v) to stop
  Please **cease** making all that noise.

- **chariot** (n) a wheeled vehicle pulled by a horse or horses and used in war
  The general rode into battle on a **chariot**.

- **conflict** (n) warfare
  The **conflict** between the two armies killed many men.

- **determine** (v) to conclude after observation
  He **determined** that the data he was looking at was wrong.

- **drought** (n) a period of time with little or no rain
  We are in the middle of a **drought** that has lasted for three years.

- **enter** (v) to begin; to start
  Most humans **entered** the Iron Age thousands of years ago.

- **famine** (n) a period of time with little or no food
  Because of the **famine**, many people starved to death.

- **fierce** (adj) warlike
  Many tribes were afraid of the **fierce** soldiers from the north.

- **force** (v) to make someone do something
  You cannot **force** me to do something that I do not want to.

- **forge** (n) a furnace used to heat metal before shaping it
  The blacksmith put the iron in the **forge** to melt it.

- **graze** (v) to eat grass in a field
  The cows are **grazing** in the field by the pond.

- **herd** (n) a large group of animals
  The rancher has hundreds of cattle in his **herd**.

- **immunity** (n) resistance; protection
  With this vaccination, you will gain **immunity** to the disease.

- **impractical** (adj) unrealistic; unworkable; not useful

  Your idea is **impractical**, so we cannot use it.

- **infect** (v) to make sick

  Do not cough on people, or you might **infect** them.

- **inhabited** (adj) lived in

  This place does not look like it is **inhabited** at all.

- **invention** (n) a creation

  The **invention** of the computer changed society.

- **literature** (n) writing, such as a novel or poem

  What is your favorite work of **literature**?

- **loom** (n) a tool that is used to weave fabric

  Some **looms** in the Industrial Revolution used water power.

- **majority** (n) the most; the greater part

  The **majority** of the group wants to go home now.

- **myth** (n) a legend; a story

  In his spare time, he reads **myths** from ancient Greece.

- **nomad** (n) a person who wanders the land and has no permanent home

  The **nomads** roam through the desert their entire lives.

- **perform** (v) to carry out; to do

  The doctor will **perform** her duties as well as she can.

- **primitive** (adj) simple; basic

  Some **primitive** tribes still live in the Amazon Rainforest.

- **ritual** (n) a kind of ceremony

  We are observing them perform an ancient **ritual** now.

- **ruins** (n) the destroyed remains of a building

  Many people visit the **ruins** of Angkor Wat in Cambodia.

- **sail** (v) to travel on a ship

  They plan to **sail** across the ocean on a yacht.

- **settle** (v) to live in

  I would like to **settle** in a warm part of the country.

- **simultaneously** (adv) at the same time

  Three people **simultaneously** called out the right answer.

- **specific** (adj) exact; precise

  You need to make a more **specific** request.

- **suffer** (v) to endure

  He **suffered** in the cold for three days, but he survived.

- **tsunami** (n) a fast-moving wall of water

  The **tsunami** killed thousands of people when it hit the coast.

- **warrior** (n) a fighter; a soldier

  The great **warrior** defeated all of his enemies in battle.

Vocabulary Review

Choose the word or phrase closest in meaning to the highlighted part of the sentence.

1   Diseases have killed countless people around the world.
 (A) numerous
 (B) several
 (C) unpleasant
 (D) sick

2   But many Europeans carried deadly diseases with them.
 (A) harmful
 (B) infectious
 (C) fatal
 (D) viral

3   Famines, droughts, earthquakes, volcanic eruptions, and tsunamis are all natural disasters.
 (A) events
 (B) explosions
 (C) weapons
 (D) catastrophes

4   Animals could move smoothly over rough terrain.
 (A) primitive
 (B) uneven
 (C) wet
 (D) grassy

5   But if they are lucky, they discover the remains of a past civilization.
 (A) patient
 (B) fortunate
 (C) kind
 (D) nervous

6   He used the *Iliad* and Homer's other famous work, the *Odyssey*, as historical documents.
 (A) papers
 (B) poems
 (C) essays
 (D) novels

7   Nomads are people who lack permanent homes.
 (A) individual
 (B) temporary
 (C) lasting
 (D) expensive

8   They hunted and tended large herds of animals.
 (A) moved
 (B) fed
 (C) opposed
 (D) raised

9   They examine the remains of buildings and artifacts from ancient cultures.
 (A) write about
 (B) construct
 (C) study
 (D) design

10   Bronze had many advantages over stone and metals such as copper.
 (A) shapes
 (B) benefits
 (C) styles
 (D) forces

11   They required more land for their animals to graze on.
 (A) found
 (B) bought
 (C) desired
 (D) needed

12   The winners forced these captives to join their own tribes.
 (A) enemies
 (B) soldiers
 (C) prisoners
 (D) guards

Part B

Chapter 04 **Chapter 04** **Education, Sociology, and Psychology**

Education, sociology, and psychology are all social sciences. The field of education focuses on learning and teaching. People in this field of study research better ways to teach students. Sociologists examine past and present human societies and how they develop, progress, and function. Psychologists study how humans think and why they think in certain ways. They also study various mental illnesses people have.

Mastering **the Question Types** A

☑ Vocabulary   ☐ Fill in a Table   ☐ Factual Information   ☐ Negative Factual Information   ☑ Prose Summary
☐ Insert Text   ☐ Reference   ☑ Rhetorical Purpose   ☐ Sentence Simplification   ☐ Inference

The Popularization of Wristwatches

The sundial was invented in Egypt more than 5,000 years ago. Much later, the water clock, the **hourglass**, and the wheel clock were made. These **timepieces** were all large though. Later, in 1673, Christiaan Huygens invented a watch with a spiral spring. He made watches smaller and portable.

²➜ It was in 1812 that the first wristwatch was made by Abraham-Louis Breguet. It was for Caroline Murat, the sister of Napoleon. During the 1800s, wristwatches became common but were mostly worn by women.

Men preferred to carry pocket watches. However, this changed in 1904. Alberto Santos Dumont, a pilot, wanted to fly with both hands but also be able to tell the time. Louis Cartier made the first men's wristwatch for him. A decade later, World War I started in 1914. Pilots needed to know the correct time. So they began wearing wristwatches. Civilians started to imitate them. Soon afterward, wristwatches became typical accessories for both men and women.

• **Glossary** •

hourglass: a tool that uses sand to tell time
timepiece: a device such as a watch that tells the time

1 In paragraph 2, why does the author mention "Caroline Murat"?

Ⓐ To describe her actions to invent the wristwatch

Ⓑ To name her as the first person to have a wristwatch

Ⓒ To discuss her relationship with Napoleon

Ⓓ To argue that she made the wristwatch popular for everyone

2 The word "imitate" in the passage is closest in meaning to

Ⓐ purchase

Ⓑ admire

Ⓒ wear

Ⓓ copy

3 *Directions*: An introductory sentence for a brief summary of the passage is provided below. Complete the summary by selecting the THREE answer choices that express the most important ideas of the passage. Some sentences do not belong because they express ideas that are not presented in the passage or are minor ideas in the passage. *This question is worth 2 points*.

The wristwatch was invented in the 1800s and became popular due to war.

-
-
-

Answer Choices

① The sundial and the hourglass were invented before the wristwatch.

② A pilot was the recipient of the first men's wristwatch.

③ Many wristwatches today can cost thousands of dollars.

④ Pilots in World War I wore wristwatches to know the precise time.

⑤ Abraham-Louis Breguet was the inventor of the wristwatch.

⑥ Men prefer to wear wristwatches much more than women do.

Checking Reading Accuracy Mark the following statements T (true) or F (false).

T   F

1 ☐ / ☐ The hourglass was invented more than 5,000 years ago.

2 ☐ / ☐ The watch invented by Christiaan Huygens could be worn by people.

3 ☐ / ☐ The sister of Napoleon wore the first women's wristwatch.

4 ☐ / ☐ Alberto Santos Dumont invented the wristwatch for men.

☐ Vocabulary   ☑ Fill in a Table   ☐ Factual Information   ☑ Negative Factual Information   ☐ Prose Summary

☐ Insert Text   ☐ Reference   ☐ Rhetorical Purpose   ☐ Sentence Simplification   ☑ Inference

Public Education

1→ Public education is a system in which students are taught in schools run by the government. It is common all around the world today. But in the past, few children attended school. Only rich upper-class children received an education. They typically studied with private **tutors** at their homes. As for lower-class children, they learned basic skills such as reading, writing, and **arithmetic** from their parents. Tutors were too expensive for them.

2→ This changed in the 1800s. During that century, mass public education began in Europe and North America. The reason for this was the need for educated people. The world was changing. It was no longer based on agriculture. Instead, it was based on industry. Factories and offices needed educated people. So many governments established schools for children. The students studied at these schools for free. This was the beginning of public education.

• **Glossary** •

tutor: a private instructor
arithmetic: math

1 In paragraph 1, the author implies that lower-class children's families

- Ⓐ worked as tutors
- Ⓑ had little money
- Ⓒ were uninterested in education
- Ⓓ studied together

2 In paragraph 2, the author's description of mass public education in the 1800s mentions all of the following EXCEPT:

- Ⓐ the subjects it taught to students
- Ⓑ the founders of schools for children
- Ⓒ the cost of attending public schools
- Ⓓ the countries it started in

3 *Directions*: Select the appropriate sentences from the answer choices and match them to the period of time to which they relate. TWO of the answer choices will NOT be used. ***This question is worth 3 points***.

Answer Choices	PERIOD OF TIME
① No fees were required for students to attend school.	**Before Public Education**
② Students in North America attended government schools.	•
③ Some parents taught their children at home.	•
④ Students were educated to work in factories.	**After Public Education**
⑤ Students in all social classes were taught by tutors.	•
⑥ Private tutors were hired for upper-class children.	•
⑦ Students mostly learned about farming techniques.	•

✒ **Checking Reading Accuracy**   Mark the following statements T (true) or F (false).

	T	**F**	
1	☐	/ ☐	In the past, only upper-class children used to attend schools.
2	☐	/ ☐	Lower-class children's parents hired private tutors for them.
3	☐	/ ☐	Mass public education began in Europe during the 1800s.
4	☐	/ ☐	Students received public educations while working in factories.

Mastering the Question Types C

☐ Vocabulary   ☐ Fill in a Table   ☑ Factual Information   ☐ Negative Factual Information   ☐ Prose Summary
☑ Insert Text   ☑ Reference   ☐ Rhetorical Purpose   ☑ Sentence Simplification   ☐ Inference

The Telephone and Modern Communications

¹➜ Alexander Graham Bell invented the telephone in 1876. **1** Ever since then, it has become a part of most people's everyday lives. **2** The first phones could only make or receive calls. **3** Nowadays, they can send messages, connect to the Internet, take pictures, and do many other functions. **4**

The main effect of the telephone was that it made communications both easier and faster. Before phones, people sent messages by letter or **telegram**. Letters were slow to be delivered. Sometimes they never reached their destinations. Getting a reply could take even longer. Telegrams were faster. But they were like letters in some ways. All long-distance contact was in writing. But phones permitted **instant** communication by talking. This let people talk to one another much faster. And it increased the speed of life for people in general. Today, thanks to mobile phones, people can connect with others instantly from virtually anywhere in the world.

• **Glossary** •

telegram: a message that is sent by telegraph
instant: immediate; at once

1 According to paragraph 1, which of the following is true of Alexander Graham Bell?

Ⓐ He was born in 1876.

Ⓑ He became a wealthy man.

Ⓒ He made the first telephone.

Ⓓ He did work with cameras.

2 Which of the sentences below best expresses the essential information in the highlighted sentence in the passage? *Incorrect* answer choices change the meaning in important ways or leave out essential information.

Ⓐ More people became interested in communicating by telephone.

Ⓑ It was easy to call people on the telephone to speak with them.

Ⓒ Some people learned how to make telephone calls to one another.

Ⓓ People could talk to others faster and easier with telephones.

3 The word "they" in the passage refers to

Ⓐ phones

Ⓑ people

Ⓒ messages

Ⓓ letters

4 Look at the four squares [■] that indicate where the following sentence could be added to the passage.

That was when he spoke the first words over a telephone line.

Where would the sentence best fit?

✎ Checking Reading Accuracy Mark the following statements T (true) or F (false).

	T	F	
1	☐	/ ☐	The telephone was invented in 1786.
2	☐	/ ☐	Modern telephones have a number of different functions.
3	☐	/ ☐	It used to take a long time to send letters to people.
4	☐	/ ☐	The invention of the telephone increased the speed of people's lives.

Mastering **the Subject** A

Language Divergence

Languages constantly undergo changes. Some are minor. Words and expressions gain new meanings. Grammar rules alter. In other cases, the changes are major. A language may diverge and become a new **tongue**. Or it may change over the course of time.

[2]→ The Roman Empire once controlled a vast territory. This included all of Western Europe. In 476, the empire fell. The **Dark Ages** then began. During them, the people of Europe had little contact even with those in nearby cities. Previously, everyone had spoken Latin. As time progressed, the Latin that people spoke began to change though. From Latin, several new languages arose. They included French, Spanish, Portuguese, Italian, and Romanian. They are called the Romance languages. These languages all have some similarities. They share an alphabet. They have many of the same root words. And they often use similar grammar. Yet they are separate languages.

A language may also change because the original speakers move to distant lands. English is one example of this. England is the home of the English language. Yet English speakers moved to places such as North America, Australia, New Zealand, and India. Over time, the English that people spoke in these places changed. **1** The local languages often adopted words from local natives. **2** The people used different expressions. **3** And they spoke with various accents. **4** Today, there are many versions of English spoken around the world.

Most languages change as time passes. English, Greek, Russian, and German have all greatly evolved over hundreds of years. Old English, Middle English, and Modern English are three separate languages. *Beowulf*, an epic poem written in Old English, uses language unintelligible to most modern speakers of English. Likewise, the ancient Greek spoken by Socrates and Plato is different from that used in modern-day Athens.

• **Glossary** •

tongue: a language
Dark Ages: the period in European history that lasted from around 476 to 1000 A.D.

118

1 In paragraph 2, the author's description of Romance languages mentions all of the following EXCEPT:

(A) where they developed

(B) how they are similar to one another

(C) what language they are related to

(D) how simple they are to learn

2 In stating that *Beowulf* "uses language unintelligible" to most modern speakers of English, the author means that people

(A) cannot understand it

(B) frequently read it

(C) dislike poetry

(D) fully comprehend the poem

3 Look at the four squares [■] that indicate where the following sentence could be added to the passage.

As an example, American English uses many words from Native American languages.

Where would the sentence best fit?

4 *Directions*: Select the appropriate phrases from the answer choices and match them to the type of language divergence to which they relate. TWO of the answer choices will NOT be used. *This question is worth 3 points*.

Answer Choices	**LANGUAGE DIVERGENCE**
1 Is what happened to the English language over time	**The Creation of a New Language**
2 Was the reason that the Dark Ages began	•
3 Was one result of the fall of the Roman Empire	•
4 Explains why modern Greeks speak a different language than Plato	**The Changing of a Language**
5 Occurred when native speakers settled in different lands	•
6 Happened because people lost contact with one another	•
7 Enabled a poet to write *Beowulf* hundreds of years ago	•

Reading Comprehension Complete the following sentences. Use the words in the box.

a. entirely new ones	b. words and expressions	c. the Greek language	d. Latin developed

1 Over time, some languages may change and become _____ .

2 _____ into several new languages after the fall of Rome.

3 English has added new _____ in several countries.

4 _____ has changed from the time of Socrates to the modern day.

Infant Perception

The age that babies begin to understand the world is hard to determine. Babies themselves cannot provide the answer. So experts look for signs that babies are perceiving the world around them. These include babies' responses to outside factors. Babies often perceive things through sight, hearing, and speech. They respond in many ways.

[2]→ Not all babies perceive the world around them at the same age. But they share some similarities. For instance, newborn babies cannot see far. They have trouble focusing. Yet they respond to lights. Most newborn babies appear more interested in black and white items than colored ones. Studies show that young infants see large areas better than small objects. A few months after being born, their vision improves. They can follow a moving object with their eyes. They can shift their eyes from one object to another. They can lock onto people's faces. They can even recognize **specific** people and things.

Babies can also perceive and respond to sounds. From birth, most of them have excellent hearing. Babies typically respond to sounds by moving their eyes to the sources of the sounds or by turning their heads. By the age of one, they can recognize when someone calls their name. They are also aware of music at a young age. Some may even move to the sound of music.

As for speaking, babies are incapable of speech right after they are born. While they make sounds, they are **nonsensical** and are not attempts to make speech. However, by around six months of age, most babies are attempting to communicate. They are starting to make meaningful sounds with their mouths. This is the first stage toward being able to speak. By around ten or eleven months after birth, most babies have spoken their first words.

• **Glossary** •
specific: exact; precise
nonsensical: not making any sense; illogical

1   Select the TWO answer choices from paragraph 2 that identify how babies use their sense of sight. *To receive credit, you must select TWO answers*.

      Ⓐ They see small objects well.   Ⓑ They can look from one thing to another.

      Ⓒ The are not able to focus well.   Ⓓ They can recognize people from birth.

2   Which of the following can be inferred from paragraph 2 about infants' sight abilities?

      Ⓐ Many of them require glasses.   Ⓑ They cannot see colors well.

      Ⓒ Their sight seldom improves after birth.   Ⓓ They have better vision than other animals.

3   Which of the sentences below best expresses the essential information in the highlighted sentence in the passage? *Incorrect* answer choices change the meaning in important ways or leave out essential information.

      Ⓐ Babies cannot hear sounds unless they are looking at the sources of the noises.

      Ⓑ Babies either move their eyes or their heads in the directions of sounds.

      Ⓒ Noises bother babies, so they move their eyes or heads away from the sounds.

      Ⓓ Unless babies hear sounds, they do not move either their eyes or head.

4   ***Directions***: An introductory sentence for a brief summary of the passage is provided below. Complete the summary by selecting the THREE answer choices that express the most important ideas of the passage. Some sentences do not belong because they express ideas that are not presented in the passage or are minor ideas in the passage. ***This question is worth 2 points***.

Babies are able to use sight, hearing, and speech to perceive the world around them.

-
-
-

Answer Choices

① Babies steadily improve their speaking abilities until they can finally make words.

② Most babies prefer to look at black and white objects than ones with colors.

③ When they are born, babies can hear very well and will often respond to sounds.

④ Most babies do not learn how to walk until they are several months old.

⑤ At birth, babies do not see well, but their sight quickly improves over time.

⑥ Babies are born with all of their senses, but some are more developed than others.

Reading Comprehension Complete the following sentences. Use the words in the box.

a. one year old	b. the vision	c. perceive the world	d. their first words

1 No one is sure how old babies are when they start to _____.

2 _____ of babies improves after they are a few months old.

3 When babies are _____, they can recognize their names being called.

4 Babies usually speak _____ around the age of ten or eleven months.

Women in the Workforce

Most people in history have worked in the field of agriculture. Both men and women did physical labor on farms. This included taking care of animals, harvesting crops, and grinding grain. When the Industrial Revolution began, the roles of women changed.

2→ Many families—fathers, mothers, and children—worked together in factories. But these places had poor working conditions. In England and other countries, laws were passed. They restricted the working hours of women and children. They were also banned from doing certain jobs. As a result, women mostly did domestic work and child care while men worked outside the house.

3→ There were some jobs that women engaged in outside the home though. Among them were working as teachers, office workers, and saleswomen. This changed due to war in the 1940s. World War II lasted from 1939 to 1945. Men were drafted to serve in their nations' **armed forces**. Factory workers were still needed to make weapons, ships, airplanes, and other things. Single women entered the workforce in great numbers then. They were often paid less than men though.

4→ When the war ended, a large number of women left the workforce. Or they returned to traditional female jobs such as teaching and nursing. Then, in the 1970s, many married women started to find jobs. Thanks to modern technology, they were able to do jobs that men had once done. For instance, jobs that no longer required physical labor became open to women.

Nowadays, women comprise around half of the workforce in many countries. This is especially true for countries that are in North America and Europe. Most women receive the same pay as men. There are also laws that prevent **discrimination** against women in the workforce.

• Glossary •

armed forces: a military; the army, navy, and air force of a country
discrimination: the act of treating a person badly due to that person's race, sex, religion, nationality, etc.

1 The word "roles" in the passage is closest in meaning to

- (A) appearances
- (B) responses
- (C) actions
- (D) opinions

2 In paragraph 2, which of the following can be inferred about women in the Industrial Revolution?

- (A) They made the same amount of money as men at factories.
- (B) They did domestic work due to laws that were passed.
- (C) They preferred working on farms to working in factories.
- (D) They were able to work all kinds of jobs in most countries.

3 In paragraph 3, the author's description of women mentions all of the following EXCEPT:

- (A) the reason they needed to work at factories
- (B) their average wages at factories
- (C) the effects of World War II on them
- (D) some jobs they did outside the house

4 According to paragraph 4, women did many of the same jobs as men in the 1970s because

- (A) there was a shortage of workers then
- (B) laws against discrimination were passed
- (C) there were improvements in technology
- (D) they had received college educations

Reading Comprehension Complete the following sentences. Use the words in the box.

| a. left the workforce | b. do domestic work | c. half the workforce | d. poor working conditions |

1 Factories in the Industrial Revolution had _____ .

2 Women started to _____ during the Industrial Revolution.

3 Many women _____ after World War II ended.

4 In many countries, women make up around _____ these days.

Types of Leaders

A presidential inauguration in the United States

¹➜ A leader is a person who makes decisions for other people. At the highest level are leaders of entire nations. For the most part, there have been three types of leaders of nations. The first are monarchs. These are kings, queens, and other nobles. Second are **charismatic** leaders who rise to power. They include dictators such as Adolf Hitler of Germany. Third are leaders elected by the people of a nation. The presidents of the United States are examples of these leaders.

²➜ For most of history, monarchs ruled the majority of nations. They often **wielded** absolute power. Those monarchs had complete control over their land. Whatever they said was law. When they died, their son—or perhaps their daughter—took over as the ruler. Some monarchs were beloved by their people. They ruled wisely and were kind leaders. In other cases, some monarchs were so bad that the people overthrew **them**. This took place in England in the 1600s. It also happened in France during the French Revolution in the late 1700s. In the 1900s, many monarchies were abolished. Others had their power taken away. Some nations, such as England, still have monarchs. Yet they are mere **figureheads** today.

³➜ Charismatic leaders are those that the people love and are willing to follow. They may be elected by the people. But they often take over through force and rule as dictators. Adolf Hitler's political party won control of the German government in the 1930s. Then, Hitler assumed power over the entire country. He and his supporters stopped anyone who got in their way. Josef Stalin of the USSR and Benito Mussolini of Italy are two other charismatic leaders from the 1900s. One advantage of these leaders is that they can easily accomplish certain goals. The legislatures and the people are often powerless to stop them. Yet their periods of rule may be unstable or violent

times. These dictators often demand too much power. They may start wars and persecute their own people. In many cases, they are overthrown by their citizens or an external power.

4→ Elected leaders are those who win elections that grant them power. The citizens of a country either vote for the person or the individual's political party. The prime minister of Great Britain and the president of the United States are two elected positions. Elected leaders hold power for a limited amount of time. **1** Then, they must win another election to maintain power. **2** This helps limit the leaders' power. **3** Countries with elected leaders often have constitutions. **4** They put specific limits on the power of their leaders. These countries rarely experience civil wars or other periods of instability.

• **Glossary** •

charismatic: having a personality that lets a person influence others easily
figurehead: a person who is the head of a group but has little or no actual power

1 In paragraph 1, the author's description of leaders mentions all of the following EXCEPT:

   (A) the name of a charismatic leader

   (B) how some people become leaders

   (C) how people become kings or queens

   (D) who some kinds of monarchs are

2 The word "wielded" in the passage is closest in meaning to

   (A) demanded

   (B) possessed

   (C) desired

   (D) approved of

3 The word "them" in the passage refers to

   (A) kind leaders

   (B) other cases

   (C) some monarchs

   (D) the people

4 According to paragraph 2, which of the following is true of monarchs throughout history?

   (A) They could usually do whatever they wanted.

   (B) They ruled jointly with their sons or daughters.

   (C) There are no longer any monarchs in the present.

   (D) The majority of them were overthrown.

5 In paragraph 3, why does the author mention "Benito Mussolini"?

   (A) To state that he was from Italy

   (B) To name a charismatic leader

   (C) To compare him to Josef Stalin

   (D) To emphasize when he lived

6 The word "persecute" in the passage is closest in meaning to

   (A) mistreat

   (B) damage

   (C) arrest

   (D) execute

7 According to paragraph 3, charismatic leaders usually gain power because

    Ⓐ they win elections in their countries

    Ⓑ they start wars with outside powers

    Ⓒ they take over their countries by force

    Ⓓ they start military coups in their countries

8 In paragraph 4, the author implies that countries with elected leaders

    Ⓐ have few major internal problems

    Ⓑ often go to war with other nations

    Ⓒ are sometimes defeated in battle

    Ⓓ are allied with the United States

9 Look at the four squares [■] that indicate where the following sentence could be added to the passage.

In the United States, the president serves a four-year term.

Where would the sentence best fit?

Click on a square [■] to add the sentence to the passage.

10 *Directions*: Select the appropriate phrases from the answer choices and match them to the type of leader to which they relate. TWO of the answer choices will NOT be used. *This question is worth 3 points*.

Drag your answer choices to the spaces where they belong.
To remove an answer choice, click on it. To review the passage, click on **View Text**.

Answer Choices	TYPE OF LEADER
① Serves a term that lasts for a few years	**Monarch**
② May sometimes be overthrown by people	•
③ Is only a figurehead in countries such as England	•
④ Frequently persecutes the people of the country	•
⑤ Rules the land as a king or queen	**Elected Leader**
⑥ Often takes over by using force	•
⑦ Has specific limits on power	•

Star Performer Word Files

- **accent** (n) a way of pronouncing words that is often unique to a region
  She speaks Spanish with a foreign **accent**.

- **agriculture** (adj) farming
  He studied **agriculture** at college to become a better farmer.

- **alphabet** (n) a system of letters or symbols that enable a language to be written
  It can be hard to learn the Greek **alphabet**.

- **arise** (v) to begin; to happen
  Some problems **arose** with the computer system.

- **attempt** (v) to try
  What is John going to **attempt** next?

- **ban** (v) to make it illegal for a person to do a certain action
  Visitors are **banned** from the laboratories in the company.

- **basic** (adj) simple
  That first grader can solve some **basic** math problems.

- **beloved** (adj) loved; favorite
  The **beloved** boss of the company retired last week.

- **charismatic** (adj) fascinating; charming; convincing
  She is a **charismatic** speaker who can convince people of her views.

- **civil war** (n) a war fought between two or more groups from the same country
  The country's **civil** war lasted for seven years.

- **contact** (n) a connection; a call
  We try to keep in **contact** at least once a week.

- **determine** (v) to establish
  They cannot **determine** the cause of the problem.

- **diverge** (v) to move away
  John's and Mark's beliefs are starting to **diverge**.

- **domestic** (adj) relating to the home
  There are all kinds of **domestic** chores people must do.

- **draft** (v) to make a person join the military
  Many men were **drafted** into the army during the war.

- **education** (n) learning; academics
  It is important to get a good **education** at school.

- **establish** (v) to found; to start some kind of group or organization
  The school was **established** in 1971.

- **evolve** (v) to change over time
  Most cultures **evolve** after many years.

- **expression** (n) a saying; a phrase; an idiom
  There are many creative **expressions** in that language.

- **factory** (n) a building in which goods are mass-produced
  The **factory** will be used to make computer chips.

- **function** (n) a use

  The computer has a great number of **functions**.

- **instantly** (adv) immediately; right away; at once

  David **instantly** realized he had made a mistake.

- **major** (adj) big; important

  Eric has a **major** influence at his company.

- **meaningful** (adj) important; significant

  That was a **meaningful** gesture you just made.

- **minor** (adj) small; of little importance

  Please make some **minor** adjustments.

- **monarch** (n) a king or queen; a royal

  The **monarch** has reigned in that country for fifty-two years.

- **native** (n) a local; a resident

  The **natives** of the country were upset with the president.

- **perceive** (v) to recognize; to identify

  You should learn to **perceive** everything around you.

- **permit** (v) to allow; to let

  Karen's mother will not **permit** her to go out on Friday night.

- **progress** (v) to advance; to move on

  They **progressed** too slowly on the project.

- **reply** (n) an answer; a response

  I have not gotten a **reply** from the college yet.

- **respond** (v) to react

  How are you going to **respond** to his question?

- **run** (v) to operate; to manage

  Harry **runs** his department better than the previous manager.

- **savings** (n) money that a person has saved

  She spent most of her **savings** while she was sick.

- **shift** (v) to move

  The headquarters is **shifting** from London to Rome.

- **tutor** (n) a private instructor

  Jack's parents hired a **tutor** to teach him math.

- **typical** (adj) normal

  He is a **typical** student who enjoys school.

- **undergo** (v) to experience; to go through

  They will **undergo** many changes in the six-week program.

- **unstable** (adj) unbalanced; uneven

  That building appears to be **unstable** and may collapse.

- **waste** (v) to misuse something; to squander

  If you **waste** time playing video games, you will not get a good education.

❗ Choose the word or phrase closest in meaning to the highlighted part of the sentence.

1   Later, in 1673, Christiaan Huygens invented a watch with a spiral spring.
  Ⓐ effective
  Ⓑ decorative
  Ⓒ rising
  Ⓓ twisting

2   A few months after being born, their vision improves.
  Ⓐ smell
  Ⓑ speech
  Ⓒ sight
  Ⓓ feeling

3   It was no longer based on agriculture.
  Ⓐ industry
  Ⓑ education
  Ⓒ tourism
  Ⓓ farming

4   At the highest level are leaders of entire nations.
  Ⓐ cities
  Ⓑ states
  Ⓒ regions
  Ⓓ continents

5   Then, Hitler assumed power over the entire country.
  Ⓐ lost
  Ⓑ considered
  Ⓒ approved of
  Ⓓ took

6   They have many of the same root words.
  Ⓐ base
  Ⓑ important
  Ⓒ foreign
  Ⓓ grammatical

7   They restricted the working hours of women and children.
  Ⓐ stopped
  Ⓑ limited
  Ⓒ encouraged
  Ⓓ approved

8   Civilians started to imitate them.
  Ⓐ Generals
  Ⓑ Soldiers
  Ⓒ Citizens
  Ⓓ Politicians

9   Today, thanks to mobile phones, people can connect with others instantly from virtually anywhere in the world.
  Ⓐ almost
  Ⓑ partially
  Ⓒ hardly
  Ⓓ fairly

10 Those monarchs had complete control over their land.
  Ⓐ final
  Ⓑ special
  Ⓒ total
  Ⓓ partial

11 Yet they are separate languages.
  Ⓐ different
  Ⓑ difficult
  Ⓒ original
  Ⓓ basic

12 Nowadays, women comprise around half of the workforce in many countries.
  Ⓐ think of
  Ⓑ consider
  Ⓒ become
  Ⓓ make up

Part B

Chapter 05 Economics

Economics is the study of the use of scarce resources that have a number of different uses. Economists focus on learning how goods and services are produced, distributed, and consumed. Microeconomics and macroeconomics are two of the major fields of study. Some economists also study the history of economics. Others look at the connections between politics and economics while some economists study finance.

Mastering **the Question Types** A

☑ Vocabulary   □ Fill in a Table   □ Factual Information   □ Negative Factual Information   ☑ Prose Summary
□ Insert Text   □ Reference   ☑ Rhetorical Purpose   □ Sentence Simplification   □ Inference

Coins

¹→ Coins are in constant use today. But coined money was rare centuries ago. Instead, most trade was done by the barter system. People traded one type of good for another. This let them **avoid** using any kind of money.

But as kingdoms and empires formed, people began to use money. This often took the form of coins. Coins had several advantages over bartering. They were smaller, weighed less, and were easier to carry than large amounts of trade goods. They could also be used to buy anything. Coins contained precious metals such as gold, silver, and copper. As a result, people understood how much the coins were worth. This made it simple for them to engage in buying and selling. It also increased the popularity of coins. Even today, while paper money and electronic **transactions** are common, people still use coins in cash transactions.

• **Glossary** •

avoid: to keep from doing something
transaction: a trade

1 In paragraph 1, why does the author mention "the barter system"?

    Ⓐ To show how people traded without money

    Ⓑ To prove it is more effective than using coins

    Ⓒ To note the historical period when it was used

    Ⓓ To explain why people prefer it to using money

2 The word "precious" in the passage is closest in meaning to

    Ⓐ rare

    Ⓑ mined

    Ⓒ melted

    Ⓓ valuable

3 *Directions*: An introductory sentence for a brief summary of the passage is provided below. Complete the summary by selecting the THREE answer choices that express the most important ideas of the passage. Some sentences do not belong because they express ideas that are not presented in the passage or are minor ideas in the passage. *This question is worth 2 points*.

People use coins for a number of reasons.

-
-
-

Answer Choices

① Many coins are made of gold, silver, and copper.

② It is easy to determine the value of the coins one has.

③ In the past, people used the barter system to trade goods.

④ Trading for goods with coins is a simple process.

⑤ Almost every country makes its own coins and paper money.

⑥ Coins weigh much less than goods people can barter.

Checking Reading Accuracy Mark the following statements T (true) or F (false).

	T	F	
1	☐	☐	The barter system involves the trading of goods for money.
2	☐	☐	Some of the first money that people used was coins.
3	☐	☐	Many coins contain valuable metals, including gold and silver.
4	☐	☐	Paper money and electronic transactions are used to trade goods today.

Mastering **the Question Types** B

☐ Vocabulary ☑ Fill in a Table ☐ Factual Information ☑ Negative Factual Information ☐ Prose Summary
☐ Insert Text ☐ Reference ☐ Rhetorical Purpose ☐ Sentence Simplification ☑ Inference

Sea Routes to Asia

¹➙ For centuries, all trade between Europe and Asia took place overland. <u>Caravans</u> laden with goods took months to travel great distances. Then, European explorers discovered sea routes to Asia. This was important since traveling by ship was both cheaper and faster to transport goods.

²➙ The Portuguese were the first to discover a sea route to Asia. They sailed south around Africa. Then, they entered the Indian Ocean and sailed north to India. Their ships returned to Europe with spices, silks, ivory, gems, and other goods. These voyages took months to complete. Yet they were still faster than land routes.

There were risks though. The ships could sink in storms. And <u>pirates</u> sometimes captured the ships. But the profits were enormous. Merchants and other wealthy individuals invested in sea trade. They were constantly looking for faster routes to Asia. This set the stage for Christopher Columbus to discover America in 1492.

• **Glossary** •

caravan: a convoy; a group of wagons, trucks, or other types of transportation that are carrying goods

pirate: a brigand; a thief who often sails ships on the ocean

1   In paragraph 1, the author implies that the Europeans

    Ⓐ built the best ships in the entire world

    Ⓑ had less wealth than people living in Asia

    Ⓒ preferred to trade by ship than by land

    Ⓓ had few valuable items to trade with others

2   According to paragraph 2, which of the following is NOT true of the Portuguese?

    Ⓐ Their sailors discovered a way to Asia.

    Ⓑ They traded for valuable goods such as gems.

    Ⓒ They took spices and silks from Europe to Asia.

    Ⓓ They managed to sail to the Indian Ocean.

3   *Directions*: Select the appropriate sentences from the answer choices and match them to the cause and effect of the discovery of a sea route to Asia to which they relate. TWO of the answer choices will NOT be used. ***This question is worth 3 points***.

Answer Choices	THE DISCOVERY OF A SEA ROUTE TO ASIA
① A voyage by sea to Asia was often dangerous.	**Cause**
② America was discovered in 1492.	•
③ Many Europeans made huge amounts of money.	•
④ The Portuguese sailed south around Africa.	**Effect**
⑤ Some pirates attacked ships with trade goods.	•
⑥ Merchants invested their money in sailing ships.	•
⑦ The Europeans wanted fast trade with Asia.	•

✒ **Checking Reading Accuracy**   Mark the following statements T (true) or F (false).

    T   **F**

1   ☐ / ☐   The Europeans and Asians used to trade only by land.

2   ☐ / ☐   Christopher Columbus discovered a sea route to Asia.

3   ☐ / ☐   The Europeans traded goods such as silks and spices.

4   ☐ / ☐   There were some dangers in trading goods by sea.

Mastering **the Question Types** C

☐ Vocabulary   ☐ Fill in a Table   ☑ Factual Information   ☐ Negative Factual Information   ☐ Prose Summary

☑ Insert Text   ☑ Reference   ☐ Rhetorical Purpose   ☑ Sentence Simplification   ☐ Inference

Maritime Trade

People have always transported goods by land and water. But in the past, moving goods on land was slow. Despite having **pack animals** and wagons, people could only carry a limited amount of goods to trade with others.

²→ Moving goods by water was much faster. This was true even when water transportation consisted of simple rafts that floated across lakes. As human civilization developed, ship technology improved. First, people built ships that could sail up and down rivers. Later, they made ships that could sail on seas and oceans. These ships, however, usually stayed in sight of land. In many places, maritime trade flourished. **❶** This happened on the Mediterranean Sea. **❷** The Phoenicians, the Greeks, the Egyptians, and the Romans sailed all around the Mediterranean thousands of years ago. **❸** Centuries later, ships that could **traverse** entire oceans were built. **❹** These enabled even more extensive waterborne trade to take place.

• **Glossary** •

pack animal: a horse, mule, or donkey used by people to carry heavy loads

traverse: to go or move across

1 Which of the sentences below best expresses the essential information in the highlighted sentence in the passage? *Incorrect* answer choices change the meaning in important ways or leave out essential information.

- Ⓐ Pack animals and wagons let people carry large amounts of trade goods.
- Ⓑ Merchants made sure to use animals and wagons to carry their possessions.
- Ⓒ With wagons and animals, it became easy to transport items to trade with.
- Ⓓ People could not carry many trade items even with animals and wagons.

2 The word "they" in the passage refers to

- Ⓐ rafts
- Ⓑ people
- Ⓒ ships
- Ⓓ rivers

3 According to paragraph 2, which of the following is true of trade on the Mediterranean Sea?

- Ⓐ It took months for ships to cross the sea.
- Ⓑ The Egyptians were the first to trade goods on it.
- Ⓒ Many groups of people traded items across it.
- Ⓓ All ships sailing on it remained in sight of land.

4 Look at the four squares [■] that indicate where the following sentence could be added to the passage.

They developed extensive maritime trade routes all over the area.

Where would the sentence best fit?

✐ Checking Reading Accuracy **Mark the following statements T (true) or F (false).**

	T	F	
1	☐	/ ☐	People could carry unlimited amounts of goods on pack animals.
2	☐	/ ☐	It was faster to trade goods by land than by water.
3	☐	/ ☐	Ship technology improved along with human civilization.
4	☐	/ ☐	Many cultures traded goods on the Mediterranean Sea.

The Master-Apprentice Relationship

1→ In Europe during <u>medieval</u> times, not everyone was a farmer. Some people were skilled artisans. There were carpenters, shoemakers, tailors, silversmiths, blacksmiths, and bakers. People skilled at these jobs were called masters. They often had apprentices. These were young boys—and sometimes girls—who trained with a master to learn his job. Apprentices studied with their masters for many years. They learned all that they could about their jobs. After a long time, they became masters themselves. Then, they trained their own apprentices. This way, skills were passed down from one generation to another.

2→ Most apprentices began their training as children or teens. They lived with their masters. Their masters provided food, clothing, and shelter. The apprentices, in turn, gave their masters free labor. They received no wages while training. Most apprentices studied for seven years. After completing their studies, they became journeymen. This meant that they were skilled but not yet qualified to be considered masters. Journeymen were able to earn money by using their talents though. They still had to practice for a few more years though. Then, they could become masters.

3→ During the Middle Ages, most places had <u>strict</u> rules concerning the standards for apprentices, journeymen, and masters. Guilds controlled these professions. Guilds were associations of tradesmen. There was usually a guild for each type of craft. Only masters could join one. To become masters, journeymen had to pass a test. This mainly involved producing an example of their work. The masters of the guild then judged the work. In this way, the guild could ensure that the quality of its members was high.

• **Glossary** •
medieval: relating to the Middle Ages
strict: severe; serious; rigid

1 The author discusses "apprentices" in paragraph 1 in order to

(A) remark that some masters had no apprentices

(B) compare them with journeymen

(C) describe how they became masters

(D) explain the kind of training they had

2 According to paragraph 2, journeymen could become masters when

(A) they practiced their trade for several more years

(B) they finished their studies as apprentices

(C) their masters believed that they were ready

(D) they had earned enough money from working

3 In paragraph 3, all of the following questions are answered EXCEPT:

(A) How did guilds control membership?

(B) Which trades had guilds during the Middle Ages?

(C) What kinds of people were members of guilds?

(D) How did journeymen become masters?

4 *Directions*: An introductory sentence for a brief summary of the passage is provided below. Complete the summary by selecting the THREE answer choices that express the most important ideas of the passage. Some sentences do not belong because they express ideas that are not presented in the passage or are minor ideas in the passage. *This question is worth 2 points*.

In the Middle Ages, apprentices could become masters in various trades after years of practice.

-
-
-

Answer Choices

1. Most apprentices lived with their masters and did work for free.

2. During an apprenticeship, a person became skilled at a certain trade.

3. After being a journeyman for many years, a person could become a master.

4. Apprentices studied with their masters for a set number of years.

5. Some guilds refused to allow more than a certain number of masters in one area.

6. There were guilds for trades such as carpenter, blacksmith, and shoemaker.

Reading Comprehension Complete the following sentences. Use the words in the box.

a. seven years of training   b. associations of tradesmen   c. their masters' skills   d. to become masters

1 Apprentices trained with masters in order to learn _____ .

2 It took _____ for an apprentice to become a journeyman.

3 Journeymen needed to learn more skills in order _____ .

4 Guilds were _____ that controlled their professions.

Mastering **the Subject** B

Colonial Trade

In the late 1400s, the Europeans began sailing around the world. One result was that many countries began to acquire colonies. They were mostly in North and South America, Africa, and Asia. Colonies became vital parts of many European empires. They were often rich in **raw materials**, which the Europeans desired. A trade system between the colonies and the home countries was set up. The colonies shipped raw materials to Europe. People in Europe made finished products. These products were then shipped back to the colonies. There, they were sold to the colonists.

2→ One example of this kind of trade involved Europe, Africa, and the Americas. The colonies in the Americas had raw materials such as sugar, tobacco, cotton, fish, wood, gold, and silver. England, France, Spain, and Portugal possessed most of the colonies in the Americas. But there was a shortage of **manpower**. Without workers, they could not get the raw materials they wanted. So they used black African slaves to do the work. Slaves were acquired from Africa. They were then shipped across the Atlantic Ocean. The slaves worked to gather or grow raw materials. These were shipped to countries in Europe. Some, including gold, silver, sugar, and tobacco, remained in Europe. Others, such as wood and cotton, were turned into furniture, clothes, and other products. Many of these goods were shipped back across the ocean for colonists to buy.

A large number of colonists believed that they were being exploited by the Europeans. The colonists wanted to keep the raw materials in their own lands so that they could make finished products of their own. This created ill will between the colonists and Europeans. Resentment between the two began to grow. Later, there were rebellions and independence movements in the colonies. Many colonies thus gained their freedom.

• **Glossary** •

raw material: any material before it is made into another form
manpower: the people who are available to work

1 The word "acquire" in the passage is closest in meaning to

(A) obtain

(B) purchase

(C) trade for

(D) battle

2 According to paragraph 2, which of the following is NOT true of trade involving Europe, Africa, and the Americas?

(A) Much of the work in the colonies was done by slave labor.

(B) Raw materials were exported from the Americas.

(C) Black slaves were sent from Africa to Europe.

(D) Some trade goods, such as sugar and gold, stayed in Europe.

3 Which of the sentences below best expresses the essential information in the highlighted sentence in the passage? *Incorrect* answer choices change the meaning in important ways or leave out essential information.

(A) Many colonists felt that the Europeans were using them.

(B) The Europeans enjoyed exploiting the colonists.

(C) The colonists did not want to work for the Europeans.

(D) Both the Europeans and the colonists profited from their exploits.

4 *Directions*: Select the appropriate phrases from the answer choices and match them to the place to which they relate. TWO of the answer choices will NOT be used. *This question is worth 3 points*.

Answer Choices	**PLACE**
1 Used slaves to do a lot of work	**Europe**
2 Created finished products to sell to others	•
3 Was the source of many raw materials	•
4 Exploited the lands that were owned	**Colony**
5 Lost many men and women to be used as slaves	•
6 Wanted to get independence and be free	•
7 Sold gems and spices to others	•

Reading Comprehension   Complete the following sentences. Use the words in the box.

a. rebelled against	b. black African slaves	c. finished products	d. acquired colonies

1 Several European countries _____ in the Americas, Africa, and Asia.

2 _____ were used to work in the Europeans' colonies.

3 The colonies shipped raw materials to Europe to be made into _____ .

4 Many colonists _____ the Europeans since they wanted independence.

Mercantilism

In the 1500s, a new type of economic system began in Europe. It would be the main system for the next 300 years. Its name was mercantilism. It was a type of economic **nationalism**. It led to countries competing against one another in many ways. It even resulted in some conflicts between them.

²➡ Mercantilism was based on a simple idea. It was that a country should try to gain economic superiority over other nations. There were many ways a country could do this. The most important way was to have a strong domestic economy. It should focus on exporting its products to other lands. In addition, a country should import as few items as possible. It should do this for two reasons. First, having a favorable **balance of trade** would give the country more gold and silver. Second, it would let the country be as self-sufficient as possible.

1 Thanks to mercantilism, many countries used trade to try to improve their economies. **2** This made them want to found colonies. **3** Some countries had colonies in Africa and Asia. **4** Others had colonies in the Americas. Spain, France, England, and Portugal all did this. Many of their strongest colonies were in North and South America.

⁴➡ In many cases, the colonies were sources of raw materials. These included timber, furs, sugar, fish, gold, and silver. They were then sent to Europe. The raw materials were often made into finished products. Then, they were exported back to the colonies or to other countries. Countries often fought wars in their colonies. England and France engaged in many battles in North America. English ships also often attacked Spanish treasure ships as well as their colonies. The ultimate goal was always to make the motherland richer in every way possible.

• **Glossary** •

nationalism: devotion to and love of one's own country; patriotism
balance of trade: the difference in the values of a country's exports and imports

1   The word "conflicts" in the passage is closest in meaning to

     Ⓐ treaties

     Ⓑ wars

     Ⓒ commerce

     Ⓓ disagreements

2   In paragraph 2, the author implies that mercantilism

     Ⓐ made countries want to avoid depending on others

     Ⓑ is still practiced by some countries today

     Ⓒ was the most successful economic system in the past

     Ⓓ ended because too many wars were fought for gold

3   According to paragraph 4, which of the following is true of European colonies?

     Ⓐ They had fairly small populations most of the time.

     Ⓑ They were major sources of finished materials.

     Ⓒ They were often richer than their mother countries.

     Ⓓ They provided raw materials for their countries.

4   Look at the four squares [■] that indicate where the following sentence could be added to the passage.

Among them were Goa in India and Malacca in modern-day Malaysia.

Where would the sentence best fit?

✎ Reading Comprehension   Complete the following sentences. Use the words in the box.

a. founded colonies	b. raw materials	c. compete against	d. strong domestic economies

1 Mercantilism caused countries in Europe to _____ one another.

2 Countries wanted _____ with a favorable balance of trade.

3 European countries _____ in places around the world.

4 Colonies sent various _____ to countries in Europe.

The Rise of Factories

An early textile factory

The majority of finished products people buy are made in factories. There are few places nowadays where people still make goods in their homes. But this was a common activity in the past. Until the 1700s, there were no factories. However, once the Industrial Revolution began, factories began to open in many places. They radically changed how economies operated.

²➜ "Cottage industry" is the term that is used to describe the act of people making things in their homes. In England prior to the Industrial Revolution, almost all products were made in cottage industries. This was especially true of textiles. Textiles are materials used to make clothing. Before the 1700s, people prepared and spun wool and cotton in their homes. This produced yarn, which the people sold to cloth makers. They made large sheets of certain types of cloth out of the yarn. They would leave the cloth plain, dye it, or imprint it. The finished textiles were then sent to tailors, who made clothing.

³➜ All of that work was done by hand. It took a long time to prepare the yarn. Carding was one job that people did to prepare the wool and cotton. To do this, the workers had to comb the fibers to remove seeds from the cotton and dirt from the wool. In addition, the workers had to straighten the fibers. This required a lot of time. Entire families were often involved in carding, spinning, and other aspects of making textiles.

⁴➜ Then, factories were founded in England in the 1700s. Textiles were the first major factory-based industry in the world. Inventors made machines that could card and spin yarn much faster than people working in their homes could. Enormous **looms** were made. These could produce cloth at rapid rates. Steam engines operated much of this machinery. The textile industry swiftly moved

from being a cottage-based industry to a factory-based one. This happened in many other industries as well.

5 ➡ Because of factories, countless people working in cottage industries lost their jobs. They often protested against these factories. Some even attacked the factories and **wrecked** their machinery. But the factories did not go away. They earned huge profits for their owners. Most people had no choice but to work in the factories, so they often moved to where the factories were located. Cities such as Manchester quickly expanded. From England, industrialization spread around the world.

6 ➡ These changes also altered the way in which people lived. In many places, standards of living rose. People earned money from working in the factories, so they could spend it on the new products being made. **1** But the rise of factories had some drawbacks. **2** People lived in crowded cities that were polluted. **3** They spent a lot of time away from their homes, worked long hours, and did dangerous jobs. **4** And the cottage industry, for the most part, completely vanished.

• **Glossary** •

loom: a type of machine that can weave yarn into cloth
wreck: to destroy, often on purpose

1   The word "radically" in the passage is closest in meaning to

      Ⓐ theoretically

      Ⓑ initially

      Ⓒ continuously

      Ⓓ drastically

2   According to paragraph 2, which of the following is NOT true of cottage industries?

      Ⓐ They existed before the Industrial Revolution.

      Ⓑ They were used by people living in England.

      Ⓒ They were common in the textile industry.

      Ⓓ They often produced clothing for people.

3   In paragraph 3, the author's description of carding mentions which of the following?

      Ⓐ The reason that people did it

      Ⓑ The way it removed dirt from cotton

      Ⓒ The fact that it was the last step in making textiles

      Ⓓ Why only experts were able to do it

4   According to paragraph 4, which of the following is true of factories in the textile industry?

      Ⓐ They used looms that worked quickly.

      Ⓑ They appeared in the seventeenth century.

      Ⓒ They used engines run by water power.

      Ⓓ There were almost none of them in England.

5   Which of the sentences below best expresses the essential information in the highlighted sentence in the passage? *Incorrect* answer choices change the meaning in important ways or leave out essential information.

      Ⓐ By living close to factories, commuting to work was easy for most people.

      Ⓑ Since people had to work in factories, they moved to places near them.

      Ⓒ It was important for factory workers all to live near their workplaces.

      Ⓓ The people who were living close to factories went to work at them.

6   According to paragraph 5, some people attacked factories because

      Ⓐ they felt that they did not earn enough money

      Ⓑ they were upset about losing their jobs

      Ⓒ they wanted the owners to share the profits

      Ⓓ they thought technology was bad for the environment

7 In paragraph 5, the author implies that Manchester

    (A) was the most important city in England

    (B) was located in the middle of England

    (C) had a large number of factories in it

    (D) had a population greater than London's

8 According to paragraph 6, which of the following is NOT true of the rise of factories?

    (A) It created pollution in many cities.

    (B) It had both advantages and disadvantages.

    (C) It helped the standard of living increase.

    (D) It made some cities become smaller.

9 Look at the four squares [■] that indicate where the following sentence could be added to the passage.

People also became more educated during this period.

Where would the sentence best fit?

> Click on a square [■] to add the sentence to the passage.

10 *Directions*: An introductory sentence for a brief summary of the passage is provided below. Complete the summary by selecting the THREE answer choices that express the most important ideas of the passage. Some sentences do not belong because they express ideas that are not presented in the passage or are minor ideas in the passage. *This question is worth 2 points*.

> Drag your answer choices to the spaces where they belong.
> To remove an answer choice, click on it. To review the passage, click on **View Text**.

The rise of factories in the Industrial Revolution resulted in the downfall of cottage industries.

-
-
-

Answer Choices

1. The number of factories increased since they made their owners rich.

2. Factories greatly changed the way in which people worked and made products.

3. Cottage industries were popular with people who worked with textiles.

4. Some upset workers tried to destroy the machines that were in factories.

5. Factories used machines that could do work much faster than people could.

6. There was an increase in pollution in a lot of the cities in England.

Star Performer Word Files

- **apprentice** (n) a person who is learning a trade
  The **apprentice** is working hard to learn to become a baker.

- **artisan** (n) a skilled worker
  There are many **artisans** looking for work nowadays.

- **barter** (v) to trade goods for one another without using money
  Some people prefer to **barter** for the goods they need.

- **carpenter** (n) a person who makes wood items
  The **carpenter** made a beautiful wooden table.

- **cash** (n) money such as paper bills and coins
  How much **cash** are you carrying with you?

- **century** (n) a period of one hundred years
  The twentieth **century** was a time of great progress.

- **colonist** (n) a person who is a member of a colony
  Many **colonists** never return to their home countries.

- **consist** (v) to be made of
  Her possessions **consist** of few items.

- **cottage** (n) a very small and simple home
  The man lived in a small **cottage** in the forest.

- **craft** (n) a skill
  She knows a lot about her **craft**.

- **desire** (v) to want; to wish for
  I **desire** to take a trip around the world.

- **dye** (v) to change the color of
  Kevin **dyed** his hair to make himself look younger.

- **engage** (v) to take part in
  They **engaged** in a debate about the upcoming election.

- **export** (v) to send goods out of a country to sell them
  Her company **exports** clothing to Europe.

- **float** (v) to move over the water
  This boat looks like it will not **float** but will sink instead.

- **fur** (n) the hairy skin of an animal
  Animal **furs** such as beaver and rabbit can be expensive.

- **gem** (n) a precious stone such as a diamond, ruby, or emerald
  Some people become rich by trading in **gems**.

- **generation** (n) an age group
  The young **generation** has a lot of potential.

- **independence** (n) freedom
  The people in the colony wanted **independence**.

- **judge** (v) to evaluate
  Do not **judge** me by my actions.

- **labor** (n) work

  He finished doing his **labors** and went home for the day.

- **maritime** (adj) related to the sea or ocean; marine; naval

  The **maritime** trade is important to that country's economy.

- **master** (n) a person who is very skilled at a certain trade

  He became a **master** after years of practicing his craft.

- **motherland** (n) a person's home country

  They will return to their **motherland** next week.

- **overland** (adv) across the land

  They went **overland** to get to the ocean.

- **pack animal** (n) an animal such as a horse or mule that is used to transport goods

  We need some **pack animals** to carry our equipment.

- **profession** (n) a line of work

  What is Judy's **profession**?

- **profit** (n) the money that a person or company earns

  They will make a big **profit** if the product becomes popular.

- **qualified** (adj) capable; skilled

  Sarah is not **qualified** for the job.

- **raft** (n) a simple boat that can float on the water

  The students went down the river in a **raft** that they built.

- **resentment** (n) a feeling of anger or bitterness

  Her feelings of **resentment** made people dislike her.

- **sail** (v) to move on the water in a ship

  Helen is going to **sail** her ship around the world.

- **self-sufficient** (adj) able to provide for oneself

  A **self-sufficient** person does not rely on others for anything.

- **skilled** (adj) talented; able

  He is highly **skilled** at making shoes.

- **slave** (n) a person who is owned by another

  The **slaves** revolted against their masters.

- **standards** (n) values; principles

  The **standards** for working at that company are high.

- **tailor** (n) a person who makes clothes

  She hired a **tailor** to make some dresses for her.

- **trade** (v) to buy and sell

  He **trades** stocks on a daily basis.

- **transaction** (n) a deal; a trade

  I only make cash **transactions** and avoid using credit cards.

- **waterborne** (adj) on the water

  Waterborne trade ended when the hurricane arrived.

Vocabulary Review

Choose the word or phrase closest in meaning to the highlighted part of the sentence.

1 The slaves worked to gather or grow raw materials.
- (A) buy
- (B) collect
- (C) sell
- (D) trade

2 Journeymen were able to earn money by using their talents though.
- (A) skills
- (B) ideas
- (C) possessions
- (D) feelings

3 The ultimate goal was always to make the motherland richer in every way possible.
- (A) basic
- (B) secret
- (C) extensive
- (D) real

4 England, France, Spain, and Portugal possessed most of the colonies in the Americas.
- (A) owned
- (B) founded
- (C) fought for
- (D) created

5 These could produce cloth at rapid rates.
- (A) fast
- (B) normal
- (C) unique
- (D) gradual

6 Later, there were rebellions and independence movements in the colonies.
- (A) wars
- (B) battles
- (C) riots
- (D) revolutions

7 After completing their studies, they became journeymen.
- (A) considering
- (B) finishing
- (C) portraying
- (D) paying for

8 They radically changed how economies operated.
- (A) excelled
- (B) failed
- (C) functioned
- (D) moved

9 Colonies became vital parts of many European empires.
- (A) minor
- (B) outer
- (C) replacement
- (D) important

10 Coins are in constant use today.
- (A) typical
- (B) partial
- (C) continual
- (D) popular

11 These included timber, furs, sugar, fish, gold, and silver.
- (A) animals
- (B) food
- (C) spices
- (D) wood

12 These enabled even more extensive waterborne trade to take place.
- (A) serious
- (B) broad
- (C) fortunate
- (D) expensive

Part B

Chapter 06 Life Sciences

Life sciences involve the study of living organisms. The life sciences include biology, marine biology, botany, physiology, zoology, and paleontology. People in these fields study plants, animals, and other organisms. They examine the physical characteristics of organisms. And they examine how organisms interact with their environments as well as with other organisms. Some people in the life sciences even study extinct animals such as dinosaurs.

Mastering **the Question Types** A

☑ Vocabulary   □ Fill in a Table   □ Factual Information   □ Negative Factual Information   ☑ Prose Summary
□ Insert Text   □ Reference   ☑ Rhetorical Purpose   □ Sentence Simplification   □ Inference

The Jellyfish

One of the oldest animal species on the Earth is the jellyfish. It has been around for hundreds of millions of years. It lived before the dinosaurs and survived after they went extinct. During that time, more than 10,000 species of jellyfish have evolved.

²➡ Despite its name, the jellyfish is not a fish. It is an <u>invertebrate</u>. It is a fairly simple animal. The jellyfish has no central nervous system or circulatory system. It also lacks a respiratory system. Its two primary features are its bell, which contains its stomach, and its tentacles. Most of the jellyfish— around ninety-five percent—is made up of water.

The <u>tentacles</u> are the most dangerous part of a jellyfish. When it hunts, it uses them to sting its prey. They release venom, which paralyzes its prey. The jellyfish can then feed on the helpless animal. Jellyfish venom can be highly potent. In some cases, it is strong enough to kill a human.

• **Glossary** •

invertebrate: an animal that lacks a backbone
tentacle: a long feeler on an animal that helps it sense things

1 In paragraph 2, the author uses "a respiratory system" as an example of

    Ⓐ a part of the jellyfish that is in its bell

    Ⓑ the primary feature of the jellyfish

    Ⓒ the system that helps the jellyfish breathe

    Ⓓ something the jellyfish does not have

2 The word "potent" in the passage is closest in meaning to

    Ⓐ fast acting

    Ⓑ powerful

    Ⓒ effective

    Ⓓ useful

3 *Directions*: An introductory sentence for a brief summary of the passage is provided below. Complete the summary by selecting the THREE answer choices that express the most important ideas of the passage. Some sentences do not belong because they express ideas that are not presented in the passage or are minor ideas in the passage. *This question is worth 2 points.*

The jellyfish is a simple predator that has been around for a long time.

-
-
-

Answer Choices

1 Jellyfish have lived on the Earth for hundreds of millions of years.

2 Some species of jellyfish can kill humans easily.

3 The jellyfish uses venom from its tentacles to catch prey.

4 There are more than 10,000 species of jellyfish.

5 The jellyfish's body is mostly its bell and tentacles.

6 A small part of the jellyfish's body is made of water.

✐ Checking Reading Accuracy   Mark the following statements T (true) or F (false).

    T   **F**

1 ☐ / ☐   Jellyfish evolved at the same time as the dinosaurs.

2 ☐ / ☐   The jellyfish is not an invertebrate but a fish.

3 ☐ / ☐   Around ninety-five percent of a jellyfish is water.

4 ☐ / ☐   Jellyfish venom can paralyze other animals.

□ Vocabulary ☑ Fill in a Table □ Factual Information ☑ Negative Factual Information □ Prose Summary
□ Insert Text □ Reference □ Rhetorical Purpose □ Sentence Simplification ☑ Inference

Natural Selection in the Peppered Moth

¹→ Charles Darwin was one of the first men to promote the theory of natural selection. It concerns how living things evolve. Organisms evolve because their living conditions change. So they respond in order to continue living. But only the strongest members of a species survive. They breed and produce new generations. These **inherit** or adapt the traits that helped previous generations survive.

²→ The peppered moth is native to England. It successfully adapted in response to changes in its environment. In the past, some moths were dark in color. Others were light. They all lived in trees. During the Industrial Revolution, many trees turned dark due to **soot** from factories. The dark peppered moths hid in the soot. But predators easily saw the light-colored moths on the dark trees. The dark moths survived. All of the light-colored moths were eaten. Within a few generations, nearly all peppered moths were dark colored.

• **Glossary** •

inherit: to receive something genetically from one's ancestors
soot: a black substance formed by the burning of coal, wood, or oil

1 According to paragraph 1, which of the following is NOT true of natural selection?

(A) It explains why the strongest animals survive.

(B) It was explained by Charles Darwin.

(C) It focuses on the evolution of living things.

(D) It concerns why some animals breed with others.

2 In paragraph 2, which of the following can be inferred about the Industrial Revolution?

(A) A lot of pollution was created during it.

(B) It started in England and then spread elsewhere.

(C) Many animal species were harmed during it.

(D) It lasted for more than one hundred years.

3 *Directions*: Select the appropriate sentences from the answer choices and match them to the cause and effect of natural selection to which they relate. TWO of the answer choices will NOT be used. *This question is worth 3 points*.

Answer Choices	NATURAL SELECTION
① Many predators hunted the peppered moth.	**Cause**
② New generations inherit preferred traits from older ones.	•
③ There is a change in the environment.	•
④ The strongest members of a species live.	**Effect**
⑤ Pollution has an effect on many animals.	•
⑥ Organisms begin to evolve.	•
⑦ An organism's living conditions change.	•

Checking Reading Accuracy Mark the following statements T (true) or F (false).

	T	F	
1	☐ /	☐	Natural selection was described by Charles Darwin.
2	☐ /	☐	The peppered moth is found in England.
3	☐ /	☐	There were once white and green peppered moths.
4	☐ /	☐	The peppered moth evolved in response to a change in its environment.

Mastering **the Question Types** C

☐ Vocabulary   ☐ Fill in a Table   ☑ Factual Information   ☐ Negative Factual Information   ☐ Prose Summary

☑ Insert Text   ☑ Reference   ☐ Rhetorical Purpose   ☑ Sentence Simplification   ☐ Inference

Protozoa

A protozoan is a tiny single-celled organism. It can move independently. It can also survive in many kinds of environments. In fact, it can live in any place with moisture. A protozoan gets its food by ingesting small molecules or cells from other living things. Scientists have identified around 60,000 types of protozoa. They expect to discover even more in the future.

²➔ Some protozoa can live by themselves. They do not require a <u>host</u>. But many do. So they live inside other organisms. These are classified as <u>parasites</u>. Parasites can cause a number of diseases in their hosts. In some cases, the diseases are fatal.

Not all protozoa are harmful. ❶ Many even make up crucial parts of the food chain. ❷ For instance, zooplankton is a protozoan species. ❸ It is a common food for many ocean animals. ❹ Without zooplankton, numerous species of fish would be deprived of a major source of food.

• **Glossary** •

host: an organism in which another organism, such as a parasite, may live

parasite: an organism that lives on the body of another and harms it in some way

1 The word "They" in the passage refers to

    (A) Small molecules

    (B) Living things

    (C) Scientists

    (D) 60,000 types of protozoa

2 According to paragraph 2, which of the following is true of parasites?

    (A) They are able to live by themselves.

    (B) They always kill their hosts after some time.

    (C) They are protozoa that need a host to survive.

    (D) They can help their hosts in some ways.

3 Which of the sentences below best expresses the essential information in the highlighted sentence in the passage? *Incorrect* answer choices change the meaning in important ways or leave out essential information.

    (A) Many fish would eat less if there were no zooplankton.

    (B) Most fish need to eat zooplankton in order to survive.

    (C) By eating zooplankton, fish can grow to be large in size.

    (D) Zooplankton provides important nutrients for all fish.

4 Look at the four squares [■] that indicate where the following sentence could be added to the passage.

Several species of whales make zooplankton a major part of their daily diets.

Where would the sentence best fit?

Checking Reading Accuracy Mark the following statements T (true) or F (false).

	T	F	
1	☐	☐	Protozoa are animals that have multiple cells.
2	☐	☐	Up to 60,000 protozoa can live in a single host.
3	☐	☐	Parasites are protozoa that need a host to survive.
4	☐	☐	Zooplankton is one species of protozoa.

Microecosystems

[1]→ An ecosystem is an area that supports many organisms. Some can be quite large. They include forests, deserts, and oceans. Others can be rather small. Scientists call them microecosystems. Examples are a puddle of water, a section of soil, an underwater **thermal** vent, and a single tree. Even the internal body of an animal can be considered one. It supports bacteria and other microorganisms. Despite being tiny, microecosystems play vital roles in the lives of many organisms.

A lot of factors can influence microecosystems. They include temperature, water content, chemical composition, salt content, and acid levels. **1** Taken together, they determine which organisms live in a microecosystem. **2** But every microecosystem is part of a larger ecosystem. **3** So any change in an ecosystem can have a great effect on a microecosystem as well. **4**

[3]→ A microecosystem can be found just about anywhere. Some, such as thermal vents, are deep beneath the ocean. They are created by undersea volcanoes. The vents produce hot water no matter how deep they are. Their warmth attracts numerous underwater life forms. They come together to form their own microecosystem. Many areas around thermal vents are **teeming** with life.

[4]→ A tree is another example of a microecosystem. Insects, birds, snakes, and people—among others—may all interact within it. For instance, insects may live in the tree. They get nutrition from eating other insects or from the tree itself. Birds can use the tree for several reasons. They may eat the insects. And they may use the tree's leaves and branches to build their nests. Predators such as snakes may eat the insects and birds in the tree. And humans may harvest the nuts or fruit from the tree. All of these creatures interact with each other in one microecosystem.

• **Glossary** •

thermal: hot; related to heat
teem: to be abundant; to abound with

1 In paragraph 1, the author uses "forests, deserts, and oceans" as examples of

    Ⓐ the Earth's most common ecosystems

    Ⓑ areas with the most organisms

    Ⓒ places where certain animals live

    Ⓓ ecosystems that are big in size

2 According to paragraph 3, thermal vents attract organisms because

    Ⓐ they produce warm water deep under the ocean

    Ⓑ they create nutrients for the organisms to eat

    Ⓒ they provide light deep beneath the surface

    Ⓓ they give animals safe places away from volcanoes

3 According to paragraph 4, which of the following is NOT true of a tree microecosystem?

    Ⓐ Several different animals may interact in it.

    Ⓑ It may have both predators and prey animals.

    Ⓒ The seeds of the tree may be useful.

    Ⓓ Some snakes eat the tree's fruit or nuts.

4 Look at the four squares [■] that indicate where the following sentence could be added to the passage.

Minor differences in all of these factors can produce numerous unique microecosystems.

Where would the sentence best fit?

Reading Comprehension Complete the following sentences. Use the words in the box.

a. is very small	b. thermal vents	c. all types of organisms	d. can affect

1 An ecosystem that _____ is known as a microecosystem.

2 The temperature and the water content of a place _____ a microecosystem.

3 _____ deep under the water are one type of microecosystem.

4 A tree may have _____ interacting in a unique microecosystem.

Predators and Prey

All ecosystems have predators and prey animals. Predators are hunters. They catch and eat prey animals. A lion hunting, killing, and eating a zebra is one example of a predator-prey relationship. These relationships are crucial in all ecosystems. They play a role in maintaining the balance of an ecosystem. If either predators or prey become too numerous, problems can arise.

Prey animals usually eat plants. Predators, however, eat prey animals. The number of predators in an area is almost always much less than the number of prey animals in the same region. An area can only support a certain number of predators. For instance, wolves often live in small **packs** of fewer than ten members. They mark the **territory** in which they live and hunt. Their area often has many deer and other small mammals. These prey animals support the local wolf population. The wolves are also territorial. They attack any other wolf that enters their land.

³→ Sometimes the balance between predators and prey gets upset. There may suddenly be too many predators and not enough prey for them to eat. There are normally two results. Some of the predators may die. Or they may move to a different area. A few species of predators actually regulate their numbers. Wolves do this by not breeding. Some male wolves simply do not mate. This ensures that the entire pack has ample food.

At other times, a region may have too many prey animals. This happens when there are few or no predators. Prey animals tend to reproduce quickly. So the animals might eat all of the vegetation in an area. This can upset the balance of an ecosystem. This has happened in Australia. The rabbit population has grown out of control since the rabbits have no natural enemies there.

• **Glossary** •

pack: a group of animals of the same kind, especially predators
territory: land, especially in which a certain animal lives

1 Which of the sentences below best expresses the essential information in the highlighted sentence in the passage? *Incorrect* answer choices change the meaning in important ways or leave out essential information.

Ⓐ Prey animals tend to outnumber a few of the predators.

Ⓑ An area usually has fewer predators than prey animals.

Ⓒ The number of predators and prey animals in one place is equal.

Ⓓ There are many more predators than prey animals.

2 The word "territorial" in the passage is closest in meaning to

Ⓐ curious   Ⓑ apparent

Ⓒ protective   Ⓓ reticent

3 According to paragraph 3, how can the balance between predators and prey animals get upset?

Ⓐ Some predators stop hunting certain animals.

Ⓑ There are too many predators in a region.

Ⓒ Prey animals move to a new ecosystem.

Ⓓ The amount of vegetation in a region increases.

4 *Directions*: An introductory sentence for a brief summary of the passage is provided below. Complete the summary by selecting the THREE answer choices that express the most important ideas of the passage. Some sentences do not belong because they express ideas that are not presented in the passage or are minor ideas in the passage. *This question is worth 2 points*.

The relationship between predators and prey animals in a region is important to the ecosystem.

-
-
-

Answer Choices

1 Wolves and lions are both predators that hunt prey animals for food.

2 Some wolves will not breed when there are too many of them in a region.

3 A lot of animals mark the territory in which they usually hunt and live.

4 When the balance between predators and prey is upset, some predators may die.

5 The prey animals in an area almost always outnumber the predators.

6 Prey animals with no natural predators often reproduce in great numbers.

Reading Comprehension Complete the following sentences. Use the words in the box.

| a. lack natural predators | b. too many predators | c. of an ecosystem | d. territorial animals |

1 The predator-prey relationship is important to the balance _____ .

2 Wolves are _____ and will attack other wolves that enter their land.

3 If there are _____ , some of them may move to another place.

4 The Australian rabbit population has increased since the rabbits _____ .

Annuals and Perennials

¹➜ The majority of plants are annuals or perennials. Annuals live for a single season and then die. Perennials live for more than two seasons. Parts of them die, but their main parts survive. Some perennials can live for centuries. Biennials are another kind of plant. They live for just two seasons. But they are the least common type of plant.

²➜ Many flowers, such as daisies and petunias, are annuals. So are wheat, corn, barley, and other crops. An annual sprouts from the ground, blooms, and then dies all in the space of one growing season. The entire plant—its roots, stems, and leaves—dies. But annuals leave behind seeds that remain **dormant** in the ground. The next year, new plants grow from these seeds. There are both summer annuals and winter annuals. Summer annuals sprout in spring and live for either weeks or months in summer. Winter annuals may start growing in fall or winter. Then, they bloom in spring and die in summer. Most winter annuals live in climates that lack cold winters.

³➜ All trees are perennials. So are potatoes, mint, garlic, strawberries, and many other plants. Perennials with flowers and leaves usually bloom in spring and become dormant in fall. Some only have flowers or **bear** fruit in their first year. After that, the flowers and the fruit never reappear even though the plant continues to live. Other perennials have flowers and fruit every year. Some perennials have adapted to live in harsh environments. They can survive in cold weather and dry conditions. They do this thanks to special structures in them. Deciduous trees, for example, shed their leaves each fall in cold climates. This helps the trees save energy and live during winter. So they are able to survive year after year.

• Glossary •
dormant: inactive; asleep
bear: to produce in a natural manner

1 In paragraph 1, the author implies that biennials

    Ⓐ produce more fruit than perennials

    Ⓑ can sometimes become perennials

    Ⓒ are less common than annuals

    Ⓓ often die in their first year

2 In paragraph 2, the author uses "daisies and petunias" as examples of

    Ⓐ two types of annuals

    Ⓑ some rare flowers

    Ⓒ flowers that bloom

    Ⓓ the most common annuals

3 In paragraph 3, the author's description of perennials mentions all of the following EXCEPT:

    Ⓐ the reason some only produce fruit in their first year

    Ⓑ the way some manage to survive during winter

    Ⓒ the environments some can live in

    Ⓓ the trees that are considered perennials

4 *Directions*: Select the appropriate sentences from the answer choices and match them to the type of plant to which they relate. TWO of the answer choices will NOT be used. ***This question is worth 3 points.***

Answer Choices	**TYPE OF PLANT**
① Survives only for two growing seasons	**Annual**
② May leave behind seeds when it dies	•
③ Includes crops such as wheat and corn	•
④ Is the least common type of plant	•
⑤ Dies after one season of growth	**Perennial**
⑥ Lives for several growing seasons	•
⑦ Includes every species of tree	•

✎ Reading Comprehension Complete the following sentences. Use the words in the box.

a. adapted to survive	b. wheat, corn, and barley	c. winter annuals	d. after one season

1 Many flowers and crops such as _____ are annuals.

2 The roots, stems, and leaves of annuals all die _____.

3 _____ start growing in fall or winter and then die in summer.

4 Perennials have _____ in a number of different conditions.

The Relationship between Dinosaurs and Birds

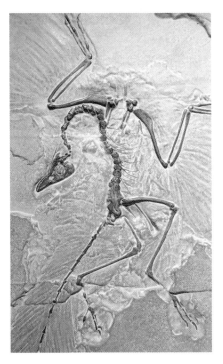

The Berlin *Archaeopteryx* fossil

The study of dinosaurs began in the 1800s. That was when people started to discover many fossilized dinosaur bones. For decades, paleontologists have thought that dinosaurs were related to modern reptiles. Yet some have a different theory. They believe that dinosaurs have a connection with birds. The basis for this idea is the similar body structures they share. There are even some experts who believe that birds evolved from dinosaurs.

²→ Thomas Huxley, a British scientist, was the first person to declare his belief that birds had evolved from dinosaurs. He noted the similarities between meat-eating dinosaurs and birds. For instance, he pointed out that the leg structures of dinosaurs were similar to those of birds. Then, a fossilized animal with feathers was found in Germany in the middle of the 1800s. Scientists called it *Archaeopteryx*. It was a known species. At that time, it was classified as a dinosaur. It had teeth, not a beak. It also had claws on its wings. Yet the fossil unearthed in Germany had feathers. This led scientists such as Huxley to believe that it was a bird since they assumed that only birds had feathers. Still, some experts claimed that *Archaeopteryx* was not a dinosaur even though it lived at the same time as they had.

³→ For the rest of the 1800s, the idea that birds evolved from dinosaurs fell out of favor. Many people came to believe that reptiles and dinosaurs were related instead. But the bird-dinosaur debate began **anew** in the 1900s. **1** In 1916, a Danish scientist published a book on birds. **2** He mentioned that birds and dinosaurs had similar bone structures. **3** Decades later in the 1960s, the bird-dinosaur theory grew stronger. **4** Many experts started to favor it. They found more fossils. These let them make more comparisons between birds and dinosaurs. One expert pointed out there were twenty-two similarities in the skeletons of carnivorous dinosaurs and birds. The fact that both had **fused** collarbones was considered a vital sign of their connection.

⁴→ In recent years, more fossilized birds have been dug up. Many of them date to times when dinosaurs lived. These fossils have given more strength to the idea that birds and dinosaurs shared a common ancestor. Yet there remain many skeptics. They believe that the ability of flight must be considered. They claim that birds evolved from a tree-climbing reptile. That, they say, is how birds learned to fly. They state that birds could not have evolved from ground-based dinosaurs. Nevertheless, the bird-dinosaur theory is becoming more popular. Perhaps one day a fossil may be found that will finally settle the debate.

• **Glossary** •

anew: again; once more
fused: merged; complex; joined

1 The word "basis" in the passage is closest in meaning to

    Ⓐ foundation

    Ⓑ proof

    Ⓒ experiment

    Ⓓ research

2 The author discusses "Thomas Huxley" in paragraph 2 in order to

    Ⓐ stress that he discovered an *Archaeopteryx* fossil with feathers

    Ⓑ explain who first mentioned that birds evolved from dinosaurs

    Ⓒ claim that he was a noted authority on birds and dinosaurs

    Ⓓ give the name of one of the most famous paleontologists

3 Which of the sentences below best expresses the essential information in the highlighted sentence in the passage? *Incorrect* answer choices change the meaning in important ways or leave out essential information.

    Ⓐ Some experts doubted *Archaeopteryx* was a dinosaur despite the two being contemporaries.

    Ⓑ It was clear to most of the experts that *Archaeopteryx* could not have been a dinosaur.

    Ⓒ *Archaeopteryx* lived at the same time as the dinosaurs, but it was not actually a dinosaur.

    Ⓓ Any animal, such as *Archaeopteryx*, that lived at that time was considered a dinosaur.

4 According to paragraph 2, which of the following is true of *Archaeopteryx*?

    Ⓐ Every fossil of it that was found had feathers.

    Ⓑ Some scientists believed it was a bird.

    Ⓒ It had both teeth and a beak.

    Ⓓ Despite having wings, it could not fly.

5 In paragraph 3, the author's description of the bird-dinosaur debate mentions all of the following EXCEPT:

    Ⓐ the way that a book influenced the debate

    Ⓑ the many similarities birds and dinosaur skeletons had

    Ⓒ the fossils that influenced the debate

    Ⓓ the time that belief in the theory became stronger

6 The word "skeptics" in the passage is closest in meaning to

    Ⓐ doubters

    Ⓑ commenters

    Ⓒ experts

    Ⓓ researchers

7 In paragraph 4, why does the author mention "a tree-climbing reptile"?

(A) To compare it with ground-based dinosaurs

(B) To describe one of the last dinosaurs that lived

(C) To name a possible animal that birds came from

(D) To describe a dinosaur that was recently discovered

8 According to paragraph 4, some people believe birds learned to fly because

(A) they inherited wings from some dinosaurs

(B) they lived in areas with many mountains

(C) they evolved from reptiles that climbed trees

(D) they were related to ground-based dinosaurs

9 Look at the four squares [■] that indicate where the following sentence could be added to the passage.

Its title was *The Origin of Birds*.

Where would the sentence best fit?

> Click on a square [■] to add the sentence to the passage.

10 *Directions*: An introductory sentence for a brief summary of the passage is provided below. Complete the summary by selecting the THREE answer choices that express the most important ideas of the passage. Some sentences do not belong because they express ideas that are not presented in the passage or are minor ideas in the passage. *This question is worth 2 points.*

> Drag your answer choices to the spaces where they belong.
> To remove an answer choice, click on it. To review the passage, click on **View Text**.

The discovery of fossils of animals like *Archaeopteryx* has led some to believe that birds evolved from dinosaurs.

-
-
-

Answer Choices

1 Many experts believe birds came from dinosaurs because of newly discovered fossils.

2 An *Archaeopteryx* fossil had feathers, so scientists considered it to be a bird.

3 Thomas Huxley was a famous paleontologist who studied both birds and dinosaurs.

4 It was in the 1800s that dinosaur bones first began to be unearthed by people.

5 There are a few skeptics who believe birds evolved from tree-climbing reptiles.

6 Many experts have noted similarities between the bones of birds and some dinosaurs.

Star Performer Word Files

- **adapt** (v) to get used to; to adjust

  You must learn to **adapt** to the cold weather.

- **bloom** (v) to flower; to blossom

  The roses are beautiful when they **bloom**.

- **branch** (n) a part of a tree that extends from the trunk; a twig

  A hawk is sitting on that tree **branch**.

- **breed** (v) to mate; to reproduce

  Rabbits **breed** constantly, so their numbers go up quickly.

- **carnivorous** (adj) meat-eating

  Dogs and wolves are both **carnivorous** animals.

- **circulatory** (adj) relating to the movement of blood in the body

  He has **circulatory** problems because he is unhealthy.

- **classify** (v) to order; to categorize

  How do scientists **classify** that animal?

- **composition** (n) a makeup

  The **composition** of that product includes several rare metals.

- **crucial** (adj) important

  The elections are a **crucial** time in the country's history.

- **debate** (n) an argument

  Kevin easily won his **debate** against Paul.

- **desert** (n) an area of land that gets little or no precipitation

  No rain has fallen in that **desert** for a century.

- **determine** (v) to decide

  The judges will **determine** the winner soon.

- **dormant** (adj) inactive; asleep

  Many reptiles become **dormant** when the weather gets cold.

- **evolve** (v) to change over the course of time

  Some scientists believe animals **evolve** due to their environments.

- **extinct** (adj) no longer alive as a species

  The dodo bird went **extinct** because people hunted it.

- **fatal** (adj) deadly; lethal

  There were three **fatal** car accidents yesterday.

- **harmful** (adj) dangerous

  Swallowing that liquid could be **harmful** to your health.

- **harvest** (v) to collect crops or other food from a field or a plant

  The farmer will **harvest** the wheat crop soon.

- **hide** (v) to conceal

  The fish began to **hide** when the shark swam by.

- **independently** (adv) freely

  Stuart works **independently** from everyone else in his group.

- **interact** (v) to act together

  Many animals **interact** with one another.

- **mammal** (n) a warm-blooded animal such as a human, ape, or elephant

  Mammals need to eat constantly to get enough energy for their bodies.

- **mark** (v) to stain; to identify

  Walter **marked** his land by building a fence around it.

- **moisture** (n) wetness; dampness

  There is too much **moisture** in this room.

- **molecule** (n) an atom; a tiny particle

  It is impossible to see a single **molecule** with the human eye.

- **numerous** (adj) great in number; many

  Numerous people complained about the noise.

- **paralyze** (v) to cause something to be unable to move

  The spider bites its prey and **paralyzes** it.

- **parasite** (n) an organism that needs a host to survive

  The **parasites** caused Lee to get sick.

- **population** (n) the number of a certain species living in an area

  What is the **population** of that city?

- **prey** (n) an animal that gets hunted by others

  Zebras are **prey** for lions and other hunters.

- **produce** (v) to make

  The scientists hope to **produce** a vaccine soon.

- **promote** (v) to sponsor; to advance

  She **promotes** her political beliefs whenever she can.

- **puddle** (n) a small hole filled with water

  Do not jump in that **puddle** and splash water on me.

- **regulate** (v) to control; to keep in order

  The government is trying to **regulate** our lives too much.

- **roots** (n) the underground part of a plant that gathers water and nutrients

  Pull the plant up by its **roots**.

- **share** (v) to have in common

  The two animals **share** a number of characteristics.

- **sprout** (v) to grow, as in a plant

  The flowers should begin to **sprout** next week.

- **structure** (n) an arrangement

  The compound has a very unique **structure**.

- **theory** (n) a hypothesis; an idea

  Please explain your **theory** one more time.

- **vegetation** (n) plant life

  There is very little **vegetation** in that desert.

Choose the word or phrase closest in meaning to the highlighted part of the sentence.

1 Without zooplankton, numerous species of fish would be deprived of a major source of food.
(A) appeared
(B) denied
(C) given
(D) accepted

2 This ensures that the entire pack has ample food.
(A) forces
(B) guarantees
(C) permits
(D) approves

3 They play a role in maintaining the balance of an ecosystem.
(A) keeping
(B) establishing
(C) making
(D) trying

4 Thomas Huxley, a British scientist, was the first person to declare his belief that birds had evolved from dinosaurs.
(A) deny
(B) think
(C) write
(D) state

5 But only the strongest members of a species survive.
(A) grow
(B) live
(C) examine
(D) move

6 Scientists have identified around 60,000 types of protozoa.
(A) studied
(B) contained
(C) named
(D) captured

7 An area can only support a certain number of predators.
(A) sustain
(B) average
(C) permit
(D) assume

8 Some perennials have adapted to live in harsh environments.
(A) severe
(B) waterless
(C) cold
(D) interesting

9 Sometimes the balance between predators and prey gets upset.
(A) transported
(B) repaired
(C) practiced
(D) unbalanced

10 These relationships are crucial in all ecosystems.
(A) animals
(B) hunters
(C) dealings
(D) awards

11 After that, the flowers and the fruit never reappear even though the plant continues to live.
(A) recur
(B) refer
(C) refute
(D) repeal

12 It successfully adapted in response to changes in its environment.
(A) apparently
(B) temporarily
(C) eventually
(D) effectively

Part B

Chapter 07 **Physical Sciences**

There are many physical sciences. They include chemistry, geology, astronomy, physics, and meteorology. The people in these fields study the characteristics, properties, and natures of nonliving things. Chemistry involves the study of elements and compounds. Geology is the study of the Earth. Astronomy is the study of outer space and the objects in it. Physics is the study of energy, matter, force, and motion. And meteorology is the study of the weather.

Mastering **the Question Types** A

☑ Vocabulary □ Fill in a Table □ Factual Information □ Negative Factual Information ☑ Prose Summary
□ Insert Text □ Reference ☑ Rhetorical Purpose □ Sentence Simplification □ Inference

Planetary Rings

¹→ Jupiter, Saturn, Uranus, and Neptune are the four biggest planets in the <u>solar system</u>. These <u>gas giants</u> share many characteristics. For example, all have planetary rings. While Saturn's are the best known, the other three also have rings orbiting them. The planets' rings differ with regard to their number, composition, and other features.

Saturn has the largest and most extensive ring system. Uranus has the next largest system. Neptune has five rings while Jupiter only has a few thin rings. Saturn's rings are primarily made of pieces of rock and ice. Some are as small as grains of sand. But others can be the size of a house. Jupiter's rings, which are difficult to see, are formed of miniscule pieces of dust.

Astronomers are not sure why rings formed. Many believe they are the remains of moons which broke apart. The remains managed to stay in orbit around the planets and then formed rings.

• **Glossary** •

solar system: all the planets, moons, and other objects that orbit the sun

gas giant: a large planet made mostly of gas

1 In paragraph 1, why does the author mention "Jupiter, Saturn, Uranus, and Neptune"?

    (A) To point out that they are gas giants

    (B) To describe how their rings appear

    (C) To mention a feature that they all share

    (D) To discuss their places in the solar system

2 The word "miniscule" in the passage is closest in meaning to

    (A) tiny

    (B) rocky

    (C) random

    (D) individual

3 *Directions*: An introductory sentence for a brief summary of the passage is provided below. Complete the summary by selecting the THREE answer choices that express the most important ideas of the passage. Some sentences do not belong because they express ideas that are not presented in the passage or are minor ideas in the passage. ***This question is worth 2 points.***

The four gas giants in the solar system all have ring systems.

-
-
-

Answer Choices

1 It is possible to see Saturn's rings with a telescope.

2 The ring systems of the planets have different sizes.

3 The rings around planets may be the remains of moons.

4 Jupiter has the smallest ring system of the planets.

5 Some pieces of rock and ice in rings are as big as a house.

6 Each planet's ring system has its own characteristics.

Checking Reading Accuracy Mark the following statements T (true) or F (false).

    T   **F**

1 ☐ / ☐ The four biggest planets in the solar system are gas giants.

2 ☐ / ☐ Saturn and Uranus have the two biggest ring systems.

3 ☐ / ☐ Most of the rings are made of large pieces of rock and ice.

4 ☐ / ☐ Astronomers are certain they know how the rings formed.

☐ Vocabulary ☑ Fill in a Table ☐ Factual Information ☑ Negative Factual Information ☐ Prose Summary
☐ Insert Text ☐ Reference ☐ Rhetorical Purpose ☐ Sentence Simplification ☑ Inference

Potential and Kinetic Energy

¹→ The measurement of how much work a force can do is energy. It is not possible to create or destroy energy. But it can be <u>converted</u> into different forms. Two of them are potential and kinetic energy.

Potential energy is the energy found in an object. The energy exists yet is not being used. The water behind a dam is one source of potential energy. Until it is <u>released</u>, its energy is not used. Because the energy is being stored, it is potential energy.

³→ Kinetic energy is energy in motion. For instance, when the water behind the dam is released, the potential energy changes into kinetic energy. Kinetic energy is what lets people create electricity from water. There are many other forms of it. A ball that is thrown, an airplane in motion, and a moving car all use kinetic energy.

• **Glossary** •

convert: to change; to alter
release: to let go

1   According to paragraph 1, which of the following is NOT true of energy?

    (A) Scientists have learned how to create energy.

    (B) Potential energy is one form that energy can take.

    (C) It is a measurement of the work a force can do.

    (D) It is possible for the form of energy to change.

2   In paragraph 3, the author implies that kinetic energy

    (A) is the most powerful in the form of water

    (B) can change into potential energy

    (C) only appears in manmade objects

    (D) can be difficult for people to utilize

3   *Directions*: Select the appropriate phrases from the answer choices and match them to the form of energy to which they relate. TWO of the answer choices will NOT be used. ***This question is worth 3 points.***

Answer Choices	FORM OF ENERGY
1 Is energy that is being stored	**Potential Energy**
2 Enables electricity to be created from water	•
3 Is the energy in water behind a dam	•
4 Can be the energy of a moving car	**Kinetic Energy**
5 Measures the amount of work that is done	•
6 Refers to energy that is in motion	•
7 May sometimes be created or destroyed	•

✍ **Checking Reading Accuracy**   Mark the following statements T (true) or F (false).

    T   **F**

1   ☐ / ☐   Energy may be both created and destroyed.

2   ☐ / ☐   The energy in an object is potential energy.

3   ☐ / ☐   Energy not yet in motion is kinetic energy.

4   ☐ / ☐   Water released from a dam has potential energy.

☐ Vocabulary ☐ Fill in a Table ☑ Factual Information ☐ Negative Factual Information ☐ Prose Summary
☑ Insert Text ☐ Reference ☐ Rhetorical Purpose ☑ Sentence Simplification ☑ Inference

Robert Boyle

Robert Boyle was born in Ireland in 1627. Since Boyle came from a wealthy family, his parents could afford to pay for him to be schooled. Boyle was interested in many subjects. But the sciences captured his attention the most.

²➜ Boyle conducted frequent experiments. These helped to establish him as a **founder** of the modern scientific method. His work also helped found the field of modern chemistry.

³➜ Boyle's most famous work was called *The Spring and Weight of Air*. ❶ He did a lot of research on air and gas for that book. ❷ In it, he described what has come to be known as Boyle's Law. ❸ It states that when the temperature is constant, there is an inverse relationship between the pressure and the volume of a **confined** gas. ❹ Boyle's Law was the first of the gas laws. Since Boyle's time, other people have discovered more gas laws.

• **Glossary** •

founder: a person who starts or establishes something
confined: restricted; trapped; limited to a certain area

1   Which of the sentences below best expresses the essential information in the highlighted sentence in the passage? *Incorrect* answer choices change the meaning in important ways or leave out essential information.

        (A) Boyle refused to go to school and study.

        (B) Boyle earned a lot of money for his parents.

        (C) Despite being rich, Boyle's family paid for no schooling.

        (D) Boyle's rich parents paid for his education.

2   In paragraph 2, the author implies that Robert Boyle

        (A) became wealthy thanks to his scientific research

        (B) was the best-known scientist during the seventeenth century

        (C) did some work alone and other work with scientists

        (D) made contributions to science that are still useful today

3   According to paragraph 3, which of the following is true of *The Spring and Weight of Air*?

        (A) It was the first book that Boyle wrote.

        (B) Boyle's Law was described in it.

        (C) It was written as a chemistry textbook.

        (D) It described several of the gas laws.

4   Look at the four squares [■] that indicate where the following sentence could be added to the passage.

It was first published in the year 1660.

Where would the sentence best fit?

✒ **Checking Reading Accuracy**   Mark the following statements T (true) or F (false).

	T	F	
1	☐ /	☐	Boyle studied many subjects, including science.
2	☐ /	☐	Boyle was one of the founders of the scientific method.
3	☐ /	☐	Boyle wrote *The Spring and Weight of Air* about gases.
4	☐ /	☐	Boyle's Law was the most difficult to discover of the gas laws.

The Layers of the Earth

The Earth has a number of layers. There are only three major ones though. They are the core, the mantle, and the crust. The innermost part is the core. The outermost part is the crust. And the <u>immense</u> area in between the two is the mantle. During the twentieth century, scientists were able to conduct research on all three layers. This enabled them finally to learn about every section of the Earth.

²➡ The core begins approximately 2,900 kilometers below the Earth's surface. It is divided into two layers: the inner core and the outer core. The inner core is solid and about 1,200 kilometers thick. Most of it is made of iron and nickel. It also contains <u>trace</u> amounts of other metals. Within the inner core, the pressure is so great that its metals cannot melt. That is not true of the outer core. It is made of molten metal and surrounds the inner core. It is more than 2,200 kilometers thick. As the Earth rotates, the outer core spins around the inner core. This creates the Earth's magnetism.

³➡ Above the core lies the mantle. In some places, it begins around ten kilometers beneath the crust under the oceans. And it begins around thirty kilometers beneath the continental crust. However, it starts at various depths around the planet. The mantle is divided into two parts: the inner mantle and the outer mantle. It comprises more than 80% of the planet's total volume.

The crust is located above the mantle. It is the Earth's hard outer shell. It is also the surface upon which humans live. Like the other two layers, the crust has two distinct parts. The oceanic crust is the part beneath the oceans. The continental crust, which is much thicker, is the part that lies beneath the continents.

• **Glossary** •

immense: very large; huge
trace: tiny; miniscule

1   The word "approximately" in the passage is closest in meaning to

    (A) precisely

    (B) somewhat

    (C) around

    (D) considerably

2   According to paragraph 2, which of the following is NOT true of the Earth's core?

    (A) The only metals in it are iron and nickel.

    (B) A part of it is made of melted metal.

    (C) There are two individual sections in it.

    (D) It is nearly 2,900 kilometers below the surface.

3   In paragraph 3, the author implies that the mantle

    (A) may burst through the crust beneath the oceans

    (B) can easily be reached by human technology

    (C) is larger than the core and the crust combined

    (D) contains a large amount of valuable minerals

4   *Directions*: Select the appropriate phrases from the answer choices and match them to the layer of the Earth to which they relate. TWO of the answer choices will NOT be used. ***This question is worth 3 points.***

Answer Choices	LAYER OF THE EARTH
1 Is the part that humans live on	**Core**
2 Is the thinnest of all three layers	•
3 Is the reason the Earth has magnetism	•
4 Contains most of the planet's volume	**Mantle**
5 Can start around ten kilometers under the oceans	•
6 Is the middle layer of the Earth	•
7 Has a lot of iron and nickel	•

Reading Comprehension   Complete the following sentences. Use the words in the box.

a. the outer core	b. the mantle starts	c. the twentieth century	d. humans live

1 Scientists began to learn about the Earth's layers in _____ .

2 The inner core is solid while _____ is made of molten metal.

3 _____ at various places beneath the oceans and the continents.

4 The crust is the part of the Earth upon which _____ .

Convection

[1]→ Convection is one of the manners in which heat may be transferred. Two other ways are radiation and conduction. Radiation does not require a **medium** to enable the transfer of heat. On the other hand, both convection and conduction need a medium to be able to transfer heat from one place to another. The two are different from each other though. Conduction involves the transfer of heat between atoms. Convection is the movement of matter from a hot area to a colder one.

Naturally occurring examples of convection can be found in many places. ❶ One is the sun. ❷ Like all stars, the sun is a huge ball of hot gas. ❸ Heat rises, so hot gases near the center of the sun rise to its surface. ❹ While they are rising, they begin to cool off. This causes the gases to retreat in the direction of the center of the sun. As they descend, they once again heat up, so they rise one more time. This is a cycle that appears to continue without end.

[3]→ Convection also takes place in the Earth's atmosphere. Hot air on the planet's surface rises into the atmosphere. When the air is near the ground, it is fairly **dense**. But as it rises, it cools off, so it becomes less dense. Then, cool air goes down as the warmer air rises. This pattern is what enables air to circulate. It also helps create the clouds, winds, and storms that are found in the atmosphere.

In the same manner, convection makes the water in the oceans circulate. Warm water rises while cooler water falls. This creates currents of water. This process of convection also helps keep the temperatures in the oceans stable.

• **Glossary** •

medium: a substance through which a force may act or produce an effect
dense: thick

1   The author discusses "radiation and conduction" in paragraph 1 in order to

    Ⓐ point out their advantages

    Ⓑ contrast them with convection

    Ⓒ show how they can be harmful

    Ⓓ focus on how they exist in nature

2   The word "descend" in the passage is closest in meaning to

    Ⓐ climb

    Ⓑ convert

    Ⓒ fall

    Ⓓ cool

3   Select the TWO answer choices from paragraph 3 that identify characteristics of convection. *To receive credit, you must select TWO answers.*

    Ⓐ It makes the air in the atmosphere move around.

    Ⓑ It only takes place in a few areas on the Earth.

    Ⓒ It happens when hot, dense air near the surface rises.

    Ⓓ It happens due to clouds, winds, and storms.

4   Look at the four squares [■] that indicate where the following sentence could be added to the passage.

So convection also takes place in stars other than the sun.

Where would the sentence best fit?

✐ Reading Comprehension   Complete the following sentences. Use the words in the box.

> a. heat is transferred   b. maintains the temperatures   c. hot gases   d. clouds, winds, and storms

1 Convection, radiation, and conduction are three ways that _____ .

2 _____ on the sun rise to the surface, cool, and then go back down to the center.

3 Convection helps create the _____ in the atmosphere.

4 Convection in the oceans _____ of the waters.

Mastering **the Subject**

Alfred Wegener and Pangaea

In 1912, a German named Alfred Wegener proposed a theory about the Earth. It concerned the formation of the continents. He believed that they had once been united. Then, they formed a supercontinent. He thought this took place around 300 million years ago. Wegener called this landmass Pangaea. He further stated that Pangaea began to break up around 200 million years ago. Over time, various parts of it formed the continents as they exist today.

Wegener came up with his idea after reading a paper in a journal. The article was about fossils of identical plants and animals that had been found on opposite sides of the Atlantic Ocean. They had been discovered in Africa and South America. Wegener was **intrigued** by this. He began to research the topic. He noticed that the coastlines of Africa and South America looked as though they could fit together. At that time, some people believed that the continents had once been joined by land bridges that had later sunk. But Wegener began to wonder whether they had actually been connected.

³→ From this, he came up with the notion of Pangaea. Wegener was not the first to believe in Pangaea. Yet he was the first to provide evidence as to how it formed. Unfortunately for him, most experts **dismissed** his theory. They pointed out that Wegener could not show how the lands had moved. During his lifetime, few people believed in his ideas. But by the late 1960s, scientists had learned about plate tectonics. Plate tectonics states that the Earth's surface is formed of several major and minor plates. They are in constant—yet slow—motion. Scientists realized that this was how Pangaea had broken up. As a result, more of them began to support Wegener's ideas.

• **Glossary** •

intrigued: interested in; fascinated by
dismiss: to disregard; to ignore; to consider to be incorrect

1 Which of the sentences below best expresses the essential information in the highlighted sentence in the passage? *Incorrect* answer choices change the meaning in important ways or leave out essential information.

- Ⓐ The paper described identical fossils that were found on both sides of the Atlantic Ocean.
- Ⓑ The article mentioned how fossils could be found on either side of the Atlantic Ocean.
- Ⓒ It provided an explanation of the search for identical fossils across the Atlantic Ocean.
- Ⓓ The study was about identical methods used to find fossils beneath the Atlantic Ocean.

2 The word "they" in the passage refers to

- Ⓐ the coastlines of Africa and South America
- Ⓑ some people
- Ⓒ the continents
- Ⓓ land bridges

3 According to paragraph 3, which of the following is true of plate tectonics?

- Ⓐ It was first described by Wegener in 1960s.
- Ⓑ It led many people to believe in Wegener's ideas.
- Ⓒ It only explains the creation of minor plates.
- Ⓓ It made Pangaea break up after only a few years.

4 *Directions*: An introductory sentence for a brief summary of the passage is provided below. Complete the summary by selecting the THREE answer choices that express the most important ideas of the passage. Some sentences do not belong because they express ideas that are not presented in the passage or are minor ideas in the passage. *This question is worth 2 points.*

Alfred Wegener believed the continents had once formed a supercontinent he called Pangaea.

- •
- •
- •

Answer Choices

1. Unlike other scientists, Wegener provided evidence for the formation of Pangaea.
2. Wegener thought that Africa and South America had once fit together.
3. Pangaea existed 300 million years ago and broke up 200 million years in the past.
4. The theory of plate tectonics was promoted by a number of geologists in the 1960s.
5. Scientists believe that the continents have moved around many times in the past.
6. Pangaea comes from a Greek term that means "all the Earth."

Reading Comprehension   Complete the following sentences. Use the words in the box.

| a. in the coastlines   b. identical fossils   c. dismissed Wegener's ideas   d. was a supercontinent |

1 Alfred Wegener thought that Pangaea _____ 300 million years ago.

2 _____ have been discovered on both sides of the Atlantic Ocean.

3 Wegener noticed the similarities _____ of Africa and South America.

4 Most people _____ until long after he had died.

The Formation of the Moon

A closeup image of the moon

¹→ Scientists have long pondered how the moon was formed. There have been countless theories on that topic. Most of them have been dismissed due to a lack of evidence. There are, however, some theories that have the support of large groups of people in the scientific world.

²→ Many people believe in the giant impact theory. It was proposed in the 1970s. It has the most support among scientists at the present time. This theory states that Earth was struck by a large **celestial** body. It was roughly as big as Mars, which is half the size of Earth. As a result of the impact, a great amount of **debris** was ejected into orbit around Earth. Over time, much of it united and formed the moon.

³→ There is a great amount of evidence that supports this theory. First is the physical evidence. The rocks on the moon are essentially the same as those found in Earth's mantle. Likewise, the moon has no hot metal core. Yet all of the other celestial bodies that formed around the same time as Earth have iron cores. These include Mercury, Venus, Mars, and Jupiter. However, there are some who question the validity of the giant impact theory. They state that a Mars-sized object impacting Earth would have greatly increased the planet's rotation. They claim that Earth's rotation would be around twelve times faster than it is today. So according to them, this theory is incorrect.

⁴→ The fission theory is another one popular with some astronomers. It imagines that a fission event caused the moon to break off from Earth. Some believe that the Pacific Ocean basin was the place on Earth where the moon broke off from. However, Earth's rotation would have to have been incredibly fast for this to have happened. This makes the fission theory unlikely as well.

A third theory claims that the moon formed independently of Earth. Some people believe that the moon was an itinerant body in the solar system. Sometime billions of years ago, the moon passed close to Earth. This caused it to get captured by Earth's gravitational field. ❶ Astronomers call this idea the capture theory. ❷ It has one major weakness: the moon's lack of an iron core. ❸ This absence indicates it was unlikely that the moon formed separately from Earth. ❹

⁶➜ There are many other theories. But they all have major problems. In all likelihood, the moon was once a part of Earth. For some reason, it then separated from the planet. Until there are more studies of the moon, the question of how it separated will remain unanswered. If men ever set foot on the moon again, perhaps they will be able to do enough research to find the answer to the question of how the moon was formed.

• **Glossary** •

celestial: relating to outer space
debris: fragments; remains

1. The word "pondered" in the passage is closest in meaning to

    (A) understood

    (B) regarded

    (C) thought about

    (D) approved of

2. In paragraph 1, the author's description of the theories of the formation of the moon mentions all of the following EXCEPT:

    (A) the fact that some theories have many supporters

    (B) the theory considered the most likely to be right

    (C) the reason some theories have been disregarded

    (D) the existence of many theories explaining it

3. According to paragraph 2, the giant impact theory states that

    (A) Mars collided with Earth many years ago

    (B) Earth and the moon formed at the same time

    (C) Earth formed from debris from a huge impact

    (D) a large object hit Earth and formed the moon

4. According to paragraph 3, the giant impact theory is doubted by some because

    (A) no other planets' moons formed this way

    (B) the moon lacks an iron core

    (C) rocks on the moon are similar to Earth rocks

    (D) Earth is currently rotating too slowly

5. In paragraph 4, why does the author mention the "Pacific Ocean basin"?

    (A) To prove that Earth rotates at the correct speed

    (B) To explain why the Mars-sized object hit Earth

    (C) To provide support for the fission theory

    (D) To show what was created by the moon

6. The word "itinerant" in the passage is closest in meaning to

    (A) sizable

    (B) magnetic

    (C) revolving

    (D) wandering

7 Which of the sentences below best expresses the essential information in the highlighted sentence in the passage? *Incorrect* answer choices change the meaning in important ways or leave out essential information.

    Ⓐ Scientists are encouraging trips to the moon to learn about its formation.

    Ⓑ Research needs to be done in person on the moon to learn more about it.

    Ⓒ By visiting the moon in person, scientists may learn how the moon formed.

    Ⓓ The best research on the moon will be done when humans return to it.

8 In paragraph 6, the author of the passage implies that the moon's formation

    Ⓐ probably took billions of years to occur

    Ⓑ can explain many mysteries of the universe

    Ⓒ may be possible to determine accurately

    Ⓓ is known only to a small number of astronomers

9 Look at the four squares [■] that indicate where the following sentence could be added to the passage.

As a result, it began to orbit the planet.

Where would the sentence best fit?

Click on a square [■] to add the sentence to the passage.

10 *Directions*: Select the appropriate phrases from the answer choices and match them to the theory on the moon's formation to which they relate. TWO of the answer choices will NOT be used. ***This question is worth 3 points***.

Drag your answer choices to the spaces where they belong.
To remove an answer choice, click on it. To review the passage, click on **View Text**.

Answer Choices	**THEORY ON THE MOON'S FORMATION**
1 Has been dismissed from a lack of evidence	**Giant Impact Theory**
2 Could have happened if Earth rotated very quickly	•
3 States that a large object hit Earth	•
4 Focuses on the importance of the Pacific Ocean basin	•
5 Explains why the moon has no iron core	**Fission Theory**
6 States that the moon formed independently of Earth	•
7 Has a lot of evidence that supports it	•

Star Performer Word Files

- **astronomer** (n) a person who studies outer space and everything in it

  The **astronomer** is using a telescope to observe the stars.

- **atmosphere** (n) the air

  Earth's **atmosphere** is mostly nitrogen and oxygen.

- **atom** (n) a molecule

  Scientists are still learning more about **atoms**.

- **capture** (v) to seize; to grab

  Try to **capture** the escaping animals.

- **celestial** (adj) from outside earth; heavenly

  Many **celestial** objects orbit the sun.

- **conduct** (v) to carry out; to do

  Dr. Smith is **conducting** some experiments in his lab.

- **circulate** (v) to flow; to move

  Open the window so that the air can **circulate**.

- **coastline** (n) the part of land next to water

  The **coastline** of that country looks beautiful.

- **continental** (adj) relating to a continent

  The **continental** climate is very warm and humid.

- **core** (n) a center

  There is a problem in the reactor's **core**.

- **cycle** (n) a series; a pattern

  The water **cycle** explains how water falls to the ground and then rises.

- **destroy** (v) to wipe out

  The bombs **destroyed** a large part of the city.

- **divide** (v) to split into two or more pieces, groups, or sections

  We will **divide** the work equally amongst ourselves.

- **dust** (n) a fine piece of powder or dirt

  There is too much **dust** on the floor.

- **eject** (v) to expel; to throw out

  The student was **ejected** from class for causing problems.

- **extensive** (adj) widespread; covering a great amount of area

  The field is **extensive** and covers a huge area of land.

- **impact** (n) a collision; a crash

  The **impact** completely destroyed both cars.

- **innermost** (adj) deepest

  Tell me your **innermost** secrets.

- **inverse** (adj) opposite

  Addition and subtraction are **inverse** operations.

- **landmass** (n) a large area of land

  Asia is the largest **landmass** in the world.

- **magnetism** (n) a force of attraction, often between metals

  Magnetism explains why some metals are attracted to iron.

- **melt** (v) to change from a solid to a liquid

  The snow is starting to **melt** because of the sun's heat.

- **method** (n) a way; a manner

  There must be another **method** that we can try.

- **motion** (n) movement

  Sue seems like she is in constant **motion**.

- **outermost** (adj) furthest; farthest

  Neptune is the **outermost** planet in the solar system.

- **orbit** (n) a complete rotation around another body

  It takes the Earth 365 days to complete one **orbit** of the sun.

- **planet** (n) a large body that orbits a star, is spherical, and has its own gravity

  There are eight **planets** in the solar system.

- **primarily** (adv) mainly; for the most part

  She is **primarily** concerned with learning more about the subject.

- **propose** (v) to suggest; to offer

  What do you **propose** that we do?

- **release** (v) to let go

  The air was **released** when the tank got a leak.

- **retreat** (v) to go backward

  We must **retreat** and find another way around the mountain.

- **rise** (v) to go up; to ascend

  The sun **rises** in the east.

- **school** (v) to teach

  You need to be **schooled** in foreign languages.

- **shell** (n) a covering

  The insect's **shell** feels very hard.

- **sink** (v) to fall beneath the water

  The ship **sank** quickly when it hit the rocks.

- **solar** (adj) relating to the sun

  Solar activity includes sunspots that appear on the sun's surface.

- **solar system** (n) the sun, the planets, and all the other celestial bodies that orbit the sun

  The **solar system** was created billions of years ago.

- **store** (v) to keep; to preserve; to save

  Please **store** this food in a dark and dry place.

- **supercontinent** (n) an extremely large continent

  There were several **supercontinents** in the Earth's past.

- **volume** (n) a quantity; an amount

  What is the **volume** of this container of water?

Vocabulary **Review**

❗ Choose the word or phrase closest in meaning to the highlighted part of the sentence.

1 Convection is one of the manners in which heat may be transferred.
   - Ⓐ ways
   - Ⓑ experiments
   - Ⓒ styles
   - Ⓓ approaches

2 It is not possible to create or destroy energy.
   - Ⓐ transfer
   - Ⓑ move
   - Ⓒ make
   - Ⓓ find

3 So according to them, this theory is incorrect.
   - Ⓐ improper
   - Ⓑ confusing
   - Ⓒ wrong
   - Ⓓ difficult

4 At that time, some people believed that the continents had once been joined by land bridges that had later sunk.
   - Ⓐ divided
   - Ⓑ connected
   - Ⓒ passed
   - Ⓓ driven

5 Since Boyle came from a wealthy family, his parents could afford to pay for him to be schooled.
   - Ⓐ comfortable
   - Ⓑ royal
   - Ⓒ important
   - Ⓓ rich

6 It was roughly as big as Mars, which is half the size of Earth.
   - Ⓐ probably
   - Ⓑ perhaps
   - Ⓒ considerably
   - Ⓓ about

7 It has one major weakness: the moon's lack of an iron core.
   - Ⓐ point
   - Ⓑ flaw
   - Ⓒ mass
   - Ⓓ idea

8 His work also helped found the field of modern chemistry.
   - Ⓐ discover
   - Ⓑ approve of
   - Ⓒ look for
   - Ⓓ establish

9 Yet he was the first to provide evidence as to how it formed.
   - Ⓐ majority
   - Ⓑ proof
   - Ⓒ theory
   - Ⓓ experiment

10 This process of convection also helps keep the temperatures in the oceans stable.
   - Ⓐ steady
   - Ⓑ above average
   - Ⓒ partial
   - Ⓓ extreme

11 They claim that Earth's rotation would be around twelve times faster than it is today.
   - Ⓐ feel
   - Ⓑ want
   - Ⓒ hope
   - Ⓓ declare

12 Boyle conducted frequent experiments.
   - Ⓐ regular
   - Ⓑ complicated
   - Ⓒ expensive
   - Ⓓ original

Part B

Chapter 08 — Environmental Sciences

Environmental sciences cover many fields. Some are biology, geology, physics, and meteorology. Environmental scientists study entire ecosystems as well as individual organisms. They may try to learn how ecosystems affect organisms and how organisms affect ecosystems. Others study ways to protect the environment. Above all, they focus on the study of the Earth and everything that exists on the planet.

☑ Vocabulary ☐ Fill in a Table ☐ Factual Information ☐ Negative Factual Information ☑ Prose Summary
☐ Insert Text ☐ Reference ☑ Rhetorical Purpose ☐ Sentence Simplification ☐ Inference

Glacier Formation

[1]→ A glacier is an enormous mass of moving ice. Most glaciers are located on mountains and in icecaps in the Polar Regions. Glaciers form over many years. There must be a sufficient amount of snowfall in an area for them to develop. This snow falls on the land. However, the temperatures are too cold for the snow to melt. So the snow later transforms into ice. Over a long period of time—sometimes centuries—the ice accumulates. It eventually becomes very heavy. Due to its weight, it gets compressed. This creates a glacier.

When a glacier forms on a mountain or some other incline, it begins moving. Most glaciers move slowly. Yet some advance several meters a day. As a glacier moves, its heavy ice can change the landscape. If a glacier reaches the ocean, pieces of it often break off and form icebergs in the oceans.

• **Glossary** •

compressed: packed together; squeezed together; solid
iceberg: a huge floating chunk of ice in the ocean

1 In paragraph 1, the author uses "the Polar Regions" as an example of

    Ⓐ zones where the temperature is cold

    Ⓑ areas that get large amounts of snow

    Ⓒ places where many glaciers are found

    Ⓓ sites that have many high mountains

2 The word "accumulates" in the passage is closest in meaning to

    Ⓐ transforms

    Ⓑ builds up

    Ⓒ moves away

    Ⓓ presses down

3 *Directions*: An introductory sentence for a brief summary of the passage is provided below. Complete the summary by selecting the THREE answer choices that express the most important ideas of the passage. Some sentences do not belong because they express ideas that are not presented in the passage or are minor ideas in the passage. *This question is worth 2 points.*

A glacier is a large sheet of ice that can move.

-
-
-

Answer Choices

① Glaciers are very heavy because they are mostly ice.

② A glacier may move several meters per day.

③ Some glaciers are currently expanding while others are melting.

④ Icebergs are parts of glaciers that have broken off.

⑤ The glaciers on the slopes of mountains often move.

⑥ It takes many years of snowfall for a glacier to form.

✎ Checking Reading Accuracy   Mark the following statements T (true) or F (false).

    T   **F**

1 ☐ / ☐   Glaciers are only found in the world's Polar Regions.

2 ☐ / ☐   Glaciers form when the temperature is too low for snow to melt.

3 ☐ / ☐   A glacier on a mountain always moves several meters a day.

4 ☐ / ☐   Glaciers that form in the ocean are called icebergs.

Mastering **the Question Types** B

☐ Vocabulary   ☑ Fill in a Table   ☐ Factual Information   ☑ Negative Factual Information   ☐ Prose Summary
☐ Insert Text   ☐ Reference   ☐ Rhetorical Purpose   ☐ Sentence Simplification   ☑ Inference

The Intertidal Zone

¹➜ The intertidal zone is found on ocean coastlines. It is the area between high and low **tide**. It may be one or two meters wide. Or it may be tens of meters wide. Its size depends on the difference between high and low tide.

²➜ An intertidal zone can be a sandy beach, a rocky shore, a **mudflat**, or the base of a cliff. It is sometimes covered by water and is exposed to the air at other times. Scientists have divided it into high, middle, and low zones. The low zone is briefly exposed to the air each day. It is the deepest part, and more fish live in it, too. The high zone is closest to shore. It is briefly covered by water each day. The intertidal zone's varied nature makes it home to many species of marine organisms. These include starfish, sponges, crabs, mussels, and numerous varieties of seaweed.

• **Glossary** •

tide: the periodic rising and falling of the water level in the ocean
mudflat: a muddy area found near the shore

1 In paragraphs 1 and 2, the author implies that the intertidal zone

     Ⓐ exists in every coastal area

     Ⓑ is the largest part of the ocean

     Ⓒ has more life than other ocean zones

     Ⓓ get polluted easily

2 The author's description of the types of areas that are found in the intertidal zone mentions all of the following EXCEPT:

     Ⓐ beaches

     Ⓑ mudflats

     Ⓒ caves

     Ⓓ rocky shores

3 *Directions*: Select the appropriate sentences from the answer choices and match them to the part of the intertidal zone to which they relate. TWO of the answer choices will NOT be used. ***This question is worth 3 points.***

Answer Choices	PART OF THE INTERTIDAL ZONE
① It has more fish that live in it.	**Low Zone**
② It can be greatly affected by the tides.	•
③ It is the deepest part of the intertidal zone.	•
④ It is covered by water for a short time.	•
⑤ It has the greatest number of shellfish in it.	**High Zone**
⑥ It is the part of the intertidal zone nearest shore.	•
⑦ It is open to air for a short time.	•

✎ **Checking Reading Accuracy** Mark the following statements T (true) or F (false).

    T   **F**

1 ☐ / ☐ The width of the intertidal zone depends on the tides.

2 ☐ / ☐ Sandy beaches and rocky areas both have intertidal zones.

3 ☐ / ☐ The low intertidal zone is the part of the zone nearest the shore.

4 ☐ / ☐ Few types of marine organisms live in the intertidal zone.

Mastering **the Question Types**   C

☐ Vocabulary   ☐ Fill in a Table   ☑ Factual Information   ☐ Negative Factual Information   ☐ Prose Summary
☑ Insert Text   ☑ Reference   ☐ Rhetorical Purpose   ☑ Sentence Simplification   ☐ Inference

Freshwater Swamps

1 A swamp is a type of <u>wetland</u>. It has spongy ground that is saturated with water. **2** In many places, it is covered with water all year round. **3** Freshwater swamps are places located near lakes and streams. **4**

In the past, most people had negative opinions of swamps. They saw swamps as places where diseases came from. People also believed swamps were useless since the land in them could not be farmed. It was also not possible—or was at least very difficult—to travel through swamps long ago.

³→ People have changed their opinions of swamps today. This is especially true of freshwater swamps. They can reduce the effects of flooding by capturing excess water. They also remove pollutants from lake and stream water. This purifies the water when it leaves the swamp. Swamps are <u>breeding grounds</u> for many fish, birds, and reptiles as well. They can safely reproduce in swamps. Due to their usefulness, many swamps are protected lands nowadays.

• **Glossary** •

wetland: land with wet soil, including swamps and marshes
breeding ground: a place where many animals have their young

1 Which of the sentences below best expresses the essential information in the highlighted sentence in the passage? *Incorrect* answer choices change the meaning in important ways or leave out essential information.

    Ⓐ People did not travel through swamps in the past.

    Ⓑ Some people thought that they could go through swamps long ago.

    Ⓒ In the past, getting through swamps was hard or could not be done.

    Ⓓ It was possible for some people to travel in swamps in the past.

2 The word "They" in the passage refers to

    Ⓐ Pollutants from lake and stream water

    Ⓑ Swamps

    Ⓒ Breeding grounds

    Ⓓ Many fish, birds, and reptiles

3 Select the TWO answer choices from paragraph 3 that identify how swamps are considered useful today. *To receive credit, you must select TWO answers.*

    Ⓐ They can make the water in streams and lakes cleaner.

    Ⓑ They can provide food for people living near them.

    Ⓒ They can act as places where animals can bear their young.

    Ⓓ They can prevent the land from being eroded during floods.

4 Look at the four squares [■] that indicate where the following sentence could be added to the passage.

They often form because these bodies of water suffer from regular flooding.

Where would the sentence best fit?

✐ Checking Reading Accuracy   Mark the following statements T (true) or F (false).

	T	F	
1	☐	/ ☐	Swamps are a type of wetland found near some streams.
2	☐	/ ☐	People had negative opinions of swamps in the past.
3	☐	/ ☐	Freshwater swamps can cause floods in some places.
4	☐	/ ☐	People protect swamps in some places these days.

Ecological Succession

Ecosystems do not always remain in the same condition. Instead, they may change. The process of change is called ecological succession. Both plant and animal life are involved. There are some stages of ecological succession that an environment may go through.

²→ Sometimes natural disasters take place. For instance, a volcano might erupt. Perhaps the eruption covers the land with lava. This causes the soil to disappear. All of the life forms in the region are killed as well. Yet the ecosystem still starts to recover. This is primary succession. It is the first stage of ecological succession. Primary succession can take years to occur. During it, simple plants, such as mosses, begin to grow. They help create new soil in the ground.

After a while, the second stage begins. This is secondary succession. It refers to the changes in a region that has soil and life forms. During this period, new forms of life gradually move into an area. The wind blows plant seeds into the region. Passing birds and other animals also drop them. **❶** These seeds sprout and grow. **❷** As they grow, the soil becomes more **fertile**. **❸** This enables more plants, as well as trees, to grow. **❹**

These plants attract insects and other small animals. Eventually, big trees grow, and animals move into the ecosystem. This may take only a few years to occur. Or it could take decades. At some point, the lifeforms in the ecosystem start to compete for survival. This **ensures** that some species die while others survive. Later, the ecosystem reaches a balance and stabilizes. This period of stability may last for thousands of years. Or another natural disaster could occur and upset the ecosystem. Then, a new round of ecological succession must begin.

• **Glossary** •

fertile: productive
ensure: to guarantee; to make sure of

1 The author discusses "natural disasters" in paragraph 2 in order to

    Ⓐ focus on an explanation of ecological succession

    Ⓑ explain how an ecosystem can lose all of its life

    Ⓒ mention that volcanoes are a common type of them

    Ⓓ note that they happen only occasionally

2 The word "them" in the passage refers to

    Ⓐ new forms of life

    Ⓑ plant seeds

    Ⓒ passing birds

    Ⓓ other animals

3 Look at the four squares [■] that indicate where the following sentence could be added to the passage.

After some time, entire forests can suddenly appear.

Where would the sentence best fit?

4 *Directions*: Select the appropriate sentences from the answer choices and match them to the stage of ecological succession to which they relate. TWO of the answer choices will NOT be used. *This question is worth 3 points.*

Answer Choices	STAGE OF ECOLOGICAL SUCCESSION
① It begins when there are no life forms in a region.	**Primary Succession**
② Oxygen begins to form in the atmosphere.	•
③ It involves changes in an area with life forms.	•
④ It is the first stage of ecological succession.	•
⑤ Humans can establish settlements during it.	**Secondary Succession**
⑥ The soil becomes more productive.	•
⑦ Simple plants begin to grow.	•

Reading Comprehension Complete the following sentences. Use the words in the box.

> **a.** plants and animals   **b.** a volcanic eruption   **c.** be in balance   **d.** ecological succession

1 Ecosystems go through various stages in a process called _____ .

2 _____ can kill all of the plants and animals in a region.

3 During secondary succession, _____ begin to appear in a region.

4 An ecosystem may _____ for thousands of years.

Weather and Crops

Farmers everywhere grow crops. However, some crops cannot be raised in certain locations. There are many factors that determine where a particular crop can grow. The climate often plays a major role. In particular, the amount of rainfall an area receives, the region's temperature, and the amount of sunshine it gets all influence which crops can grow in a place.

² ➔ Rainfall is one of the most important factors involved in the growing of crops. All crops require water. But some need it more than others. Rice, for instance, needs a lot of water to grow. Rice requires several centimeters of rain in the paddies where it grows. As a result, areas that get heavy rainfall in a short period of time are ideal for growing rice. That is why rice grows well in places in Asia that have summer **monsoon** rains. However, too much water is bad for some crops. Wheat and corn, for example, do not grow well if they receive the same amount of water that rice plants do.

³ ➔ Temperature and sunshine also play important roles in growing crops. Some crops are native to regions that have high temperatures and get a lot of sunshine. These are warm-weather crops. Some of them are eggplants, beans, corn, peppers, and tomatoes. Other plants are cool-weather crops. They prosper in areas with cooler climates. These are primarily leafy green and root plants. Some include carrots, cabbage, lettuce, onions, radishes, and turnips.

In cooler climates, farmers need to take sudden temperature changes into account. For instance, there may be late spring frosts and early fall snows. These can kill crops very easily. So farmers cannot plant too early. Nor can they **harvest** too late. In these cases, the temperature is the most important factor they must consider.

• Glossary •

monsoon: a downpour; a heavy rainstorm that happens seasonally in some regions
harvest: to gather crops from a field

1 Which of the sentences below best expresses the essential information in the highlighted sentence in the passage? *Incorrect* answer choices change the meaning in important ways or leave out essential information.

Ⓐ A region's climate determines which crops may be grown in it.

Ⓑ Areas that have high temperatures are ideal for growing crops.

Ⓒ Sunshine and rainfall can affect the crops raised in an area.

Ⓓ Hot, sunny places are highly desired by farmers who grow crops.

2 According to paragraph 2, rice is grown in Asia because

Ⓐ many places in Asia have short growing periods

Ⓑ the monsoon rains that fall help water the rice plants

Ⓒ rice requires fewer nutrients from the soil than wheat and corn

Ⓓ the combination of sunshine and rain in Asia is ideal for it

3 In paragraph 3, why does the author mention "eggplants, beans, corn, peppers, and tomatoes"?

Ⓐ To describe some cool-weather crops   Ⓑ To note they are leafy green plants

Ⓒ To explain the temperatures they grow at   Ⓓ To name some warm-weather crops

4 *Directions*: An introductory sentence for a brief summary of the passage is provided below. Complete the summary by selecting the THREE answer choices that express the most important ideas of the passage. Some sentences do not belong because they express ideas that are not presented in the passage or are minor ideas in the passage. **This question is worth 2 points.**

The climate helps determine which crops grow in which areas.

-
-
-

Answer Choices

① When snow falls early in the year, it can cause damage to many crops.

② Cool-weather crops can grow in places with cold climates.

③ Hot places that get much sunshine are good for warm-weather plants.

④ Some crops need much more rainfall to grow than others do.

⑤ Rice is one crop that is commonly grown in a number of Asian countries.

⑥ Turnips, cabbage, and lettuce are all leafy green plants.

Reading Comprehension Complete the following sentences. Use the words in the box.

| a. the climate | b. warm-weather crops | c. late spring frosts | d. summer monsoon rains |

1 _____ in a region often determines which crops can be grown in it.

2 Rice usually grows well in Asia thanks to the _____ .

3 Some _____ include eggplants, beans, corn, and peppers.

4 Crops can often be killed because of _____ .

The Effect of Volcanic Eruptions

1→ Some of the most devastating events on the planet are volcanic eruptions. They can expel massive amounts of lava and ash into the air and onto the surrounding land. This may damage the local area. It may take decades for a region to recover from the **aftermath** of a volcano. A volcano's effects are not just local either. In some cases, they can result in regional or even global changes.

2→ In 1980, Mount St. Helens, a volcano in Washington in the United States, erupted. It was a huge eruption. It was so powerful that it blew off part of the mountain. It shot out lava and ash over a wide area. The lava and ash blocked rivers and filled in lakes. In the volcano's immediate vicinity, all life was killed. Entire forests were knocked down, burned, or covered by ash. Most of the local animals were killed, too. Those that survived fled the area. After the eruption, the area was a wasteland. Thirty years later, some places affected by the eruption have begun to recover. But other areas are still barren and contain very little life.

3→ The Mount St. Helens eruption was very powerful. But it only affected a small area. This was different from the eruption of Krakatoa in 1883. Krakatoa was a volcano in Indonesia. When it erupted, the strength of the explosion totally destroyed the volcano. The eruption caused a **tsunami** that killed thousands of people on various islands. It also sent a gigantic ash cloud into the air. The ash spread around the world. It caused global temperatures to drop. This led to crop failures in distant lands. People in some lands starved to death because of Krakatoa.

• Glossary •

aftermath: a result; an aftereffect; a consequence

tsunami: a fast-moving wave often caused by an underwater earthquake

1 According to paragraph 1, which of the following is NOT true of volcanic eruptions?

(A) They can affect places around the world.

(B) They shoot ash into the air.

(C) They only affect the area right around them.

(D) They may damage an area for several decades.

2 The word "barren" in the passage is closest in meaning to

(A) infertile

(B) quiet

(C) dangerous

(D) abandoned

3 According to paragraph 2, rivers near Mount St. Helens were blocked because

(A) many trees were knocked down into the rivers

(B) huge stones were sent down the mountain

(C) landslides caused the rivers to be dammed

(D) so much lava and ash was ejected

4 According to paragraph 3, which of the following can be inferred about the Krakatoa eruption?

(A) The eruption only affected people living in Asia.

(B) It was stronger than the Mount St. Helens eruption.

(C) The eruption took place for more than one day.

(D) It was the most powerful eruption in history.

Reading Comprehension   Complete the following sentences. Use the words in the box.

a. knocked down	b. the Krakatoa eruption	c. the local environment	d. contain little life

1 Volcanoes may damage _____ for a very long time.

2 Mount St. Helens _____ and burned many forests around it.

3 Many of the places around Mount St. Helens still _____ .

4 _____ affected the temperature of the entire planet.

The Changing Atmosphere

The Earth's atmosphere seen from space

¹➜ The Earth's surface is surrounded by the atmosphere. It protects all life on the planet from the sun's radiation. It also holds the gases that living things breathe. The atmosphere today is much different from how it was in the past. In fact, it has changed a great deal since the Earth was formed. In the beginning, there was hardly any oxygen in it. Since then, the oxygen content has risen and fallen depending on certain events. The levels of oxygen are <u>critical</u> for one main reason: They have played a role in how life began and grew on the planet.

At present, the atmosphere is around twenty-one percent oxygen. But when the Earth formed more than four billion years ago, there was hardly any of it. Instead of oxygen, helium and hydrogen comprised most of the atmosphere. This was the planet's first atmosphere. As time passed, Earth's crust became more solid. Volcanic activity began. That sent carbon dioxide and water vapor into the air. The atmosphere became dense and had high pressure. That formed the second atmosphere. But there was still no oxygen.

³➜ In the oceans, however, there was oxygen in the water molecules. Slowly, some of it leaked into the air. This was a result of the action of <u>algae</u> in the oceans. They used solar energy to process water molecules. One effect was to release oxygen into the air. Another was to remove carbon dioxide from the air. This caused some life forms that relied on high levels of carbon dioxide to die.

⁴➜ This third atmosphere had low levels of oxygen for an <u>eon</u>. The oxygen level in the air was less than five percent for about 400 million years. Some of the oxygen turned into ozone. The ozone moved high into the atmosphere. It helped protect the planet from solar radiation. This allowed more life forms to evolve and survive on the Earth. For instance, the first plants began to appear on land.

They mostly grew near lakes and ocean shores. After a while, forests appeared. As the number of plants increased, so too did the oxygen level. The reason is that plants use photosynthesis to produce food. One byproduct of it is the release of oxygen molecules into the air. After more oxygen was released, more oxygen-breathing land animals appeared.

5→ Scientists refer to this event as the Cambrian Explosion. In a relatively short time, vast numbers of oxygen-breathing lifeforms arose on the planet. **1** This happened around 580 to 530 million years ago. **2** Many of these lifeforms were complex compared to the life forms that had previously existed. **3** Some experts theorize that the rise of the oxygen level is one reason for the Cambrian Explosion. **4**

6→ After it occurred, the oxygen level continued to rise. At some times in the past, it was even greater than it currently is. Scientists further believe that, over millions of years, the planet's oxygen level will change again. Whether it will increase or decrease, however, is not known.

• Glossary •

critical: very important; crucial
eon: an extremely long period of time, often lasting millions or billions of years vast: great; large

1 According to paragraph 1, which of the following is true of the Earth's atmosphere?

Ⓐ The majority of the atmosphere is oxygen.

Ⓑ It has undergone several changes over time.

Ⓒ It was created because of the sun's radiation.

Ⓓ It extends hundreds of miles above the planet.

2 The word "dense" in the passage is closest in meaning to

Ⓐ breathable

Ⓑ expanded

Ⓒ normal

Ⓓ thick

3 Why does the author mention "algae" in paragraph 3?

Ⓐ To explain its role in creating oxygen in the air

Ⓑ To note why it grew well in the Earth's oceans

Ⓒ To discuss how solar energy made it grow

Ⓓ To state that it caused some life forms to die

4 In paragraph 4, the author implies that solar radiation

Ⓐ created the ozone layer

Ⓑ is harmful to life

Ⓒ is constantly decreasing

Ⓓ affects plants more than animals

5 In paragraph 4, the author's description of the third atmosphere mentions which of the following?

Ⓐ It had more oxygen than other elements.

Ⓑ It lasted for almost one billion years.

Ⓒ Solar radiation harmed the Earth at that time.

Ⓓ Plants began to grow on land during it.

6 The word "theorize" in the passage is closest in meaning to

Ⓐ speculate

Ⓑ promise

Ⓒ hope

Ⓓ research

7 In paragraph 5, the author's description of the Cambrian Explosion mentions all of the following EXCEPT:

(A) how long ago it happened

(B) what may have caused it to happen

(C) which mammals lived during that time

(D) what kinds of lifeforms began appearing

8 According to paragraph 6, which of the following is true of the planet's oxygen level?

(A) It will no longer change in the future.

(B) It is going to steadily decrease soon.

(C) It will take millions of years to change.

(D) It is going to increase due to solar radiation.

9 Look at the four squares [■] that indicate where the following sentence could be added to the passage.

In fact, more animals appeared then than during any other period in Earth's history.

Where would the sentence best fit?

> Click on a square [■] to add the sentence to the passage.

10 *Directions*: Select the appropriate phrases from the answer choices and match them to the atmosphere to which they relate. TWO of the answer choices will NOT be used. *This question is worth 4 points*.

> Drag your answer choices to the spaces where they belong.
> To remove an answer choice, click on it. To review the passage, click on **View Text**.

Answer Choices	ATMOSPHERE
1 Had some oxygen transform into ozone	**First Atmosphere**
2 Was affected by the actions of algae in the oceans	•
3 Had its oxygen level increased by plants on land	•
4 Lasted for only about one million years	**Second Atmosphere**
5 Was mostly helium and hydrogen	•
6 Was affected by the actions of humans	•
7 Had carbon dioxide removed from it	**Third Atmosphere**
8 Contained virtually no oxygen	•
9 Held enough oxygen to support land animals	•

Star Performer Word Files

- **attract** (v) to draw; to pull toward
  The eclipse will **attract** many viewers who want to see it.

- **cliff** (n) a rocky overhang
  The climbers are trying to go up that **cliff**.

- **climate** (n) the typical weather in a place
  How is the **climate** in your country?

- **content** (n) a substance; a makeup; a composition
  The **content** of the book was pleasing to the readers.

- **decade** (n) a period lasting ten years
  Sara lived in Europe for more than one **decade**.

- **decrease** (v) to go down; to decline
  Decrease the amount of pressure you are applying.

- **devastating** (adj) destructive
  The earthquake had a **devastating** effect on the city.

- **distant** (adj) far
  He does not want to go to a **distant** place today.

- **enormous** (adj) huge; very large
  The blue whale is an **enormous** animal.

- **erupt** (v) to explode, as in a volcano
  It appears that the volcano will **erupt** sometime soon.

- **eventually** (adv) over time; after a while
  Eventually, you will understand how to solve the problem.

- **excess** (adj) extra; more than is necessary
  The **excess** dirt from the mine will be moved to another area.

- **expel** (v) to eject
  The volcano **expelled** lava for several hours.

- **exposed** (adj) open; uncovered; bare
  Deforestation caused the soil to be **exposed** to the wind.

- **frost** (n) a time when the temperature suddenly drops below freezing
  The early October **frost** killed many vegetables in the garden.

- **incline** (n) a slope, like on a mountain
  I do not like to drive up and down steep **inclines**.

- **increase** (v) to go up
  Please **increase** the speed that you are working.

- **iceberg** (n) a large mass of floating ice
  An **iceberg** caused the *Titanic* to sink.

- **landscape** (n) the appearance of the land; scenery
  I always enjoy looking at the **landscape** in this region.

- **mass** (n) an accumulation; a collection
  There is a huge **mass** of garbage in this room.

- **occasionally** (adv) sometimes

  We **occasionally** go for long walks in the forest.

- **organism** (n) a living creature

  What is the smallest **organism** that exists?

- **paddy** (n) a rice field

  The rice **paddy** has water in it for almost the entire summer.

- **photosynthesis** (n) the process by which plants create their own food

  The plant uses **photosynthesis** when there is sunlight.

- **plant** (v) to put a seed or plant into the ground in the hope that it will grow

  She will **plant** tomatoes and carrots in her garden this year.

- **pollutant** (n) anything that harms the air, land, or water

  The factory is releasing too many **pollutants** into the air.

- **prosper** (v) to do well

  The country is beginning to **prosper** after the long war.

- **recover** (v) to improve in condition

  It took John three weeks to **recover** from his illness.

- **remain** (v) to stay

  You can **remain** here while I am gone.

- **reproduce** (v) to make young; to have babies

  Many birds **reproduce** in winter when they are in warm places.

- **sandy** (adj) having a large amount of sand

  She prefers to visit **sandy** beaches instead of rocky ones.

- **shore** (n) the coast; land

  The fisherman is standing on the **shore**.

- **shoot out** (v) to expel; to push out

  Ash **shot out** high from the volcano.

- **soil** (n) earth or dirt that is fertile

  This **soil** is rich, so it will be good for farming.

- **sudden** (adj) instant

  I felt a **sudden** pain in my back just now.

- **sufficient** (adj) enough

  Do you have a **sufficient** amount of money for your trip?

- **sunshine** (n) the light from the sun

  She will lay out in the **sunshine** to get a suntan.

- **water vapor** (n) steam

  When you boil water, some of it becomes **water vapor**.

- **varied** (adj) diverse; mixed

  Varied amounts of spices are used in this recipe.

- **wasteland** (adj) a barren area with no life

  The moon is a **wasteland** that supports no living creatures.

🔲 Choose the word or phrase closest in meaning to the highlighted part of the sentence.

1   In these cases, the temperature is the most important factor they must consider.
    Ⓐ watch out for
    Ⓑ think about
    Ⓒ record
    Ⓓ transfer

2   This caused some life forms that relied on high levels of carbon dioxide to die.
    Ⓐ stood for
    Ⓑ breathed in
    Ⓒ depended on
    Ⓓ ate up

3   So the snow later transforms into ice.
    Ⓐ moves
    Ⓑ feels
    Ⓒ changes
    Ⓓ melts

4   There are some stages of ecological succession that an environment may go through.
    Ⓐ phases
    Ⓑ examples
    Ⓒ theories
    Ⓓ formulas

5   It also sent a gigantic ash cloud into the air.
    Ⓐ serious
    Ⓑ deadly
    Ⓒ huge
    Ⓓ thick

6   Slowly, some of it leaked into the air.
    Ⓐ froze
    Ⓑ returned
    Ⓒ escaped
    Ⓓ tried

7   Wheat and corn, for example, do not grow well if they receive the same amount of water that rice plants do.
    Ⓐ get
    Ⓑ drink
    Ⓒ find
    Ⓓ want

8   The intertidal zone is found on ocean coastlines.
    Ⓐ waves
    Ⓑ shores
    Ⓒ tides
    Ⓓ islands

9   The reason is that plants use photosynthesis to produce food.
    Ⓐ consume
    Ⓑ locate
    Ⓒ enjoy
    Ⓓ make

10 This purifies the water when it leaves the swamp.
    Ⓐ floods
    Ⓑ evaporates
    Ⓒ reduces
    Ⓓ cleans

11 These are primarily leafy green and root plants.
    Ⓐ nearly
    Ⓑ hardly
    Ⓒ mainly
    Ⓓ fairly

12 In the volcano's immediate vicinity, all life was killed.
    Ⓐ area
    Ⓑ mountain
    Ⓒ rocks
    Ⓓ lava

Part C

Experiencing the TOEFL iBT Actual Tests

CONTINUE

Reading Section Directions

This section measures your ability to understand academic passages in English. You will have **54 minutes** to read and answer questions about **3 passages**. A clock at the top of the screen will show you how much time is remaining.

Most questions are worth 1 point but the last question for each passage is worth more than 1 point. The directions for the last question indicate how many points you may receive.

Some passages include a word or phrase that is **underlined** in blue. Click on the word or phrase to see a definition or an explanation.

When you want to move to the next question, click on **Next**. You may skip questions and go back to them later. If you want to return to previous questions, click on **Back**. You can click on **Review** at any time, and the review screen will show you which questions you have answered and which you have not answered. From this review screen, you may go directly to any question you have already seen in the Reading section.

Click on **Continue** to go on.

Thebes

The ancient temple of Karnak

Thebes was a city in ancient Egypt. It was located 675 kilometers south of Cairo. It sat in the area where modern-day Luxor exists. Thousands of years ago, Thebes was a political, religious, and trade center. It was the site of many religious festivals. It was also Egypt's capital at times. Today, it is a famous city of ancient Egypt due to the many ruins there.

Thebes was one of the most populated cities in ancient times. It had a population that ranged from 30,000 to 75,000 people. Most of the city was located along the eastern bank of the Nile River. The western bank was used for the <u>necropolis</u>—the city of the dead. It got that name due to the many royal tombs and burial grounds located there. Some people resided on the western bank. They were primarily those in the employ of the pharaohs and included priests, soldiers, and laborers. They worked on the extensive series of tombs and monuments around the city.

The city was first inhabited around 3200 B.C. Thebes later became a minor trading outpost during the Old Kingdom Period of Egyptian history. It lasted from 2316 B.C. to 2181 B.C. At that time, the city of Herakleopolis was the center of Egyptian rule. But its leaders were weak and ineffectual, and the Thebans disliked their rule. In 2055 B.C., the Theban leader Mentuhotep defeated the rulers of Herakleopolis. He then united Egypt under one ruler. Mentuhotep worshiped the god Amun. He turned Thebes into the capital of Egypt and the center of a cult worshiping Amun that would last for thousands of years. At the height of their power, the Theban rulers built numerous tombs and monuments. Many of them have survived—in varying states—until modern times. Among the more famous are the temple complexes of Karnak and Luxor, the Valley of the Kings, and the Valley of the Queens.

Karnak was a complex with many temples. The largest and most important one was the Temple of Amun. Construction on it lasted from 2000 to 300 B.C. Rulers added pieces to it over the centuries until it became one of the world's largest temples. The most vivid place inside the temple is a vast hall about 5,000 square meters in size with a roof upheld by twelve massive stone columns. Each one is around twenty-four meters in height. Reliefs carved into the temple's stone walls show the history of Egypt. Near the Temple of Amun is the temple complex of Luxor. It is connected to the Temple of Amun by an avenue lined with stone sphinxes. The Luxor complex was also built by different rulers over the centuries. Most of it lies in ruins today. Some of it was looted by invaders. Other sections were converted to Coptic churches after Christianity came to Egypt in more modern times.

The Valley of the Kings is an ancient burial site. It lies in a long, narrow valley near Thebes. It serves as the final resting place of every pharaoh of the eighteenth, nineteenth, and twentieth **dynasties**, which lasted from 1539 B.C. to 1075 B.C. There are sixty-two known tombs there. They include pharaohs, some wives and children, and a few high-ranking officials. Most of the tombs were well concealed. The pharaohs feared that their tombs would be subject to looting after their deaths. So they had the tombs designed to stop thieves. The Valley of the Queens is similar in purpose and design. It serves as a burial place for the queens of Egypt of the nineteenth and twentieth dynasties and their children. More than ninety tombs have been found there. Both valleys are located on the western bank of the Nile River.

• Glossary •

necropolis: a large cemetery from ancient times
dynasty: a series of members of the same family that rule a land

1 In paragraph 1, the author's description of Thebes mentions all of the following EXCEPT:

Ⓐ the time it was founded

Ⓑ the reason for its fame

Ⓒ its importance in the past

Ⓓ its general location

2 The word "**those**" in the passage refers to

Ⓐ royal tombs

Ⓑ burial grounds

Ⓒ the pharaohs

Ⓓ priests, soldiers, and laborers

3 In paragraph 2, which of the following can be inferred about Thebes?

Ⓐ Most of the people living there were farmers.

Ⓑ More people lived on its eastern side than its western side.

Ⓒ Many robbers broke into the tombs located there.

Ⓓ It was a bigger city than Cairo during ancient times.

Thebes

1→ Thebes was a city in ancient Egypt. It was located 675 kilometers south of Cairo. It sat in the area where modern-day Luxor exists. Thousands of years ago, Thebes was a political, religious, and trade center. It was the site of many religious festivals. It was also Egypt's capital at times. Today, it is a famous city of ancient Egypt due to the many ruins there.

2→ Thebes was one of the most populated cities in ancient times. It had a population that ranged from 30,000 to 75,000 people. Most of the city was located along the eastern bank of the Nile River. The western bank was used for the necropolis—the city of the dead. It got that name due to the many royal tombs and burial grounds located there. Some people resided on the western bank. They were primarily those in the employ of the pharaohs and included priests, soldiers, and laborers. They worked on the extensive series of tombs and monuments around the city.

• **Glossary** •

necropolis: a large cemetery from ancient times

4 According to paragraph 3, which of the following is NOT true of Herakleopolis?

Ⓐ It was important during the Old Kingdom Period.

Ⓑ It existed thousands of years ago.

Ⓒ One of its rulers was Mentuhotep.

Ⓓ Its rulers were disliked by Thebes.

5 The word "converted" in the passage is closest in meaning to

Ⓐ renovated

Ⓑ developed

Ⓒ changed

Ⓓ designed

6 According to paragraph 4, which of the following is true of the Temple of Amun?

Ⓐ It was built 5,000 years ago.

Ⓑ It was located in Karnak.

Ⓒ It is mostly ruins today.

Ⓓ It became a Coptic church later.

³→ The city was first inhabited around 3200 B.C. Thebes later became a minor trading outpost during the Old Kingdom Period of Egyptian history. It lasted from 2316 B.C. to 2181 B.C. At that time, the city of Herakleopolis was the center of Egyptian rule. But its leaders were weak and ineffectual, and the Thebans disliked their rule. In 2055 B.C., the Theban leader Mentuhotep defeated the rulers of Herakleopolis. He then united Egypt under one ruler. Mentuhotep worshiped the god Amun. He turned Thebes into the capital of Egypt and the center of a cult worshiping Amun that would last for thousands of years. At the height of their power, the Theban rulers built numerous tombs and monuments. Many of them have survived—in varying states—until modern times. Among the more famous are the temple complexes of Karnak and Luxor, the Valley of the Kings, and the Valley of the Queens.

⁴→ Karnak was a complex with many temples. The largest and most important one was the Temple of Amun. Construction on it lasted from 2000 to 300 B.C. Rulers added pieces to it over the centuries until it became one of the world's largest temples. The most vivid place inside the temple is a vast hall about 5,000 square meters in size with a roof upheld by twelve massive stone columns. Each one is around twenty-four meters in height. Reliefs carved into the temple's stone walls show the history of Egypt. Near the Temple of Amun is the temple complex of Luxor. It is connected to the Temple of Amun by an avenue lined with stone sphinxes. The Luxor complex was also built by different rulers over the centuries. Most of it lies in ruins today. Some of it was looted by invaders. Other sections were converted to Coptic churches after Christianity came to Egypt in more modern times.

7 The author discusses "The Valley of the Queens" in paragraph 5 in order to

(A) name some queens buried there

(B) focus on its location

(C) describe its contents

(D) state when it was first used

8 According to paragraph 5, the pharaohs hid their tombs because

(A) they did not want robbers to find them

(B) they wanted to rest in peace

(C) they thought it was bad luck to be found

(D) they did not want their bodies dug up

⁵→ The Valley of the Kings is an ancient burial site. It lies in a long, narrow valley near Thebes. It serves as the final resting place of every pharaoh of the eighteenth, nineteenth, and twentieth **dynasties**, which lasted from 1539 B.C. to 1075 B.C. There are sixty-two known tombs there. They include pharaohs, some wives and children, and a few high-ranking officials. Most of the tombs were well concealed. The pharaohs feared that their tombs would be subject to looting after their deaths. So they had the tombs designed to stop thieves. The Valley of the Queens is similar in purpose and design. It serves as a burial place for the queens of Egypt of the nineteenth and twentieth dynasties and their children. More than ninety tombs have been found there. Both valleys are located on the western bank of the Nile River.

• **Glossary** •

dynasty: a series of members of the same family that rule a land

9 Look at the four squares [■] that indicate where the following sentence could be added to the passage.

Many priceless relics were taken and either melted down for their gold and silver or sold to collectors.

Where would the sentence best fit?

> Click on a square [■] to add the sentence to the passage.

Karnak was a complex with many temples. The largest and most important one was the Temple of Amun. Construction on it lasted from 2000 to 300 B.C. Rulers added pieces to it over the centuries until it became one of the world's largest temples. The most vivid place inside the temple is a vast hall about 5,000 square meters in size with a roof upheld by twelve massive stone columns. Each one is around twenty-four meters in height. Reliefs carved into the temple's stone walls show the history of Egypt. Near the Temple of Amun is the temple complex of Luxor. It is connected to the Temple of Amun by an avenue lined with stone sphinxes. The Luxor complex was also built by different rulers over the centuries. **1** Most of it lies in ruins today. **2** Some of it was looted by invaders. **3** Other sections were converted to Coptic churches after Christianity came to Egypt in more modern times. **4**

10 *Directions*: An introductory sentence for a brief summary of the passage is provided below. Complete the summary by selecting the THREE answer choices that express the most important ideas of the passage. Some sentences do not belong because they express ideas that are not presented in the passage or are minor ideas in the passage. *This question is worth 2 points.*

> Drag your answer choices to the spaces where they belong.
> To remove an answer choice, click on it. To review the passage, click on **View Text**.

The Egyptian city of Thebes was important in ancient times.

-
-
-

Answer Choices

1. Thebes was a trade center and capital of Egypt at times.

2. The Valley of the Kings is located close to the ruins of Thebes.

3. Many ruins from ancient Thebes have been found recently.

4. Many pharaohs and their wives were buried near Thebes.

5. The body of King Tut was found close to the Thebes.

6. The Temple of Amun was a major complex in the city.

Temporary Ponds

A pond is a small body of water. It can be located in almost any type of <u>terrain</u>, including deserts. Some ponds are permanent. So they have water all year round. Other ponds are temporary. They grow, shrink, and even disappear depending on a number of factors. These include the amount of rainfall, the range of temperatures and the evaporation rate in a region, and the actions of people. Temporary ponds are important parts of many ecosystems. They support a wide range of organisms. Some of them depend on the waters of the ponds for their survival. And others consume smaller organisms that live in these ponds.

A pond often forms in a place with shallow land. The area usually gets lots of rainfall or snow melt. Given enough water, as well as low temperatures and low evaporation rates, a pond may become permanent. Yet many dry up as the seasons change. Typically, they have plenty of water in spring and fall but dry up during the summer heat. They may also freeze in winter. In deserts and other dry lands, most ponds are short lived. They appear only during the rainy season. Then, they vanish quickly because deserts have such high evaporation rates. People can sometimes affect whether a pond is permanent or temporary. Farmers may use a pond's water to irrigate their crops or to provide water for their animals. This can drain ponds of their water.

Temporary ponds form unique ecosystems. They are bodies of water with no fish. Since they are dry for part of the year, fish cannot survive in them. This gives other organisms better chances at survival. For instance, fish often eat insects and amphibians. But without fish in a temporary pond, these animals not only survive but also thrive. When the ponds dry up, they can still survive out of the water. These insects and amphibians also provide rich sources of food for animals higher on the food chain. Birds and bats, for instance, eat many of the insects and other small creatures that live in temporary ponds. This is all made possible due to the absence of fish from the water.

These ponds also provide some organisms with safe places to lay eggs. <u>Amphibians</u>, for example, lay their eggs in water. Frogs and toads live their early lives in water. When there are more temporary ponds, more frogs, toads, and other amphibians can hatch and grow. This is of particular importance in the desert. The spadefoot toad lives in the arid southwestern United States. It stays underground most of the year. When heavy rains fall, the toads come to the surface. They mate and find temporary ponds. There, the females lay hundreds of eggs in the ponds' waters. What happens next is a race against time. The eggs must hatch before the water evaporates. Another danger is that many predators find the eggs and eat them. Still, every year, enough toads hatch and live to adulthood so that the species can survive.

Temporary ponds support a wide range of plant life. One unique aspect of many ponds is how they form rings of flowers and other plants. They grow at the edges of the pond during the rainy season. Once the pond dries up, all that is left is a beautiful ring of flowers that shows the outline of where the pond was. Many rare species of plants grow near temporary ponds. This happens due to the unusual mix of acids and salts in the soil caused by the changes in water levels. This creates the conditions necessary for some rare plants to grow. The mesa mint is a rare plant that only grows near temporary ponds around San Diego in the United States. There are many other unique plants that grow near these ponds in other places around the country as well.

• Glossary •

terrain: a piece of land
amphibian: a cold-blooded animal such as a frog or toad that can live in the water or on land

11 In paragraph 1, the author's description of temporary ponds mentions all of the following EXCEPT:

Ⓐ how many organisms live in them

Ⓑ how people's actions can affect them

Ⓒ how they may have fresh or salt water

Ⓓ what environments they can be found in

12 Which of the following can be inferred from paragraph 2 about temporary ponds?

Ⓐ They last for the shortest amount of time in deserts.

Ⓑ It is possible for them to become permanent ponds.

Ⓒ The largest of these ponds are used by humans.

Ⓓ They contain the greatest amount of water in winter.

13 According to paragraph 2, which of the following is true of farmers?

Ⓐ They sometimes dig holes to make temporary ponds.

Ⓑ They may use temporary ponds for their animals.

Ⓒ They like temporary ponds because they provide free water.

Ⓓ They prefer to grow crops on land that has temporary ponds.

Temporary Ponds

1➜ A pond is a small body of water. It can be located in almost any type of <u>terrain</u>, including deserts. Some ponds are permanent. So they have water all year round. Other ponds are temporary. They grow, shrink, and even disappear depending on a number of factors. These include the amount of rainfall, the range of temperatures and the evaporation rate in a region, and the actions of people. Temporary ponds are important parts of many ecosystems. They support a wide range of organisms. Some of them depend on the waters of the ponds for their survival. And others consume smaller organisms that live in these ponds.

2➜ A pond often forms in a place with shallow land. The area usually gets lots of rainfall or snow melt. Given enough water, as well as low temperatures and low evaporation rates, a pond may become permanent. Yet many dry up as the seasons change. Typically, they have plenty of water in spring and fall but dry up during the summer heat. They may also freeze in winter. In deserts and other dry lands, most ponds are short lived. They appear only during the rainy season. Then, they vanish quickly because deserts have such high evaporation rates. People can sometimes affect whether a pond is permanent or temporary. Farmers may use a pond's water to irrigate their crops or to provide water for their animals. This can drain ponds of their water.

• **Glossary** •

terrain: a piece of land

14 The author discusses "fish" in paragraph 3 in order to

ⓐ argue that some fish are able to survive in temporary ponds

ⓑ explain the difference between fish, insects, and amphibians

ⓒ prove that they are necessary for a pond's ecosystem

ⓓ show how temporary ponds are affected by their absence

15 In paragraph 3, the author implies that insects and amphibians

ⓐ multiply in great numbers in temporary ponds

ⓑ never get eaten by animals in temporary ponds

ⓒ cannot survive when a temporary pond dries up

ⓓ must avoid fish in most of the places they live

16 The word "arid" in the passage is closest in meaning to

ⓐ dry

ⓑ warm

ⓒ extensive

ⓓ unpopulated

17 According to paragraph 4, the spadefoot toad mates when

ⓐ the summer heat ends

ⓑ temporary ponds evaporate

ⓒ there is a lot of rain falling

ⓓ desert predators are nearby

³→ Temporary ponds form unique ecosystems. They are bodies of water with no fish. Since they are dry for part of the year, fish cannot survive in them. This gives other organisms better chances at survival. For instance, fish often eat insects and amphibians. But without fish in a temporary pond, these animals not only survive but also thrive. When the ponds dry up, they can still survive out of the water. These insects and amphibians also provide rich sources of food for animals higher on the food chain. Birds and bats, for instance, eat many of the insects and other small creatures that live in temporary ponds. This is all made possible due to the absence of fish from the water.

⁴→ These ponds also provide some organisms with safe places to lay eggs. **Amphibians**, for example, lay their eggs in water. Frogs and toads live their early lives in water. When there are more temporary ponds, more frogs, toads, and other amphibians can hatch and grow. This is of particular importance in the desert. The spadefoot toad lives in the arid southwestern United States. It stays underground most of the year. When heavy rains fall, the toads come to the surface. They mate and find temporary ponds. There, the females lay hundreds of eggs in the ponds' waters. What happens next is a race against time. The eggs must hatch before the water evaporates. Another danger is that many predators find the eggs and eat them. Still, every year, enough toads hatch and live to adulthood so that the species can survive.

• **Glossary** •

amphibian: a cold-blooded animal such as a frog or toad that can live in the water or on land

18 According to paragraph 5, the mesa mint grows
around temporary ponds because

Ⓐ it can only grow in soil with a lot of water

Ⓑ no animals live nearby to eat the plant

Ⓒ there is no salt in the ground to kill it

Ⓓ the water levels of the ponds affect the soil

⁵→ Temporary ponds support a wide range of
plant life. One unique aspect of many ponds is how
they form rings of flowers and other plants. They
grow at the edges of the pond during the rainy
season. Once the pond dries up, all that is left is a
beautiful ring of flowers that shows the outline of
where the pond was. Many rare species of plants
grow near temporary ponds. This happens due to
the unusual mix of acids and salts in the soil caused
by the changes in water levels. This creates the
conditions necessary for some rare plants to grow.
The mesa mint is a rare plant that only grows near
temporary ponds around San Diego in the United
States. There are many other unique plants that
grow near these ponds in other places around the
country as well.

19 Look at the four squares [■] that indicate where the following sentence could be added to the passage.

Among these hunters are snakes and various species of birds.

Where would the sentence best fit?

> Click on a square [■] to add the sentence to the passage.

These ponds also provide some organisms with safe places to lay eggs. **Amphibians**, for example, lay their eggs in water. Frogs and toads live their early lives in water. When there are more temporary ponds, more frogs, toads, and other amphibians can hatch and grow. This is of particular importance in the desert. The spadefoot toad lives in the arid southwestern United States. It stays underground most of the year. When heavy rains fall, the toads come to the surface. They mate and find temporary ponds. There, the females lay hundreds of eggs in the ponds' waters. What happens next is a race against time. **1** The eggs must hatch before the water evaporates. **2** Another danger is that many predators find the eggs and eat them. **3** Still, every year, enough toads hatch and live to adulthood so that the species can survive. **4**

• Glossary •

amphibian: a cold-blooded animal such as a frog or toad that can live in the water or on land

20 *Directions*: An introductory sentence for a brief summary of the passage is provided below. Complete the summary by selecting the THREE answer choices that express the most important ideas of the passage. Some sentences do not belong because they express ideas that are not presented in the passage or are minor ideas in the passage. *This question is worth 2 points*.

> Drag your answer choices to the spaces where they belong.
> To remove an answer choice, click on it. To review the passage, click on **View Text**.

Temporary ponds create unique ecosystems that affect both plants and animals.

-
-
-

Answer Choices

1. Numerous insects and amphibians live near ponds because of the lack of fish.

2. Many animals lay their eggs in temporary ponds whenever they form.

3. Temporary ponds often have water during the rainy season but dry up later.

4. A temporary pond may evaporate because of the weather or a lack of rain.

5. Some rare plants only grow by temporary ponds due to the water's effect on the soil.

6. The spadefoot toad is an animal that comes aboveground when temporary ponds form.

Types of Stars

An image of NML Cygni, a hypergiant

Stars are enormous balls of gas that fill galaxies throughout the universe. There are many types of stars. Astronomers classify them in various ways. The most common ways are by their size, color, and **luminosity**. One system is called the Yerkes spectral classification. Three American scientists developed it in the 1940s. In it, stars are classified as hypergiants, supergiants, bright giants, normal giants, subgiants, dwarf stars, subdwarfs, and white, red, and brown dwarfs.

The largest stars in the universe are hypergiants. They also have the greatest luminosity. It can be millions of times greater than the Earth's sun. Hypergiants are rare and have relatively short lives. They live for only a few million years. This is short compared to the sun, which has a lifetime of around ten billion years. Hypergiants may appear blue, red, white, or yellow in color. Supergiants are next in size and luminosity. They can be around 100,000 times brighter than the sun. They are commonly red or blue in color. Thus people sometimes call them red or blue supergiants. Bright giants are slightly smaller in size and less luminous than supergiants. They vary in color and can be white, orange, red, yellow-white, and blue-white.

Giant stars are midway in size between stars like the sun and the larger giants. Giant stars are usually ten to one hundred times bigger than the sun and are ten to one thousand times brighter as well. They were once stars like the sun. But they changed once they expended all of the hydrogen in their **cores**. Then, their cores contracted while their surfaces expanded. They became brighter and turned into giant stars. Midway between giant stars and stars such as the sun are the subgiants. Astronomers believe that subgiants have no more hydrogen but have not yet expanded.

Most stars in the universe are classified as dwarf stars. They are among the youngest stars in existence. They are either at the beginning of their lives or are partway through them. Eventually, many will use all of their fuel and become giants. They are also known as main sequence stars. The reason is that they have the same range of size, color, and luminosity in most star classification systems. Some dwarf stars are similar to the sun. Yet they can be bigger or smaller than it. Many are white or yellow in color. Subdwarfs are smaller and less luminous than dwarf stars.

The final three types of stars are red, white, and brown dwarfs. The vast majority of stars in the universe are red dwarfs. They have about half the mass of the sun and have low surface temperatures. Their luminosity is always low, which makes them difficult to observe. Red dwarfs burn their hydrogen at a very slow rate. It may take hundreds of billions of years for a red dwarf to run out of fuel. Since the universe is only around fourteen billion years old, all red dwarfs are at the beginning of their life cycles.

Among the smallest stars in the universe are white dwarfs. Both their mass and luminosity are low. Astronomers believe that the white dwarf stage is the final one in a star's life. A white dwarf is the core that remains after a giant star dies. It contains no hydrogen, helium, or any other source of energy. Its heat and luminosity remain from its life as a giant star. Over time, a white dwarf will grow dimmer and become cooler. As for brown dwarfs, they are stars that lack enough mass to begin the chain reaction necessary to burn their fuel. So they have the structure of a star but never become hot or bright. They may remain in that state forever.

• **Glossary** •
luminosity: brightness
core: a center

21 According to paragraph 1, which of the following can be inferred about the Yerkes classification system?

   Ⓐ It was the first star classification system to be created.

   Ⓑ The only people who use it are American scientists.

   Ⓒ It was created due to the advances in astronomy in the 1940s.

   Ⓓ It is one of the most accepted star classification systems.

22 The word "relatively" in the passage is closest in meaning to

   Ⓐ comparatively

   Ⓑ simply

   Ⓒ partially

   Ⓓ hardly

Types of Stars

[1]→ Stars are enormous balls of gas that fill galaxies throughout the universe. There are many types of stars. Astronomers classify them in various ways. The most common ways are by their size, color, and **luminosity**. One system is called the Yerkes spectral classification. Three American scientists developed it in the 1940s. In it, stars are classified as hypergiants, supergiants, bright giants, normal giants, subgiants, dwarf stars, subdwarfs, and white, red, and brown dwarfs.

The largest stars in the universe are hypergiants. They also have the greatest luminosity. It can be millions of times greater than Earth's sun. Hypergiants are rare and have relatively short lives. They live for only a few million years. This is short compared to the sun, which has a lifetime of around ten billion years. Hypergiants may appear blue, red, white, or yellow in color. Supergiants are next in size and luminosity. They can be around 100,000 times brighter than the sun. They are commonly red or blue in color. Thus people sometimes call them red or blue supergiants. Bright giants are slightly smaller in size and less luminous than supergiants. They vary in color and can be white, orange, red, yellow-white, and blue-white.

• Glossary •

luminosity: brightness

23 Which of the sentences below best expresses the essential information in the highlighted sentence in the passage? *Incorrect* answer choices change the meaning in important ways or leave out essential information.

ⓐ The sun is nearly as bright as giant stars are.

ⓑ The brightness and the size of giant stars are the same as the sun.

ⓒ Giant stars are much larger and brighter than the sun.

ⓓ The sun is considerably smaller than all giant stars.

24 The word "expended" in the passage is closest in meaning to

ⓐ converted

ⓑ spent

ⓒ transferred

ⓓ made

25 In paragraph 3, the author implies that the sun

ⓐ is the same size as a giant star

ⓑ has nearly expended all of its fuel

ⓒ has a core that totally lacks hydrogen

ⓓ may become a giant star one day

26 According to paragraph 4, which of the following is NOT true of dwarf stars?

ⓐ They are younger than many other stars.

ⓑ All of them are larger than the sun.

ⓒ Another name for them is main sequence stars.

ⓓ They comprise the greatest number of stars.

³→ Giant stars are midway in size between stars like the sun and the larger giants. Giant stars are usually ten to one hundred times bigger than the sun and are ten to one thousand times brighter as well. They were once stars like the sun. But they changed once they expended all of the hydrogen in their cores. Then, their cores contracted while their surfaces expanded. They became brighter and turned into giant stars. Midway between giant stars and stars such as the sun are the subgiants. Astronomers believe that subgiants have no more hydrogen but have not yet expanded.

⁴→ Most stars in the universe are classified as dwarf stars. They are among the youngest stars in existence. They are either at the beginning of their lives or are partway through them. Eventually, many will use all of their fuel and become giants. They are also known as main sequence stars. The reason is that they have the same range of size, color, and luminosity in most star classification systems. Some dwarf stars are similar to the sun. Yet they can be bigger or smaller than it. Many are white or yellow in color. Subdwarfs are smaller and less luminous than dwarf stars.

• **Glossary** •

core: a center

27 According to paragraph 5, which of the following is true of red dwarfs?

  Ⓐ They have a low level of brightness.

  Ⓑ They are around the same size as the sun.

  Ⓒ They are less common than hypergiants.

  Ⓓ They give off more heat than most stars.

28 According to paragraph 6, a giant star becomes a white dwarf because

  Ⓐ the star has entered its final stage of life

  Ⓑ the star contains too much hydrogen

  Ⓒ the mass of the star increases

  Ⓓ the star failed to become a red dwarf

29 Look at the four squares [■] that indicate where the following sentence could be added to the passage.

A telescope is necessary to see many of them from the Earth.

Where would the sentence best fit?

Click on a square [■] to add the sentence to the passage.

5→ The final three types of stars are red, white, and brown dwarfs. The vast majority of stars in the universe are red dwarfs. They have about half the mass of the sun and have low surface temperatures. **1** Their luminosity is always low, which makes them difficult to observe. **2** Red dwarfs burn their hydrogen at a very slow rate. **3** It may take hundreds of billions of years for a red dwarf to run out of fuel. **4** Since the universe is only around fourteen billion years old, all red dwarfs are at the beginning of their life cycles.

6→ Among the smallest stars in the universe are white dwarfs. Both their mass and luminosity are low. Astronomers believe that the white dwarf stage is the final one in a star's life. A white dwarf is the core that remains after a giant star dies. It contains no hydrogen, helium, or any other source of energy. Its heat and luminosity remain from its life as a giant star. Over time, a white dwarf will grow dimmer and become cooler. As for brown dwarfs, they are stars that lack enough mass to begin the chain reaction necessary to burn their fuel. So they have the structure of a star but never become hot or bright. They may remain in that state forever.

30 *Directions*: Select the appropriate sentences from the answer choices and match them to the type of star to which they relate. TWO of the answer choices will NOT be used. *This question is worth 3 points*.

Drag your answer choices to the spaces where they belong.
To remove an answer choice, click on it. To review the passage, click on **View Text**.

Answer Choices	**TYPE OF STAR**
① It has expanded after using its hydrogen.	**Supergiant**
② It is the most common type of star.	•
③ It only lives for a few million years.	•
④ It is the second brightest star in the universe.	**Dwarf Star**
⑤ It is a star that is similar to the sun.	•
⑥ It usually appears red or blue in color.	•
⑦ It is one of the universe's youngest stars.	•

CONTINUE

Reading Section Directions

This section measures your ability to understand academic passages in English. You will have **54 minutes** to read and answer questions about **3 passages**. A clock at the top of the screen will show you how much time is remaining.

Most questions are worth 1 point but the last question for each passage is worth more than 1 point. The directions for the last question indicate how many points you may receive.

Some passages include a word or phrase that is **underlined** in blue. Click on the word or phrase to see a definition or an explanation.

When you want to move to the next question, click on **Next**. You may skip questions and go back to them later. If you want to return to previous questions, click on **Back**. You can click on **Review** at any time, and the review screen will show you which questions you have answered and which you have not answered. From this review screen, you may go directly to any question you have already seen in the Reading section.

Click on **Continue** to go on.

Film Editing

When films are created, they go through three major stages of editing. They are preproduction, principle photography, and postproduction. Preproduction involves writing the screenplay and selecting the actor and the locations. Sets are also built then. Principle photography is the shooting of the film with cameras. Postproduction involves editing the **film footage** into a story. Special effects, music, and color timing are also done in this stage. All three aspects are very important. But it is the final editing process that makes the story come together as a whole from many separate pieces.

For most of the history of film, editing was a long and tedious process. Editors had to cut and paste long strips of film into a coherent story. Today, there are much faster and simpler ways. Computer editing platforms do much of the work. In addition, the existence of digital cameras means that the use of film may soon disappear altogether. No matter which method is used, film editing has three main stages. They are the initial assembly, the first rough cut, and the final cut.

The initial assembly takes place during principle photography. A producer hires an editor to take the footage that was shot and to piece it together. During principle photography, the director takes many shots of the same scene. They are filmed from different angles and often with different line readings from the actors. Each scene shot is called a take. As the shooting occurs, the director decides which bits of film to save and print. Printing fewer takes saves money. The editor then takes those scenes and assembles the initial cut. As each scene is printed and edited, the editor makes short clips to view. These clips, called dailies, let the director see how the film is coming together.

When principle photography is done, postproduction begins. The editor and the director work together to make the first rough cut. This is the whole film as they wish to present it. But there is no musical score, special efforts, or color timing. Sometimes the editor may use a temporary score of old music. This can give the viewer an idea of what the final score may be like. Temporary images are also used to represent special effects of scenes not yet shot. For example, the rough cut of *Star Wars* (1977) had World War II aerial **dogfight** footage. It represented a space battle that had not been shot yet.

A wide group of people see the rough cut. These include the studio heads, the producers, the director, and other trusted people. At this point, the film may be approved or not. The editors may be asked to assemble the footage in a different way. That can make the story better or clear up any confusion. The producers may want to test the film with an audience. So they may ask a group of people to watch the film and to rate it. If the audience reacts negatively, changes may be needed.

If the film is liked, it heads to the last bit of editing: the final cut. The editor and the director work with a composer to make the final score. This is usually done with a full orchestra. It times the music to fit the film as it plays on screen. Special effects and sound effects are then added. Once the music and the effects are added, the film is locked. Then, it is sent to the color timer. This is a specialist who adjusts the color of the final film to the desired tones and hues. Once that is done, the film is complete. Then, it can be released for people to see.

• **Glossary** •

film footage: scenes that are recorded for a movie

dogfight: a battle between two or more aircraft

Film Editing

1➤ When films are created, they go through three major stages of editing. They are preproduction, principle photography, and postproduction. Preproduction involves writing the screenplay and selecting the actor and the locations. Sets are also built then. Principle photography is the shooting of the film with cameras. Postproduction involves editing the **film footage** into a story. Special effects, music, and color timing are also done in this stage. All three aspects are very important. But it is the final editing process that makes the story come together as a whole from many separate pieces.

2➤ For most of the history of film, editing was a long and tedious process. Editors had to cut and paste long strips of film into a coherent story. Today, there are much faster and simpler ways. Computer editing platforms do much of the work. In addition, the existence of digital cameras means that the use of film may soon disappear altogether. No matter which method is used, film editing has three main stages. They are the initial assembly, the first rough cut, and the final cut.

---

1 In paragraph 1, all of the following questions are answered EXCEPT:

(A) What is involved in principle photography?

(B) Which editing stage takes the most time?

(C) What are the names of the stages of editing?

(D) When are music and special effects added to a film?

2 The word "tedious" in the passage is closest in meaning to

(A) appealing

(B) difficult

(C) dull

(D) important

3 In paragraph 2, the author uses "Computer editing platforms" as an example of

(A) reasons special effects look so real

(B) applications that work with digital cameras

(C) processes used by editors in the past

(D) tools that save time in editing

• **Glossary** •

film footage: scenes that are recorded for a movie

4 According to paragraph 3, which of the following is true of principle photography?

    Ⓐ Multiple shots of the same scenes are taken.

    Ⓑ It lasts longer when a director has more money.

    Ⓒ The final cut takes place during it.

    Ⓓ Most scenes are shot with a single take.

5 Which of the following can be inferred from paragraph 3 about dailies?

    Ⓐ Parts of them appear in the completed film.

    Ⓑ They are made by the director to help the editor.

    Ⓒ The score is added to them by the editor.

    Ⓓ Some of them can last for more than one hour.

6 In paragraph 4, why does the author mention "*Star Wars*"?

    Ⓐ To describe some of the battle scenes in it

    Ⓑ To state the year it was released

    Ⓒ To compare it with the fighting in World War II

    Ⓓ To note that its rough cut had temporary images

[3]➙ The initial assembly takes place during principle photography. A producer hires an editor to take the footage that was shot and to piece it together. During principle photography, the director takes many shots of the same scene. They are filmed from different angles and often with different line readings from the actors. Each scene shot is called a take. As the shooting occurs, the director decides which bits of film to save and print. Printing fewer takes saves money. The editor then takes those scenes and assembles the initial cut. As each scene is printed and edited, the editor makes short clips to view. These clips, called dailies, let the director see how the film is coming together.

[4]➙ When principle photography is done, postproduction begins. The editor and the director work together to make the first rough cut. This is the whole film as they wish to present it. But there is no musical score, special efforts, or color timing. Sometimes the editor may use a temporary score of old music. This can give the viewer an idea of what the final score may be like. Temporary images are also used to represent special effects of scenes not yet shot. For example, the rough cut of *Star Wars* (1977) had World War II aerial **dogfight** footage. It represented a space battle that had not been shot yet.

• Glossary •

dogfight: a battle between two or more aircraft

7 According to paragraph 5, many people watch the rough cut because

   Ⓐ they must create the film's final score

   Ⓑ they decide to release the film or not

   Ⓒ they point out negative parts of the film

   Ⓓ they will provide the film to theaters

8 The word "who" in the passage refers to

   Ⓐ the music and the effects

   Ⓑ the color timer

   Ⓒ the color

   Ⓓ the final film

9 Look at the four squares [■] that indicate where the following sentence could be added to the passage.

Changes to the film may be made if it does not match the music.

Where would the sentence best fit?

> Click on a square [■] to add the sentence to the passage.

⁵→ A wide group of people see the rough cut. These include the studio heads, the producers, the director, and other trusted people. At this point, the film may be approved or not. The editors may be asked to assemble the footage in a different way. That can make the story better or clear up any confusion. The producers may want to test the film with an audience. So they may ask a group of people to watch the film and to rate it. If the audience reacts negatively, changes may be needed.

If the film is liked, it heads to the last bit of editing: the final cut. The editor and the director work with a composer to make the final score. This is usually done with a full orchestra. **1** It times the music to fit the film as it plays on screen. **2** Special effects and sound effects are then added. **3** Once the music and the effects are added, the film is locked. **4** Then, it is sent to the color timer. This is a specialist who adjusts the color of the final film to the desired tones and hues. Once that is done, the film is complete. Then, it can be released for people to see.

10 *Directions*: Select the appropriate statements from the answer choices and match them to the stage of editing to which they relate. TWO of the answer choices will NOT be used. *This question is worth 3 points.*

> Drag your answer choices to the spaces where they belong.
> To remove an answer choice, click on it. To review the passage, click on **View Text**.

Answer Choices	**STAGE OF EDITING**
① Audiences are asked to rate the film.	**Principle Photography**
② Scenes in films are recorded.	•
③ An orchestra creates the music score.	•
④ Dailies are created by the editor.	•
⑤ The screenplay is written.	**Postproduction**
⑥ Performers and locations are chosen.	•
⑦ The rough cut is created.	•

The Relationship between Plants and Animals

Acacia ants on an acacia tree

Many organisms eat others. They do this to get energy and to survive. Plants are eaten by large numbers of other organisms. To protect themselves, plants have evolved. They have developed defenses that stop other organisms from eating them. There are many kinds of defenses. Some plants use physical defenses. Others utilize chemical defenses, such as poison. And a few plants develop special relationships with other organisms. In return for food and shelter, these organisms protect the plants from outside attacks. Still, plants do not always repel animals. In fact, they often need animals to survive.

The primary defense of many plants is their composition. These are physical defenses. For instance, most trees have tough bark. The bark is difficult for the majority of animals to chew through. It protects the more sensitive parts of the plants. Many plants, such as roses, have sharp thorns. These can injure animals and insects. Certain seeds and fruits may be too difficult for animals and insects to open. Coconuts are one example. A coconut has a tough outer shell that is hard to open. And the leaves of some plants are very waxy. So it is hard for animals or insects to eat them. Some leaves are highly sensitive and close when they are touched. As a result, animals become afraid of these plants and shun them. Finally, the fruits and the leaves of some plants are found at heights out of the reach of many animals.

Chemical defenses are another common method plants use. Some plants contain poisons that can harm animals. So they make attackers sick or even kill them at times. Poison ivy, for instance, produces a chemical that causes rashes when touched. Some poisonous plants <u>paralyze</u> their attackers. The poison eventually wears off. But it makes the paralyzed attacker easy prey for predators. Over time, animals learn to identify these harmful plants. So they do not go near those plants.

Other plants do not use poisons but still employ chemical defenses. These plants may have leaves that taste bad to animals. Milkweed has leaves that contain a white sap. This sap tastes bitter to most animals. So they do not feed on milkweed leaves. Some plants release bad smells that repel animals. Peonies and salvias are two such plants. The smell of their leaves keeps deer away. Deer eat large amounts of vegetation every day. So these plants have evolved to prevent deer from eating them.

A third plant defensive method is to get a living organism to protect it. Some plants develop relationships with insects. The plant provides food such as nectar as well as shelter for the insects. The insects then protect the plant from other animals. The acacia tree and the acacia ant have this kind of relationship. The acacia tree has **hollow** thorns. These serve as homes for the ants. The tree also produces sweet nectar, which the ants eat. In return, the ants attack all other insects that try to eat any part of the acacia tree. This enables the tree to survive and not be harmed by other organisms.

Despite having many defenses to protect themselves from animals, plants may need assistance from them. For example, pollination requires insects and other animals to spread pollen inside plants' flowers. This lets the plants reproduce. Many plants attract animals with their colorful flowers and nectar. The animals suck the nectar from the flowers. While doing so, some pollen gets stuck to the insects. As they visit other flowers, the pollen rubs off. It then spreads to the eggs in the flowers. This helps produce seeds and fruit. In addition, plants need animals to spread their seeds. Many animals eat the fruits and the seeds of plants. These pass through the animals' digestive systems. The seeds then land on the ground in new areas. Many seeds germinate and then grow to become mature plants.

• Glossary •

paralyze: to cause someone or something to be unable to move; to freeze
hollow: having a hole in the middle

11 According to paragraph 1, which of the following is NOT true of plant defenses?

Ⓐ Plants have several kinds of defenses.

Ⓑ Some plants have other organisms defend them.

Ⓒ Plants have evolved to develop defenses.

Ⓓ They are used to keep all animals away.

12 In paragraph 2, the author uses "bark" as an example of

Ⓐ a primary form of plant defense

Ⓑ the most effective plant defense

Ⓒ a plant defense involving poison

Ⓓ a defense that is used by roses

13 According to paragraph 2, which of the following is true of coconuts?

Ⓐ They are located very high on coconut trees.

Ⓑ The leaves of coconut trees feel waxy.

Ⓒ Their shells are difficult for animals to open.

Ⓓ Some of them have thorns that can hurt animals.

The Relationship between Plants and Animals

1→ Many organisms eat others. They do this to get energy and to survive. Plants are eaten by large numbers of other organisms. To protect themselves, plants have evolved. They have developed defenses that stop other organisms from eating them. There are many kinds of defenses. Some plants use physical defenses. Others utilize chemical defenses, such as poison. And a few plants develop special relationships with other organisms. In return for food and shelter, these organisms protect the plants from outside attacks. Still, plants do not always repel animals. In fact, they often need animals to survive.

2→ The primary defense of many plants is their composition. These are physical defenses. For instance, most trees have tough bark. The bark is difficult for the majority of animals to chew through. It protects the more sensitive parts of the plants. Many plants, such as roses, have sharp thorns. These can injure animals and insects. Certain seeds and fruits may be too difficult for animals and insects to open. Coconuts are one example. A coconut has a tough outer shell that is hard to open. And the leaves of some plants are very waxy. So it is hard for animals or insects to eat them. Some leaves are highly sensitive and close when they are touched. As a result, animals become afraid of these plants and shun them. Finally, the fruits and the leaves of some plants are found at heights out of the reach of many animals.

14 In paragraph 3, the author's description of plant poison mentions all of the following EXCEPT:

  Ⓐ the kind of a defense it is

  Ⓑ its effects on some animals

  Ⓒ the name of a plant that utilizes it

  Ⓓ the reason jungle plants often use it

15 The word "repel" in the passage is closest in meaning to

  Ⓐ reject

  Ⓑ enrage

  Ⓒ enhance

  Ⓓ drive off

16 According to paragraph 4, which of the following can be inferred about peonies and salvias?

  Ⓐ They may be eaten by some animals.

  Ⓑ Deer will eat them if they are very hungry.

  Ⓒ Their leaves are poisonous to some animals.

  Ⓓ They have thick sap in their leaves.

³→ Chemical defenses are another common method plants use. Some plants contain poisons that can harm animals. So they make attackers sick or even kill them at times. Poison ivy, for instance, produces a chemical that causes rashes when touched. Some poisonous plants **paralyze** their attackers. The poison eventually wears off. But it makes the paralyzed attacker easy prey for predators. Over time, animals learn to identify these harmful plants. So they do not go near those plants.

⁴→ Other plants do not use poisons but still employ chemical defenses. These plants may have leaves that taste bad to animals. Milkweed has leaves that contain a white sap. This sap tastes bitter to most animals. So they do not feed on milkweed leaves. Some plants release bad smells that repel animals. Peonies and salvias are two such plants. The smell of their leaves keeps deer away. Deer eat large amounts of vegetation every day. So these plants have evolved to prevent deer from eating them.

• **Glossary** •

paralyze: to cause someone or something to be unable to move; to freeze

17 According to paragraph 5, acacia ants protect acacia trees because

   Ⓐ it is their instinct to guard the trees

   Ⓑ the trees give them food and shelter

   Ⓒ they would die without support from the trees

   Ⓓ other insects could kill the trees

18 According to paragraph 6, plants need animals because

   Ⓐ animals spread the pollen that lets plants reproduce

   Ⓑ animals can fertilize the ground in which the plants grow

   Ⓒ animals eat the flowers that grow on most plants

   Ⓓ animals bury seeds that can germinate at a later time

19 Look at the four squares [■] that indicate where the following sentence could be added to the passage.

This provides nourishment for the ants.

Where would the sentence best fit?

> Click on a square [■] to add the sentence to the passage.

---

⁵➡ A third plant defensive method is to get a living organism to protect it. Some plants develop relationships with insects. The plant provides food such as nectar as well as shelter for the insects. The insects then protect the plant from other animals. The acacia tree and the acacia ant have this kind of relationship. The acacia tree has **hollow** thorns. These serve as homes for the ants. **1** The tree also produces sweet nectar, which the ants eat. **2** In return, the ants attack all other insects that try to eat any part of the acacia tree. **3** This enables the tree to survive and not be harmed by other organisms. **4**

⁶➡ Despite having many defenses to protect themselves from animals, plants may need assistance from them. For example, pollination requires insects and other animals to spread pollen inside plants' flowers. This lets the plants reproduce. Many plants attract animals with their colorful flowers and nectar. The animals suck the nectar from the flowers. While doing so, some pollen gets stuck to the insects. As they visit other flowers, the pollen rubs off. It then spreads to the eggs in the flowers. This helps produce seeds and fruit. In addition, plants need animals to spread their seeds. Many animals eat the fruits and the seeds of plants. These pass through the animals' digestive systems. The seeds then land on the ground in new areas. Many seeds germinate and then grow to become mature plants.

• Glossary •

hollow: having a hole in the middle

20 *Directions*: An introductory sentence for a brief summary of the passage is provided below. Complete the summary by selecting the THREE answer choices that express the most important ideas of the passage. Some sentences do not belong because they express ideas that are not presented in the passage or are minor ideas in the passage. ***This question is worth 2 points***.

> Drag your answer choices to the spaces where they belong.
> To remove an answer choice, click on it. To review the passage, click on **View Text**.

Plants have evolved to develop a variety of defenses to protect themselves from animals.

-
-
-

Answer Choices

1. A lot of animals avoid poison ivy once they learn how to identify it.

2. Tough bark and sharp thorns are external types of protection for plants.

3. Some plants form relationships with organisms that help protect them.

4. Acacia ants are rewarded with nectar from the acacia trees they guard.

5. Many plants rely on insects to spread pollen when their flowers bloom.

6. There are some plants that repel animals by using forms of poison.

The Dividing of the Roman Empire

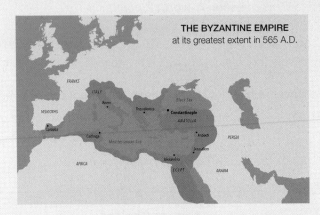

The Byzantine Empire at its greatest extent in 565 A.D.

    At its height, the Roman Empire covered all of southern Europe, most of Britain, the Middle East, and North Africa. For many years, the Romans successfully controlled this vast region. But then the situation began to change. They found it necessary to split the empire into two parts. These became the Western Roman Empire and the Eastern Roman Empire. Each half had its own emperor. This division happened for several reasons. First, it was easier to administer the empires since they were smaller. Second, a long period of civil war had made the Roman Empire unstable. Lastly, Diocletian, the emperor who made the split, wanted to move the seat of power to the much richer eastern part. In the end, this move failed to save the Western Roman Empire. It was overcome in 476. But the Eastern Roman Empire lived for almost another <u>millennium</u>. It became the Byzantine Empire and did not fall until 1453.

    Rome was the largest empire of its time. Its size made managing the empire difficult. While the Romans had an excellent system of roads, running the empire was still hard. In the provinces, orders from Rome were often ignored. Provincial governors controlled local areas. They usually did as they pleased. Money was sent to them from Rome. It was for building roads and supporting troops. Taxes were also collected in these areas. But the locals often disliked paying them. So there were many minor rebellions against the rulers in Rome. To ease these problems, Diocletian split the empire in 284.

    Diocletian came to power during a time of turmoil. In the third century, there had been a number of civil wars. They took place over fifty years. During that time, twenty-five men had been emperors. Most lived a short time and were assassinated. During this troubled period, Rome became much weaker. The non-Roman people living on its borders recognized this weakness. They wanted the land and the riches of Rome for themselves. Diocletian saw these problems. He realized that splitting the empire could make defending it easier. Communications would be shorter. And soldiers would have to move shorter distances to protect each empire's borders.

Diocletian therefore made the momentous decision to move the seat of Roman power to the east. He became the Eastern Roman emperor. His close friend Maximian became the Western Roman emperor. But they were not equals. Diocletian was the supreme ruler. He chose to rule the eastern empire since it was wealthier. He quickly began making changes in his territory. He reformed the bureaucracy and increased the number of <u>bureaucrats</u>. He created more local seats of government. He increased tax collection. Diocletian also went to war with troublesome locals. And he defended the empire's borders and put down rebellions.

Diocletian was a great reformer. But his reforms did not last long after he died. Following his death, there was a period when attempts to reunite the empire were made. In 305, Constantine the Great became the emperor of the west. Another civil war erupted. Constantine emerged victorious. He believed that the west was in decline. So he moved to the east and built the great city of Constantinople. It became the capital of the Eastern Roman Empire. The power of Rome was now firmly in the east. Still, in the late 300s, Emperor Theodosius reunited the two empires for some time. But he died in 395. Once he died, the split became permanent. His two sons inherited one empire each. The Eastern Roman Empire prospered. The Western Roman Empire declined further. Germanic tribes increased their attacks on its borders. Eventually, they overran the defenders and captured Rome itself. This began the period in Western Europe known as the Dark Ages.

• Glossary •

millennium: a period of time lasting 1,000 years
bureaucrat: a person who works in a government office; a civil servant

21 According to paragraph 1, Diocletian divided the Roman Empire because

   Ⓐ he had no desire to preserve the western half of the empire

   Ⓑ the division would make managing the empire easier

   Ⓒ he was interested in creating the Byzantine Empire

   Ⓓ there were enough men capable of running both empires

22 In paragraph 2, the author implies that roads

   Ⓐ were always in need of being expanded

   Ⓑ connected every city in the Roman Empire

   Ⓒ cost a small amount of money to maintain

   Ⓓ were important to managing an empire

23 According to paragraph 2, which of the following is true of provincial governors in the Roman Empire?

   Ⓐ They always obeyed orders from Rome.

   Ⓑ They were chosen from wealthy Roman families.

   Ⓒ They were the leaders of many rebellions.

   Ⓓ They were sent money from Rome for roads.

The Dividing of the Roman Empire

1→ At its height, the Roman Empire covered all of southern Europe, most of Britain, the Middle East, and North Africa. For many years, the Romans successfully controlled this vast region. But then the situation began to change. They found it necessary to split the empire into two parts. These became the Western Roman Empire and the Eastern Roman Empire. Each half had its own emperor. This division happened for several reasons. First, it was easier to administer the empires since they were smaller. Second, a long period of civil war had made the Roman Empire unstable. Lastly, Diocletian, the emperor who made the split, wanted to move the seat of power to the much richer eastern part. In the end, this move failed to save the Western Roman Empire. It was overcome in 476. But the Eastern Roman Empire lived for almost another <u>millennium</u>. It became the Byzantine Empire and did not fall until 1453.

2→ Rome was the largest empire of its time. Its size made managing the empire difficult. While the Romans had an excellent system of roads, running the empire was still hard. In the provinces, orders from Rome were often ignored. Provincial governors controlled local areas. They usually did as they pleased. Money was sent to them from Rome. It was for building roads and supporting troops. Taxes were also collected in these areas. But the locals often disliked paying them. So there were many minor rebellions against the rulers in Rome. To ease these problems, Diocletian split the empire in 284.

• **Glossary** •

millennium: a period of time lasting 1,000 years

24 The word "turmoil" in the passage is closest in meaning to

Ⓐ chaos

Ⓑ indecision

Ⓒ prosperity

Ⓓ rebellion

25 The word "assassinated" in the passage is closest in meaning to

Ⓐ murdered

Ⓑ deposed

Ⓒ exiled

Ⓓ kidnapped

26 According to paragraph 4, the author's description of Maximian mentions which of the following?

Ⓐ The reason he ruled the eastern half of the Roman Empire

Ⓑ His relative lack of power compared to Diocletian

Ⓒ How his family relationship to Diocletian was important

Ⓓ His attempts to reform the Roman bureaucracy

Diocletian came to power during a time of turmoil. In the third century, there had been a number of civil wars. They took place over fifty years. During that time, twenty-five men had been emperors. Most lived a short time and were assassinated. During this troubled period, Rome became much weaker. The non-Roman people living on its borders recognized this weakness. They wanted the land and the riches of Rome for themselves. Diocletian saw these problems. He realized that splitting the empire could make defending it easier. Communications would be shorter. And soldiers would have to move shorter distances to protect each empire's borders.

⁴→ Diocletian therefore made the momentous decision to move the seat of Roman power to the east. He became the Eastern Roman emperor. His close friend Maximian became the Western Roman emperor. But they were not equals. Diocletian was the supreme ruler. He chose to rule the eastern empire since it was wealthier. He quickly began making changes in his territory. He reformed the bureaucracy and increased the number of bureaucrats. He created more local seats of government. He increased tax collection. Diocletian also went to war with troublesome locals. And he defended the empire's borders and put down rebellions.

• **Glossary** •

bureaucrat: a person who works in a government office; a civil servant

27 In paragraph 5, why does the author mention "Constantinople"?

Ⓐ To declare it was the capital of the Eastern Roman Empire

Ⓑ To explain why the Byzantine Empire became so wealthy

Ⓒ To discuss how long it took to construct the city

Ⓓ To state that Constantine was the first emperor to live there

28 According to paragraph 5, the split in the Roman Empire became permanent in 395 because

Ⓐ Germanic invaders captured and destroyed the city of Rome

Ⓑ the Byzantine Empire no longer protected the western half of the empire

Ⓒ there was a civil war that made the two halves fight one another

Ⓓ the two sons of Theodosius each inherited one half of the empire

29 Look at the four squares [■] that indicate where the following sentence could be added to the passage.

This greatly increased the amount of money the empire had access to.

Where would the sentence best fit?

Click on a square [■] to add the sentence to the passage.

Diocletian therefore made the momentous decision to move the seat of Roman power to the east. He became the Eastern Roman emperor. His close friend Maximian became the Western Roman emperor. But they were not equals. Diocletian was the supreme ruler. He chose to rule the eastern empire since it was wealthier. He quickly began making changes in his territory. He reformed the bureaucracy and increased the number of **bureaucrats**. **1** He created more local seats of government. **2** He increased tax collection. **3** Diocletian also went to war with troublesome locals. **4** And he defended the empire's borders and put down rebellions.

⁵➙ Diocletian was a great reformer. But his reforms did not last long after he died. Following his death, there was a period when attempts to reunite the empire were made. In 305, Constantine the Great became the emperor of the west. Another civil war erupted. Constantine emerged victorious. He believed that the west was in decline. So he moved to the east and built the great city of Constantinople. It became the capital of the Eastern Roman Empire. The power of Rome was now firmly in the east. Still, in the late 300s, Emperor Theodosius reunited the two empires for some time. But he died in 395. Once he died, the split became permanent. His two sons inherited one empire each. The Eastern Roman Empire prospered. The Western Roman Empire declined further. Germanic tribes increased their attacks on its borders. Eventually, they overran the defenders and captured Rome itself. This began the period in Western Europe known as the Dark Ages.

• **Glossary** •

bureaucrat: a person who works in a government office; a civil servant

30 ***Directions***: An introductory sentence for a brief summary of the passage is provided below. Complete the summary by selecting the THREE answer choices that express the most important ideas of the passage. Some sentences do not belong because they express ideas that are not presented in the passage or are minor ideas in the passage. ***This question is worth 2 points***.

> Drag your answer choices to the spaces where they belong.
> To remove an answer choice, click on it. To review the passage, click on **View Text**.

The Emperor Diocletian divided the Roman Empire into two halves for a number of reasons.

-
-
-

Answer Choices

1. Splitting the empire made it easier to defend the borders from invading armies.

2. Constantine the Great built the city Constantinople to be the capital of his empire.

3. Twenty-five men ruled the Roman Empire in a fifty-year period in the third century.

4. The permanent split between the eastern and western halves took place in 395.

5. Diocletian hoped to reform the empire in order to make it stronger than it was.

6. The Roman Empire was too unstable because of the many civil wars it endured.

MEMO

MEMO

MEMO

TOEFL® MAP

New TOEFL® Edition

Reading

Basic

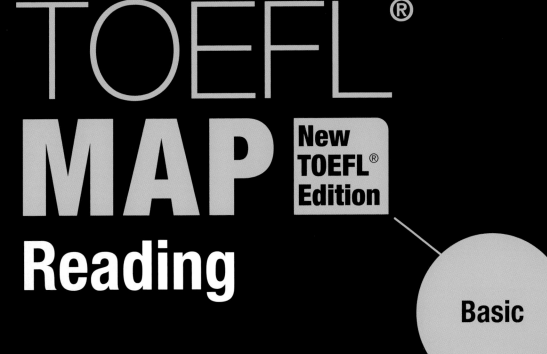

Answers and Explanations

TOEFL® MAP Reading

New TOEFL® Edition

Basic

Answers and Explanations

Part A

Understanding Reading Question Types

Question Type | 01 Vocabulary

Exercises with Vocabulary Questions

Exercise 1 D

When topsoil and land get carried away, they get removed from the area where they are.

Exercise 2 C

Something that is extremely dark is highly dark. It is very difficult to see anything if a place is extremely dark.

Exercise 3 B

The surrounding land in a city is the land that is nearby it.

Exercise 4 D

Imprints of plants and animals on stone are only traces of the plants and animals. They are not complete fossils.

Question Type | 02 Reference

Exercises with Reference Questions

Exercise 1 A

The "it" that a large number of plants and animals cannot survive in is the desert.

Exercise 2 C

The "ones" that are common are taxes.

Exercise 3 D

The "it" that the Greeks defeated was the city of Troy.

Exercise 4 B

The "they" who prefer to homeschool their children are many American parents.

Question Type | 03 Factual Information

Exercises with Factual Information Questions

Exercise 1 A

The author writes, "Many people know about Armstrong for his trumpet playing."

Exercise 2 D

It is written, "These people rarely socialize in person. Instead, they prefer to meet and speak with others online."

Exercise 3 C

The author notes, "Most sailors preferred to stay in sight of land at all times. So ships were built for rivers or lakes."

Exercise 4 A

The author mentions, "And there are all sorts of statues depicting other figures as well."

Question Type | 04 Negative Factual Information

Exercises with Negative Factual Information Questions

Exercise 1 B

The author notes that there are many dikes in the region of northwestern Holland. So it is not true that there are few dikes in that area.

Exercise 2 B

The passage does not include anything about how flying squirrels are able to glide.

Exercise 3 C

About alternative energy, the author comments, "They are fairly clean sources of energy as well. They do not pollute the air like burning coal, oil, and gas does."

Exercise 4 A

The author does not include anything about predicting earthquakes in the passage.

Question Type | 05 Sentence Simplification

Exercises with Sentence Simplification Questions
p.28

Exercise 1 (B)

The highlighted sentence notes that inventors still own the products if the inventions get licensed. This is best explained in answer choice (B).

Exercise 2 (A)

The highlighted sentence notes that chlorophyll causes a reaction that changes water and carbon dioxide into glucose and oxygen. This is best explained in answer choice (A).

Question Type | 06 Inference

Exercises with Inference Questions
p.32

Exercise 1 (B)

The author notes, "When movies began to add sound, most silent movie actors could not make the transition to this new form." In the previous sentences, the author mentioned the style of acting that performers used. So the author implies that silent movies required a different acting style than movies with sound.

Exercise 2 (B)

First, the author remarks, "They are native to Africa and Asia and thrive in desert conditions." Then, the author comments, "However, camels' humps contain fat. They use this fat to provide sustenance when food and water are in short supply." It can be inferred that camels' humps help them survive in the desert.

Exercise 3 (A)

The author writes, "Black holes are among the most mysterious bodies in the universe." Something mysterious is often unknown or little known.

Exercise 4 (D)

The author comments, "He also painted the famous *The Birth of Venus*. He made other paintings with mythological themes as well." By writing "as well" when describing paintings with mythological themes, the author implies that *The Birth of Venus* itself had a mythological theme.

Question Type | 07 Rhetorical Purpose

Exercises with Rhetorical Purpose Questions
p.36

Exercise 1 (B)

The author mentions, "Darwin came to believe in gradualism because of his trip to the Galapagos Islands."

Exercise 2 (D)

In the paragraph, the author provides a lot of information about lunar eclipses.

Exercise 3 (C)

The author mentions that the cave in Chauvet has the oldest paintings on its walls. It is written, "The oldest have been found at Chauvet in France."

Exercise 4 (A)

The author comments, "There are vaccines for a number of deadly viruses. These include polio, cholera, and typhoid."

Question Type | 08 Insert Text

Exercises with Insert Text Questions
p.40

Exercise 1 1

The sentence before the first square notes that suburbs are safer than big cities. The sentence to be inserted gives an example of how safe suburban areas are.

Exercise 2 2

The sentence before the second square mentions that the saguaro cactus may live for up to 200 years. The sentence to be inserted explains how the saguaro cactus usually dies.

Question Type | 09 Prose Summary

Exercises with Prose Summary Questions
p.44

Exercise 1 4, 5, 6

According to the passage, every person in the feudal system had responsibilities that were owed to other people. For example, the nobles gave the king both money and soldiers. Serfs worked their lords' lands and gave them crops. And the king gave land to nobles that were loyal to him.

 **Exercise 2** ② , ④ , ⑥

According to the passage, there are many differences between mammals and reptiles. For example, mammals get warm from food while reptiles use the sun. Mammals have hair, but reptiles do not. And reptiles do not eat as often as mammals.

Question Type | **10** **Fill in a Table**

Exercises with Fill in a Table Questions
p.48

Exercise 1 Advantage: ② , ④ , ⑤   Disadvantage: ③ , ⑥

According to the passage, the advantages of dams are that they give people places to go fishing and boating, they stop floods, and they can provide electricity. As for their disadvantages, they force some people to move, and they stop silt from moving downriver.

Exercise 2 Cause: ① , ④ , ⑦   Effect: ② , ⑤

According to the passage, the causes of the Boston Tea Party were the facts that no Americans were represented in Parliament, France and Britain had fought in America, and the Tea Act was passed. As for its effects, America fought a war against Britain, and Britain tried to punish the people of Boston.

Part B

Building Background Knowledge of TOEFL Topics

● Chapter | **01** **History**

Mastering the Question Types A
p.52

 1 Ⓑ   2 Ⓐ   3 ③ , ⑤ , ⑥

1 [Rhetorical Purpose Question]

The author writes, "In the past, they were the homes of kings, queens, and high-ranking nobles."

2 [Vocabulary Question]

A place that is opulent looks magnificent.

3 [Prose Summary Question]

According to the passage, people made palaces for protection and to give them more prestige. For example, some palaces showed off the wealth of their owners. Other palaces had big walls to prevent enemies from getting in. And soldiers often guarded castles.

✏ **Checking Reading Accuracy**

1 T   2 F   3 T   4 F

Mastering the Question Types B
p.54

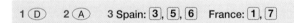 1 Ⓓ   2 Ⓐ   3 Spain: ③ , ⑤ , ⑥   France: ① , ⑦

1 [Inference Question]

The author writes, "Christopher Columbus found the New World in 1492. After that, many other explorers from Europe went across the Atlantic Ocean." This implies that Columbus was the first European to go to the Americas.

2 [Negative Factual Question]

The author does not mention how much gold and silver the Spanish found in the New World. It is only mentioned that the Spanish wanted to find gold and silver.

3 [Fill in a Table Question]

According to the passage, the Spanish wanted to become wealthy, they had colonies in South America, and they enslaved many natives. As for the French, they got along well with the natives and wanted animal furs.

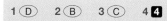
1 T   2 F   3 T   4 T

Mastering the Question Types C   p.56

1 ⒟   2 Ⓑ   3 Ⓒ   4 **4**

1 [Sentence Simplification Question]

The highlighted sentence notes that there was a lot of great writing during the Nara Period. This is best explained in answer choice ⒟.

2 [Reference Question]

The "they" that copied Chinese fashions and architecture were the Japanese.

3 [Factual Question]

The writer notes, "This was particularly true of some families. The Fujiwara family was one. A few Fujiwara daughters married emperors. So their children became quite powerful. In fact, the Fujiwara family influenced Japan for more than 300 years after the Nara Period ended."

4 [Insert Text Question]

The sentence before the fourth square notes that many families tried to sway the emperor. The sentence to be inserted mentions that some of these families were successful, so they achieved their goals.

1 T   2 F   3 T   4 F

Mastering the Subject A   p.58

1 Ⓑ   2 Ⓒ   3 Ⓑ   4 The Italian Peninsula
Homeland: ④, ⑧ The Senatorial Provinces: ①, ⑤, ⑥
The Imperial Provinces: ③, ⑨

1 [Factual Question]

About the Roman Empire, the author writes, "It controlled land in most of Europe and parts of the Middle East and North Africa. Millions of people lived within its borders. Yet most of them had been conquered in battle."

2 [Inference Question]

The passage reads, "The number of soldiers in a region depended on its danger level." Then, the author writes, "The third region included the imperial provinces. These were on the empire's borders. The emperor directly ruled them. Many soldiers, known as legionaries, were

posted in the imperial provinces in units called legions." So it can be inferred that the imperial provinces were the most dangerous ones.

3 [Rhetorical Purpose Question]

The author writes, "They also offered citizenship to people in the provinces. This gave people many rights and privileges. At first, local leaders were made citizens. Over time, others became citizens, too. This helped the people feel that they were Romans. This system proved to be effective. The Pax Romana, or 'Roman Peace,' was a result of these policies."

4 [Fill in a Table Question]

According to the passage, the Italian peninsula homeland was the most secure area and had the fewest troops in the empire. The senatorial provinces had people used to Roman rule, had been in the empire for a long time, and included Spain. The imperial provinces had large numbers of legionaries and were directly controlled by the emperor.

1 b   2 c   3 a   4 d

Mastering the Subject B   p.60

1 Ⓐ   2 Ⓑ   3 **2**   4 ①, ②, ⑤

1 [Vocabulary Question]

Aid that is vital is critical.

2 [Inference Question]

The author writes, "Dom Pedro was ordered home. He refused and remained in Brazil. He became the leader of the rebellion." Thus it can be inferred that Dom Pedro, by rebelling against his own family, considered himself to be Brazilian instead of Portuguese.

3 [Insert Text Question]

The sentence before the second square notes that the Portuguese royal family fled to Brazil to escape from the forces of Napoleon. The sentence to be inserted mentions the reason why: The king thought that escaping was better than fighting.

4 [Prose Summary Question]

According to the passage, until Dom Pedro helped Brazil get its independence, Brazil was a colony of Portugal. For example, the rebellion was successful partly because of some foreigners who provided aid to Brazil. In addition, Dom Pedro became the emperor of Brazil once the revolution ended. And Brazil, before it became independent, had been a colony of Portugal's for more than 300 years.

1 b   **2** c   **3** d   **4** a

Mastering the Subject C   p.62

1 Ⓒ   **2** Ⓑ   **3** Ⓒ   **4** Ⓓ

1 [Sentence Simplification Question]

The highlighted sentence notes that Sumerian farmers learned how to grow enough food that would support the people all year long. This is best explained in answer choice Ⓒ.

2 [Factual Question]

The author comments, "Yet both the kings and priests needed support. This led to the formation of a bureaucracy."

3 [Inference Question]

It is written, "The Sumerians also had their own religion. They worshipped many gods from temples they built in their city-states." This implies that religion was important to the Sumerians.

4 [Negative Factual Question]

The author mentions the changing climate, but there is no mention of cold temperatures causing problems for the Sumerians.

1 d   **2** b   **3** a   **4** c

TOEFL Practice Test   p.64

1 Ⓓ   **2** Ⓓ   **3** Ⓒ   **4** Ⓒ   **5** Ⓓ
6 Ⓐ   **7** Ⓐ   **8** Ⓐ   **9** **4**
10 **1**, **4**, **5**

1 [Rhetorical Purpose Question]

The author writes, "In 1607, Jamestown, Virginia, was founded. It was the first permanent British settlement in North America."

2 [Vocabulary Question]

When there are roughly two and a half million people somewhere, there are approximately that many people. It is not an exact number.

3 [Factual Question]

The author writes, "They were all located on the east coast next to the Atlantic Ocean." So the colonies were all next to water.

4 [Negative Factual Question]

There is no mention in the passage of who won the Thirty Years' War.

5 [Factual Question]

It is written, "But in America, land was free to anyone who settled it. This appealed to a large number of people. They eagerly sailed to America to claim land for themselves."

6 [Inference Question]

The author writes, "In addition, the king and other nobles owned much of the land. But in America, land was free to anyone who settled it. This appealed to a large number of people. They eagerly sailed to America to claim land for themselves. They built homes and farmed their land." This implies that the people were unhappy with the distribution of land in Britain since they wanted to own land for themselves.

7 [Vocabulary Question]

The prospect of improving one's personal welfare is the hope of doing that.

8 [Factual Question]

The author comments, "People born into noble families often led lives of leisure and wealth."

9 [Insert Text Question]

The sentence before the fourth square notes that Maryland was a place for Catholics to live in safety. The sentence to be inserted mentions that other people were also allowed to live there. The word "however" provides a connection between the two sentences.

10 [Prose Summary Question]

According to the passage, there were three main reasons people left Britain to go to the American colonies. First, they thought that they could improve their lives. They wanted the opportunity to own land. They also wanted to have the freedom to practice the religion that they believed in.

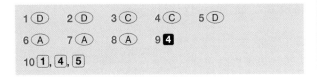

Vocabulary **Review**   p.70

1 Ⓐ	2 Ⓑ	3 Ⓓ	4 Ⓐ
5 Ⓓ	6 Ⓑ	7 Ⓑ	8 Ⓒ
9 Ⓒ	10 Ⓒ	11 Ⓑ	12 Ⓓ

Mastering the Question Types A

p.72

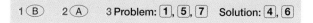

1 ⓒ   2 Ⓐ   3 ② , ⑤ , ⑥

1   [Rhetorical Question]

The author writes, "This is called stage blocking. It is used for plays, operas, musicals, and ballets."

2   [Vocabulary Question]

Gestures that people make are movements.

3   [Prose Summary Question]

According to the passage, stage blocking is very important to any kind of stage production. For example, it shows the actors where to stand on stage. Stage blocking lets the audience see the performers' facial expressions. It also lets people hear the actors' voices.

✓ **Checking Reading Accuracy**

1 F   2 F   3 T   4 T

Mastering the Question Types B

p.74

1 Ⓑ   2 Ⓐ   3 Problem: ① , ⑤ , ⑦   Solution: ④ , ⑥

1   [Inference Question]

The author notes, "Second, they were small, so only one person could view the film strip at a time." So it can be inferred that large audiences could not see films on early movie projectors.

2   [Negative Factual Question]

Videocassette recorders were invented in the 1970s. So people could not watch movies on videotape with early movie projectors.

3   [Fill in a Table Question]

According to the passage, some of the problems with early movie projectors were that they often broke down, only one person could watch them at a time, and they showed short films. As for the solutions, projectors were made that could show movies on screens, and inventors made better projectors.

✓ **Checking Reading Accuracy**

1 F   2 F   3 T   4 T

Mastering the Question Types C

p.76

1 ⓒ   2 Ⓑ   3 Ⓑ   4 **④**

1   [Sentence Simplification Question]

The highlighted sentence notes that the Egyptians made great buildings as well as a large amount of art. This is best explained in answer choice ⓒ.

2   [Reference Question]

The "They" that know what clothes people wore then are experts.

3   [Factual Question]

The passage reads, "Very much Egyptian art from the past has survived to the present day. This is due to the hot, dry climate in Egypt."

4   [Insert Text Question]

The two sentences before the fourth square note two styles that Egyptian artists used. The sentence to be inserted mentions that the two styles combine to make images that are easy for people to identify as Egyptian art.

✓ **Checking Reading Accuracy**

1 T   2 F   3 F   4 T

Mastering the Subject A

p.78

1 Ⓐ   2 Ⓓ   3 ⓒ   4 ① , ⑤ , ⑥

1   [Inference Question]

The author mentions, "Instead, he entered the insurance business, which was quite profitable for him." This implies that Charles Ives became a wealthy man.

2   [Reference Question]

The "them" that were difficult for musicians to play were Charles Ives's compositions.

3   [Negative Factual Question]

It is written, "He did, however, record some of his works before his death."

4   [Prose Summary Question]

According to the passage, Charles Ives created original music but was mostly unknown while he was alive. For example, he did not often perform his own music, so this kept him unknown. He used church music and European music to create original music of his own. And he was unpopular with many musicians because his music was hard to play.

1 c   2 a   3 d   4 b

Mastering the Subject B   p.80

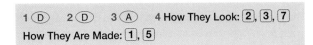

1 Ⓓ   2 Ⓓ   3 Ⓐ   4 How They Look: ②, ③, ⑦
How They Are Made: ①, ⑤

1 [Vocabulary Question]

A portrait that is flattering is pleasing to look at.

2 [Rhetorical Purpose Question]

The author writes, "In some cases though, an individual
may have a slight smile. The *Mona Lisa*, Leonardo da
Vinci's masterpiece, is one such painting."

3 [Sentence Simplification Question]

The highlighted sentence notes that even though
cameras were new, they were still cheaper to use than
hiring a portrait painter was. This is best explained in
answer choice Ⓐ.

4 [Fill in a Table Question]

According to the passage, portraits show the head, the
face, and the upper body of a person, may be a picture
of the actual artist, and often show a neutral expression
on the person's face. As for how they are made, they
may be taken by a photographer or be painted by an
artist.

1 c   2 b   3 d   4 a

Mastering the Subject C   p.82

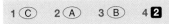

1 Ⓒ   2 Ⓐ   3 Ⓑ   4 **2**

1 [Factual Question]

The author writes, "It became popular during the 1740s.
This was when the ancient Roman towns of Pompeii
and Herculaneum were discovered. In the first century
A.D., an eruption of the volcano Mt. Vesuvius buried
both towns under a layer of ash. When the towns were
unearthed, they were mostly intact. This included their
paintings, sculptures, and architecture. Images of them
rapidly spread across Europe. This led to the creation of
Neoclassical Art."

2 [Rhetorical Purpose Question]

About Neoclassical art, the author explains, "It also
arose as a reaction to Rococo and Baroque Art."

3 [Factual Question]

It is written, "One of the greatest artists of the period
was Jacque-Louis David. His works always featured
heroic subjects. His most famous painting is *Napoleon
Bonaparte Crossing the Alps*."

4 [Insert Text Question]

The sentence before the second square notes that
Neoclassical Art lasted throughout the 1800s. The
sentence to be inserted mentions that it lost a lot of
influence all throughout that time period.

1 c   2 a   3 d   4 b

TOEFL Practice Test   p.84

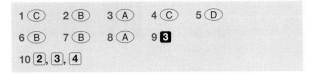

1 Ⓒ   2 Ⓑ   3 Ⓐ   4 Ⓒ   5 Ⓓ
6 Ⓑ   7 Ⓑ   8 Ⓐ   9 **3**
10 ②, ③, ④

1 [Factual Question]

The author notes, "To do this, they required a better
understanding of the world."

2 [Vocabulary Question]

When humanist ideas initiated the Renaissance, they
helped start it.

3 [Inference Question]

The author mentions, "During the Middle Age, artists
and musicians were seen as merely workers." This
implies that artists in the Middle Ages had a low status.

4 [Negative Factual Question]

Art and music experienced a renewal in the
Renaissance, not the Middle Ages.

5 [Factual Question]

The author comments, "The Renaissance was a crucial
time for artists. They rediscovered old ways of painting.
They developed more depth in their works. They also
learned how to draw people that were anatomically
correct."

6 [Factual Question]

The author notes, "So during the Renaissance, many
merchants became wealthy. Some of them were
interested in acquiring works of art for themselves. They
hired struggling artists."

7 [Rhetorical Purpose Question]

The author writes, "Through the Renaissance, most

music was still made for the Church. This trend continued even after that period came to an end. But in the 1600s and 1700s, music slowly became more secular. There were many popular composers during this time. Johann Sebastian Bach was one of them."

8 [Factual Question]

The author states, "Music, on the other hand, was not influenced by humanism as quickly as was art. Through the Renaissance, most music was still made for the Church."

9 [Insert Text Question]

The sentence before the third square notes that artists developed depth in their work. The sentence to be inserted mentions that doing this allowed artists to make their works look three dimensional.

10 [Prose Summary Question]

According to the passage, humanism made the Renaissance and the time after it more secular, and this affected both art and music. For example, humanists studied many different fields to try to understand the world. Music became popular during the 1600s and 1700s because there were many popular composers during that time. And artists in the Renaissance learned new techniques by studying artwork that was made in the past.

⊙ Vocabulary Review　　　　　　　　　p.90

1	Ⓑ	2	Ⓑ	3	Ⓓ	4	Ⓐ
5	Ⓒ	6	Ⓐ	7	Ⓐ	8	Ⓑ
9	Ⓓ	10	Ⓒ	11	Ⓐ	12	Ⓒ

● Chapter | 03 Archaeology and Anthropology

Mastering the Question Types A　　　　p.92

1 Ⓑ　　2 Ⓒ　　3 ②, ③, ⑤

1 [Rhetorical Purpose Question]

About Iran, the author notes, "The oldest bronze tools discovered date to 3800 B.C. They were found in Iran."

2 [Vocabulary Question]

When someone tries to shape bronze, the person is trying to form it.

3 [Prose Summary Question]

According to the passage, humans learned how to make bronze tools and weapons during the Bronze Age. For example, they learned that bronze was more useful than stone and copper for many reasons. The Bronze Age also ended in many places around 1000 B.C. And most societies entered the Bronze Age around 3000 B.C.

✓ Checking Reading Accuracy

1 F　　　　2 F　　　　3 T　　　　4 T

Mastering the Question Types B　　　　p.94

1 Ⓒ　　2 Ⓒ　　3 Worshiping Gods: ①, ⑤　Farming: ③, ⑥, ⑦

1 [Inference Question]

The writer remarks, "In fall, farmers thought that some rituals would make their harvests bountiful." This implies that farmers believed that their rituals were effective.

2 [Negative Factual Question]

The author does not mention anything about where rituals were held in the paragraphs.

3 [Fill in a Table Question]

According to the passage, some rituals for worshiping gods involved sacrificing animals, and sacrifices were also done by the Aztecs. As for rituals for farming, they were done to bring rain, they were done to make the soil good, and some of them took place in spring.

✓ Checking Reading Accuracy

1 T　　　　2 F　　　　3 T　　　　4 T

Mastering the Question Types C　　　　p.96

1 Ⓓ　　2 Ⓓ　　3 Ⓑ　　4 ❸

1 [Factual Question]

The author writes, "It was long believed that the Vikings had visited North America centuries before the Europeans sailed there in the 1490s," and, "Finally, in the 1960s, a Viking site was discovered. It was in Newfoundland, Canada."

2 [Reference Question]

The "Some" that included nails, a loom, and a forge were artifacts.

3 [Sentence Simplification Question]

The highlighted sentence notes that the artifacts found make archaeologists believe that both men and women lived there. This is best explained in answer choice Ⓑ.

4 [Insert Text Question]

The sentence before the third square notes that the Vikings were only there for up to ten years. The sentence to be inserted mentions that they may have only been there for three years.

⏶ **Checking Reading Accuracy**

1 F   2 T   3 F   4 T

Mastering the Subject A   p.98

1 Ⓒ   2 Ⓒ   3 Ⓓ   4 ⓵, ⓷, ⓹

1 [Factual Question]

The author states, "A tablet with a picture of a potter's wheel was found in its ruins. The tablet has been dated to around 3500 B.C."

2 [Rhetorical Purpose Question]

The author writes, "First, people used it to make pottery. The potter's wheel enabled artisans to make better ceramics."

3 [Vocabulary Question]

Terrain is another word for land.

4 [Prose Summary Question]

According to the passage, people mostly used the wheel for pottery and transportation after it was invented. For example, some wheels were attached to carts with two and four wheels. The wheel was also used more often as soon as better roads were made. And the wheel was used in the potter's wheel, which made ceramics become better.

⏶ **Reading Comprehension**

1 a   2 d   3 b   4 c

Mastering the Subject B   p.100

1 Ⓐ   2 Ⓓ   3 Ⓒ   4 Disease: ⓷, ⓸   Natural Disaster: ⓵, ⓶, ⓹

1 [Rhetorical Question]

The author states, "In the 1500s, European explorers started to visit the Americas. But many Europeans carried deadly diseases with them. The Native

Americans had no natural immunity to these illnesses. This made them get sick easily. As a result, some diseases infected millions of people. Most of them died. Entire tribes of people were sometimes wiped out."

2 [Sentence Simplification Question]

The highlighted sentence notes that the winners of battles usually just killed all of the losers. This is best explained in answer choice Ⓓ.

3 [Inference Question]

The author writes, "In ancient Crete, the Minoan civilization may have ended when a tsunami hit it. The huge wave could have been caused by an erupting volcano." If a huge wave destroyed Minoan civilization, then it must have been located near the sea.

4 [Fill in a Table Question]

According to the passage, disease was one way that the Europeans killed many people, and diseases also killed many Native American tribes. As for natural disasters, one killed the Anasazi, earthquakes could often destroy entire cultures, and a natural disaster killed the Minoans, too.

⏶ **Reading Comprehension**

1 b   2 a   3 d   4 c

Mastering the Subject C   p.102

1 Ⓑ   2 Ⓐ   3 Ⓒ   4 ⓶

1 [Negative Factual Question]

The author writes, "But there have been groups of nomads all throughout history." This means that there are still nomads living today.

2 [Vocabulary Question]

When nomads ventured into either Europe or the Middle East, they moved there.

3 [Factual Question]

That author writes, "Genghis Khan was their most famous leader. In the thirteenth century, he led armies of Mongols across the Eurasian plains. He conquered land as far away as Europe. And he created the world's largest empire."

4 [Insert Text Question]

The sentence before the second square notes that Genghis Khan created the largest empire in the world. The sentence to be inserted mentions the endpoints of the empire that he founded.

1 a   2 c   3 b   4 d

TOEFL Practice Test
p.104

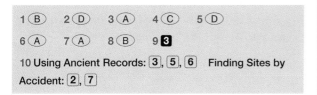

1 Ⓑ   2 Ⓓ   3 Ⓐ   4 Ⓒ   5 Ⓓ

6 Ⓐ   7 Ⓐ   8 Ⓑ   9 **3**

10 Using Ancient Records: **3**, **5**, **6**   Finding Sites by
Accident: **2**, **7**

1 [Factual Question]

About ancient sites, the author writes, "Many old
settlements have disappeared. They have been
swallowed by jungles or buried beneath deserts. Wars
and natural disasters have destroyed many as well."

2 [Sentence Simplification Question]

The highlighted sentence notes that the *Iliad* describes
how the Greeks defeated the Trojans. This is best
explained in answer choice Ⓓ.

3 [Rhetorical Purpose Question]

It is written, "One man, Heinrich Schliemann, did not.
He used the *Iliad* and Homer's other famous work, the
Odyssey, as historical documents. Schliemann went to
the place in Turkey where Homer said that Troy was. He
began digging. He found the remains of several ancient
cities. One of them was later determined to have been
the historical Troy." The author focuses on mentioning
Schliemann's role in the finding of Troy.

4 [Negative Factual Question]

The author does not state which language the *Iliad* was
written in.

5 [Inference Question]

The author states, "Sometimes people who are digging
may find sites by accident. This often happens in cities
such as Rome, Athens, and Jerusalem. They are among
the oldest cities in the world that are still inhabited."
This implies that the three cities contain the ruins of
many ancient sites.

6 [Factual Question]

The author mentions, "In the present, builders may
uncover them. When this happens, construction there
ceases immediately."

7 [Vocabulary Question]

When the author notes that archaeologists may search
in vain, it means that they find nothing.

8 [Factual Question]

The author writes, "First, they make a plot of the area.
It can cover a small amount of space. Or it can cover a
large area of land."

9 [Insert Text Question]

The sentence before the third square notes that some
people, such as farmers and construction workers, find
ancient ruins while they are digging. The sentence to
be inserted mentions that these are acts of good luck
that have resulted in some important archaeological
discoveries.

10 [Fill in a Table Question]

According to the passage, archaeologists using ancient
records discovered Troy. Some archaeologists also
rely on researching works of literature, which was the
method used by Heinrich Schliemann. As for finding
sites by accident, this can happen in very old cities,
and these sites can sometimes be unearthed by
construction workers.

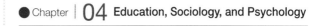 Vocabulary **Review**
p.110

1 Ⓐ   2 Ⓒ   3 Ⓓ   4 Ⓑ

5 Ⓑ   6 Ⓐ   7 Ⓒ   8 Ⓓ

9 Ⓒ   10 Ⓑ   11 Ⓓ   12 Ⓒ

● Chapter | **04** Education, Sociology, and Psychology

Mastering the Question Types A
p.112

1 Ⓑ   2 Ⓓ   3 **2**, **4**, **5**

1 [Rhetorical Purpose Question]

The author notes, "It was in 1812 that the first
wristwatch was made by Abraham-Louis Breguet. It
was for Caroline Murat, the sister of Napoleon."

2 [Vocabulary Question]

People who imitate others copy their actions.

3 [Prose Summary Question]

According to the passage, the first wristwatch was
made in the 1800s, and the watches later became
popular during a war. For example, a pilot received the
first men's wristwatch. Pilots in World War I also wore
wristwatches to know the correct time. And Abraham-
Louis Breguet made the first wristwatch.

1 F   2 T   3 T   4 F

Mastering the Question Types B   p.114

> 1 Ⓑ   2 Ⓐ   3 Before Public Education: ③, ⑥
> After Public Education: ①, ②, ④

1 [Inference Question]

The author writes, "As for lower-class children, they learned basic skills such as reading, writing, and arithmetic from their parents. Tutors were too expensive for them." This implies that the families had little money.

2 [Negative Factual Question]

The passage does not mention anything about which subjects students were taught at schools in the 1800s.

3 [Fill in a Table Question]

According to the passage, before public education existed, some parents taught their children at home while upper-class children were taught by private tutors. As for the time after public education began, students went to school for free, North American students went to government schools, and students got educated so that they would be able to work in factories.

1 T   2 F   3 T   4 F

Mastering the Question Types C   p.116

> 1 Ⓒ   2 Ⓓ   3 Ⓓ   4 ❶

1 [Factual Question]

The author writes, "Alexander Graham Bell invented the telephone in 1876."

2 [Sentence Simplification Question]

The highlighted sentence notes that telephones made talking to people both easier and faster. This is best explained in answer choice Ⓓ.

3 [Reference Question]

The "they" that sometimes never reached their destinations were letters.

4 [Insert Text Question]

The sentence before the first square notes the year that Alexander Graham Bell invented the telephone. The sentence to be inserted mentions that this was the time when he spoke the first words over the phone.

1 F   2 T   3 T   4 T

Mastering the Subject A   p.118

> 1 Ⓓ   2 Ⓐ   3 ❷   4 The Creation of a New
> Language: ③, ⑥   The Changing of a Language:
> ①, ④, ⑤

1 [Negative Factual Question]

The author does not mention anything about how easy or difficult it is to learn a Romance language.

2 [Vocabulary Question]

When something is unintelligible to people, then they cannot understand it.

3 [Insert Text Question]

The sentence before the second square notes that local languages have taken words from the local natives. The sentence to be inserted mentions the example of American English using many words taken from Native American languages.

4 [Fill in a Table Question]

According to the passage, the fall of the Roman Empire resulted in the creating of some new languages. In addition, when people lose contact with one another, a new language may be created. As for a language changing, this has happened to the English language. It is also the reason why Plato spoke a different form of Greek than people in modern Greece. And it happens when native speakers in one place settle in new lands.

1 a   2 d   3 b   4 c

Mastering the Subject B   p.120

> 1 Ⓑ, Ⓒ   2 Ⓑ   3 Ⓑ   4 ①, ③, ⑤

1 [Factual Question]

First, the author writes, "They have trouble focusing." Then, the author points out, "They can shift their eyes from one object to another."

2 [Inference Question]

The author writes, "Most newborn babies appear more interested in black and white items than colored ones." This implies that babies cannot see colors very well.

3 [Sentence Simplification Question]

The highlighted sentence notes that babies move their eyes or heads in the direction of the sounds that they hear. This is best explained in answer choice Ⓑ.

4 [Prose Summary Question]

According to the passage, babies use sight, hearing, and speech to perceive the world. For example, their speaking abilities improve over time until they can finally make words. They have good hearing and can respond to sounds. And while their sight is bad at birth, it improves over time.

✔ **Reading Comprehension**

1 c   **2** b   **3** a   **4** d

Mastering the Subject C   p.122

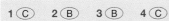
1 Ⓒ   **2** Ⓑ   **3** Ⓑ   **4** Ⓒ

1 [Vocabulary Question]

The roles of women are the actions that they take.

2 [Inference Question]

The author writes, "In England and other countries, laws were passed. They restricted the working hours of women and children. They were also banned from doing certain jobs. As a result, women mostly did domestic work and child care while men worked outside the house." Therefore, the passing of the laws resulted in women mostly doing domestic work.

3 [Negative Factual Question]

There is no mention in the passage about what the average wages at factories were for women.

4 [Factual Question]

The passage notes, Then, in the 1970s, many married women started to find jobs. Thanks to modern technology, they were able to do jobs that men had once done."

✔ **Reading Comprehension**

1 d   **2** b   **3** a   **4** c

TOEFL Practice Test   p.124

1 Ⓒ   **2** Ⓑ   **3** Ⓒ   **4** Ⓐ   **5** Ⓑ

6 Ⓐ   **7** Ⓒ   **8** Ⓐ   **9** ▮1▮

10 Monarch: ▢2, ▢3, ▢5   Elected Leader: ▢1, ▢7

1 [Negative Factual Question]

The author mentions nothing about how people become kings or queens.

2 [Vocabulary Question]

When monarchs wielded absolute power, they possessed it.

3 [Reference Question]

The "them" that were overthrown by the people were some monarchs.

4 [Factual Question]

About monarchs, it is written, "They often wielded absolute power. Those monarchs had complete control over their land. Whatever they said was law."

5 [Rhetorical Purpose Question]

The author remarks, "Josef Stalin of the USSR and Benito Mussolini of Italy are two other charismatic leaders from the 1900s."

6 [Vocabulary Question]

Leaders who persecute their own people mistreat them.

7 [Factual Question]

The author notes, "Charismatic leaders are those that the people love and are willing to follow. They may be elected by the people. But they often take over through force and rule as dictators."

8 [Inference Question]

The author comments, "These countries rarely experience civil wars or other periods of instability." This implies that countries with elected leaders have few major internal problems.

9 [Insert Text Question]

The sentence before the first square notes that elected leaders serve for a limited amount of time. The sentence to be inserted mentions how long the president of the United States gets to serve for.

10 [Fill in a Table Question]

According to the passage, a monarch may be overthrown by the people, is just a figurehead in countries such as England, and rules as a king or queen. As for an elected leader, that person serves a term that lasts a limited number of years and has specific limits on the power that he possesses.

1	Ⓓ	2	Ⓒ	3	Ⓓ	4	Ⓑ
5	Ⓓ	6	Ⓐ	7	Ⓑ	8	Ⓒ
9	Ⓐ	10	Ⓒ	11	Ⓐ	12	Ⓓ

● Chapter | 05 **Economics**

Mastering the Question Types A   p.132

1 Ⓐ   2 Ⓓ   3 ②, ④, ⑥

1   [Rhetorical Purpose Question]

The author declares, "But coined money was rare centuries ago. Instead, most trade was done by the barter system."

2   [Vocabulary Question]

A precious metal such as gold, silver, or copper is valuable.

3   [Prose Summary Question]

According to the passage, there are many reasons why people use coins. For example, it is easy to determine the value of a person's coins. It is simple to trade coins for goods. And coins weigh less than goods for barter.

✎ **Checking Reading Accuracy**

1 F   2 T   3 T   4 T

Mastering the Question Types B   p.134

1 Ⓒ   2 Ⓒ   3 Cause: ④, ⑦   Effect: ②, ③, ⑥

1   [Inference Question]

The author writes, "This was important since traveling by ship was both cheaper and faster to transport goods." Because ships were fast and cheap, the author implies that the Europeans preferred to trade by using them.

2   [Negative Factual Question]

The passage reads, "Their ships returned to Europe with spices, silks, ivory, gems, and other goods." So it is not true that they took spices and silks from Europe to Asia.

3   [Fill in a Table Question]

According to the passage, the cause of the discovery of a sea route to Asia was that the Portuguese sailed south around Africa. In addition, the Europeans wanted to engage in fast trade with Asia. As for its effects, America was discovered in 1492, many Europeans became wealthy, and some merchants invested money in sailing ships.

✎ **Checking Reading Accuracy**

1 T   2 F   3 T   4 T

Mastering the Question Types C   p.136

1 Ⓓ   2 Ⓑ   3 Ⓒ   4 ❸

1   [Sentence Simplification Question]

The highlighted sentence notes that even with wagons and pack animals, people could not carry a large amount of trade goods. This is best explained in answer choice Ⓓ.

2   [Reference Question]

The "they" that made ships that could sail on seas and oceans were people.

3   [Factual Question]

The author writes, "This happened on the Mediterranean Sea. The Phoenicians, the Greeks, the Egyptians, and the Romans sailed all around the Mediterranean thousands of years ago."

4   [Insert Text Question]

The sentence before the third square notes that many groups of people sailed on the Mediterranean Sea. The sentence to be inserted mentions that these groups of people had numerous trade routes on the sea.

✎ **Checking Reading Accuracy**

1 F   2 F   3 T   4 T

Mastering the Subject A   p.138

1 Ⓒ   2 Ⓐ   3 Ⓑ   4 ②, ③, ④

1   [Rhetorical Question]

In paragraph 1, the author spends many words describing how apprentices became masters.

2   [Factual Question]

It is written, "Journeymen were able to earn money by using their talents though. But they still had to practice for a few more years."

3   [Negative Factual Question]

There is no mention in the paragraph about which

trades had guilds during the Middle Ages.

4 [Prose Summary Question]

According to the passage, in the Middle Ages, it took many years of practice for apprentices to become masters. For example, apprentices first had to become skilled at their trade. As journeymen, they had to train for years before becoming masters. And apprentices had to study with their masters for a certain number of years to learn all of the required skills.

Reading Comprehension

1 c   **2** a   **3** d   **4** b

Mastering the Subject B
p.140

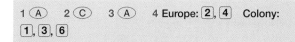

1 Ⓐ   **2** Ⓒ   **3** Ⓐ   **4** Europe: ⓶, ⓸   Colony: ⓵, ⓷, ⓺

1 [Vocabulary Question]

When countries began to acquire colonies, they obtained them.

2 [Negative Factual Question]

The author notes that black slaves were sent from Africa to America. But there is no mention of them being sent from Africa to Europe.

3 [Sentence Simplification Question]

The highlighted sentence notes that a lot of colonists believed that they were being used by the Europeans. This is best explained in answer choice Ⓐ.

4 [Fill in a Table Question]

According to the passage, people in Europe created finished products and exploited the lands that they owned. As for people in colonies, they used slaves to do a lot of their work. In addition, the colonies were sources of raw materials. And the colonists themselves wanted to be free from European rule.

Reading Comprehension

1 d   **2** b   **3** c   **4** a

Mastering the Subject C
p.142

1 Ⓑ   **2** Ⓐ   **3** Ⓓ   **4** ⓸

1 [Vocabulary Question]

When there were conflicts between countries, there were wars between them.

2 [Inference Question]

The passage reads, "In addition, a country should import as few items as possible. It should do this for two reasons. First, having a favorable balance of trade would give the country more gold and silver. Second, it would let the country be as self-sufficient as possible." Thus the author implies that countries did not want to depend on others.

3 [Factual Question]

The author writes, "In many cases, the colonies were sources of raw materials. These included timber, furs, sugar, fish, gold, and silver. They were then sent to Europe."

4 [Insert Text Question]

The sentence before the fourth square notes that some countries in Europe had colonies in Africa and Asia. The sentence to be inserted mentions two of these colonies that were established.

Reading Comprehension

1 c   **2** d   **3** a   **4** b

TOEFL Practice Test
p.144

1 Ⓓ   **2** Ⓓ   **3** Ⓐ   **4** Ⓐ   **5** Ⓑ
6 Ⓑ   **7** Ⓒ   **8** Ⓓ   **9** ❶
10 ⓵, ⓶, ⓹

1 [Vocabulary Question]

Something that is radically changed is drastically changed.

2 [Negative Factual Question]

The passage reads, "The finished textiles were then sent to tailors, who made clothing." So cottage industries did not produce clothing. Tailors did that.

3 [Factual Question]

The author notes, "Carding was one job that people did to prepare the wool and cotton."

4 [Factual Question]

It is mentioned, "Enormous looms were made. These could produce cloth at rapid rates."

5 [Sentence Simplification Question]

The highlighted sentence notes that people moved to where the factories were since they had to work in them. This is best explained in answer choice Ⓑ.

6 [Factual Question]

The author writes, "Because of factories, countless people working in cottage industries lost their jobs. They often protested against these factories. Some even attacked the factories and wrecked their machinery."

7 [Inference Question]

The passage reads, "Most people had no choice but to work in the factories, so they often moved to where the factories were located. Cities such as Manchester quickly expanded." It can be inferred that, since Manchester expanded quickly, there were many factories in it.

8 [Negative Factual Question]

The author points out that many cities got bigger. They did not get smaller.

9 [Insert Text Question]

The sentence before the first square notes that people were earning more money, which they could spend on new products. The sentence to be inserted mentions that they were also getting educated at the same time. The word "also" is an important linking word for the two sentences.

10 [Prose Summary Question]

According to the passage, cottage industries ended because of the rise of factories. One reason was that factory owners became rich. In addition, factories changed how people worked. And factories that had machines could do work much faster than people without machines.

 **Vocabulary Review**   p.150

1	B	2	A	3	A	4	A
5	A	6	D	7	B	8	C
9	D	10	C	11	D	12	B

● Chapter | **06 Life Sciences**

Mastering the Question Types A   p.152

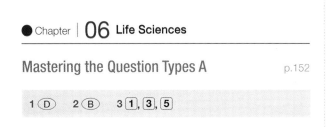

1 D   2 B   3 [1], [3], [5]

1 [Rhetorical Purpose Question]

The author writes, "The jellyfish has no central nervous system or circulatory system. It also lacks a respiratory system."

2 [Vocabulary Question]

Venom that is potent is powerful.

3 [Prose Summary Question]

According to the passage, the jellyfish is an old, simple predator. For example, it has been around for hundreds of millions of years. It uses venom to catch prey. And most of its body is its bell and tentacles.

Checking Reading Accuracy

1 F   2 F   3 T   4 T

Mastering the Question Types B   p.154

1 D   2 A   3 Cause: [3], [7]   Effect: [2], [4], [6]

1 [Negative Factual Question]

The author mentions nothing about why animals breed with other animals.

2 [Inference Question]

The author writes about how soot on trees caused the peppered moth to evolve. It can be inferred that there was a lot of pollution during the Industrial Revolution since it caused a species to evolve like that.

3 [Fill in a Table Question]

According to the passage, one cause of natural selection is that the environment changes. Another is that the living conditions for an organism change. As for the effects of natural selection, new generations of organisms inherit preferred traits from older ones. In addition, the strongest members of a species live while some organisms begin to evolve.

Checking Reading Accuracy

1 T   2 T   3 F   4 T

Mastering the Question Types C   p.156

1 C   2 C   3 A   4 **4**

1 [Reference Question]

The "They" that expect to discover more protozoa in the future are scientists.

2 [Factual Question]

The author writes, "Some protozoa can live by themselves. They do not require a host. But many do. So they live inside other organisms. These are classified as parasites."

3 [Sentence Simplification Question]

The highlighted sentence notes that without zooplankton, a large number of species of fish would eat less. This is best explained in answer choice Ⓐ.

4 [Insert Text Question]

The sentence before the fourth square notes that zooplankton is a common food for many ocean animals. The sentence to be inserted mentions some of the animals that feed on zooplankton.

Checking Reading Accuracy

1 F   2 F   3 T   4 T

Mastering the Subject A   p.158

1 Ⓓ   2 Ⓐ   3 Ⓓ   4 **1**

1 [Rhetorical Purpose Question]

The author writes, "An ecosystem is an area that supports many organisms. Some can be quite large. They include forests, deserts, and oceans."

2 [Factual Question]

The passage reads, "The vents produce hot water no matter how deep they are. Their warmth attracts numerous underwater life forms."

3 [Negative Factual Question]

The passage reads, "Predators such as snakes may eat the insects and birds in the tree. And humans may harvest the nuts or fruit from the tree." So it is not true that snakes eat fruits or nuts from the tree.

4 [Insert Text Question]

The sentence before the first square notes some of the factors that can influence microecosystems. The sentence to be inserted mentions that even minor differences in these factors can result in unique microecosystems being formed.

Reading Comprehension

1 a   2 d   3 b   4 c

Mastering the Subject B   p.160

1 Ⓑ   2 Ⓒ   3 Ⓑ   4 ④, ⑤, ⑥

1 [Sentence Simplification Question]

The highlighted sentence notes that prey animals usually outnumber predators in a region. This is best

explained in answer choice Ⓑ.

2 [Vocabulary Question]

Wolves that are territorial are protective of the land that they consider their own.

3 [Factual Question]

The author notes, "Sometimes the balance between predators and prey gets upset. There may suddenly be too many predators and not enough prey for them to eat."

4 [Prose Summary Question]

According to the passage, the predator-prey relationship is important to an ecosystem. For example, predators may die when the balance is upset. Prey animals also typically outnumber the predators. And prey animals with no natural predators can upset the ecosystem by reproducing too much.

Reading Comprehension

1 c   2 d   3 b   4 a

Mastering the Subject C   p.162

1 Ⓒ   2 Ⓐ   3 Ⓐ   4 Annual: ②, ③, ⑤
Perennial: ⑥, ⑦

1 [Inference Question]

The author states, "Biennials are another kind of plant. They live for just two seasons. But they are the least common type of plant." So it can be inferred that biennials are less common than annuals.

2 [Rhetorical Purpose Question]

The author writes, "Many flowers, such as daisies and petunias, are annuals."

3 [Negative Factual Question]

The author remarks that some perennials only produce fruit in their first year of growth, but there is no mention of why they do that.

4 [Fill in a Table Question]

According to the passage, annuals may leave seeds behind when they die, can be crops such as wheat and corn, and die after growing for one season. As for perennials, they live for several growing seasons, and all trees are considered perennials.

Reading Comprehension

1 b   2 d   3 c   4 a

TOEFL Practice Test

p.164

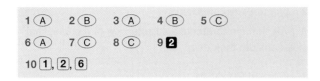

1 Ⓐ　2 Ⓑ　3 Ⓐ　4 Ⓑ　5 Ⓒ
6 Ⓐ　7 Ⓒ　8 Ⓒ　9 **2**
10 **1**, **2**, **6**

1 [Vocabulary Question]

The basis for an idea is its foundation.

2 [Rhetorical Purpose Question]

The author writes, "Thomas Huxley, a British scientist, was the first person to declare his belief that birds had evolved from dinosaurs."

3 [Sentence Simplification Question]

The highlighted sentence notes that despite *Archaeopteryx* and dinosaurs being contemporaries, some experts doubted that *Archaeopteryx* was a dinosaur. This is best explained in answer choice Ⓐ.

4 [Factual Question]

It is written, "Scientists called it *Archaeopteryx*. It was a known species. At that time, it was classified as a dinosaur. It had teeth, not a beak. It also had claws on its wings. Yet the fossil unearthed in Germany had feathers. This led scientists such as Huxley to believe that it was a bird since they assumed that only birds had feathers."

5 [Negative Factual Question]

The author mentions nothing about which fossils influenced the debate.

6 [Vocabulary Question]

Skeptics are doubters. They do not believe that something is true.

7 [Rhetorical Purpose Question]

The author notes, "Yet there remain many skeptics. They believe that the ability of flight must be considered. They claim that birds evolved from a tree-climbing reptile."

8 [Factual Question]

The author writes, "They claim that birds evolved from a tree-climbing reptile. That, they say, is how birds learned to fly."

9 [Insert Text Question]

The sentence before the second square notes that a Danish scientist wrote a book about birds. The sentence to be inserted mentions the title of that book.

10 [Prose Summary Question]

According to the passage, the discovery of *Archaeopteryx* fossils made some people believe that birds evolved from dinosaurs. For example, after studying some newly discovered fossils, experts came to have this belief. In addition, some *Archaeopteryx* fossils had feathers, so people thought that it was a bird. And the similarity between the bones of birds and dinosaurs was noted by many experts.

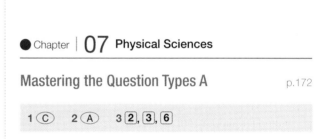

Vocabulary **Review**

p.170

1 Ⓑ　　2 Ⓑ　　3 Ⓐ　　4 Ⓓ
5 Ⓑ　　6 Ⓒ　　7 Ⓐ　　8 Ⓐ
9 Ⓓ　　10 Ⓒ　　11 Ⓐ　　12 Ⓓ

● Chapter | **07** Physical Sciences

Mastering the Question Types A

p.172

1 Ⓒ　　2 Ⓐ　　3 **2**, **3**, **6**

1 [Rhetorical Purpose Question]

The entire first paragraph focuses on the ring systems of the four planets, which they all share.

2 [Vocabulary Question]

Miniscule pieces of dust are tiny pieces.

3 [Prose Summary Question]

According to the passage, the four gas giants in the solar system have rings. For example, their ring systems all have different sizes. Their rings may be the remains of moons. And each ring system has its own characteristics.

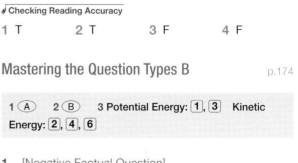

✎ Checking Reading Accuracy

1 T　　　2 T　　　3 F　　　4 F

Mastering the Question Types B

p.174

1 Ⓐ　　2 Ⓑ　　3 Potential Energy: **1**, **3**　Kinetic Energy: **2**, **4**, **6**

1 [Negative Factual Question]

The passage reads, "It is not possible to create or destroy energy."

2 [Inference Question]

The author states, "For instance, when the water behind the dam is released, the potential energy changes into kinetic energy." Since energy can change in form from potential energy to kinetic energy, it can be inferred that kinetic energy can also change into potential energy.

3 [Fill in a Table Question]

According to the passage, potential energy is energy that is being stored, such as the water that is behind a dam. As for kinetic energy, it is what lets electricity get created from moving water. In addition, it can be the energy of a moving car, and it refers to energy that is in motion.

♪ **Checking Reading Accuracy**

1 F	2 T	3 F	4 F

Mastering the Question Types C   p.176

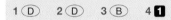

1 Ⓓ   2 Ⓓ   3 Ⓑ   4 **1**

1 [Sentence Simplification Question]

The highlighted sentence notes that Boyle had rich parents who paid for him to be educated. This is best explained in answer choice Ⓓ.

2 [Inference Question]

The passage reads, "These helped to establish him as a founder of the modern scientific method. His work also helped found the field of modern chemistry." Since Boyle's work founded "the modern scientific method" and since he founded "the field of modern chemistry," it can be inferred that he made useful contributions to modern-day science.

3 [Factual Question]

It is written, "Boyle's most famous work was called *The Spring and Weight of Air*. He did a lot of research on air and gas for that book. In it, he described what has come to be known as Boyle's Law."

4 [Insert Text Question]

The sentence before the first square notes the title of Robert Boyle's most famous work. The sentence to be inserted mentions the year in which it was published for the first time.

♪ **Checking Reading Accuracy**

1 T	2 T	3 T	4 F

Mastering the Subject A   p.178

1 Ⓒ   2 Ⓐ   3 Ⓒ   4 Core: ③, ⑦   Mantle: ④, ⑤, ⑥

1 [Vocabulary Question]

A distance that is measured approximately is not an exact distance. Instead, the number that is given is only around the exact number.

2 [Negative Factual Question]

About the core, the author notes, "Most of it is made of iron and nickel. It also contains trace amounts of other metals."

3 [Inference Question]

The author writes, "The mantle is divided into two parts: the inner mantle and the outer mantle. It comprises more than 80% of the planet's total volume." It can therefore be inferred that the mantle is larger than the crust and the core combined.

4 [Fill in a Table Question]

According to the passage, the core gives the Earth its magnetism and has a lot of iron and nickel. As for the mantle, it contains most of the planet's volume, it can begin ten kilometers beneath the ocean in some places, and it is the Earth's middle layer.

♪ **Reading Comprehension**

1 c	2 a	3 b	4 d

Mastering the Subject B   p.180

1 Ⓑ   2 Ⓒ   3 Ⓐ, Ⓒ   4 **3**

1 [Rhetorical Purpose Question]

The author comments, "On the other hand, both convection and conduction need a medium to be able to transfer heat from one place to another. The two are different from each other though. Conduction involves the transfer of heat between atoms. Convection is the movement of matter from a hot area to a colder one."

2 [Vocabulary Question]

When gases in the sun descend, they fall.

3 [Factual Question]

The passage reads, "This pattern is what enables air to circulate," and, "Hot air on the planet's surface rises into the atmosphere. When the air is near the ground, it is fairly dense."

4 [Insert Text Question]

The sentence before the third square reads, "Like all stars, the sun is a huge ball of gas." The sentence to be added begins with "so" and focuses on both the sun and other stars. Thus, the two sentences go well together.

Reading Comprehension

1 a   **2** c   **3** d   **4** b

Mastering the Subject C
p.182

1 Ⓐ   **2** Ⓒ   **3** Ⓑ   **4** ①, ②, ③

1 [Sentence Simplification Question]

The highlighted sentence notes that a paper discussed some fossils that were identical and had been found on both sides of the Atlantic Ocean. This is best explained in answer choice Ⓐ.

2 [Reference Question]

The "they" that were actually connected were the continents.

3 [Factual Question]

It is noted, "Plate tectonics states that the Earth's surface is formed of several major and minor plates. They are in constant—yet slow—motion. Scientists realized that this was how Pangaea had broken up. As a result, more of them began to support Wegener's ideas."

4 [Prose Summary Question]

According to the passage, Alfred Wegener thought that the continents had once combined to form the supercontinent Pangaea. For example, Wegener provided evidence as to how Pangaea had formed. He believed that Africa and South America had once fit together. In addition, he thought that Pangaea existed 300 million years ago and then broke up around 200 million years ago.

Reading Comprehension

1 d   **2** b   **3** a   **4** c

TOEFL Practice Test
p.184

1 Ⓒ   **2** Ⓑ   **3** Ⓓ   **4** Ⓓ   **5** Ⓒ

6 Ⓓ   **7** Ⓒ   **8** Ⓒ   **9** ❶

10 Giant Impact Theory: ③, ⑤, ⑦   **Fission Theory:** ②, ④

1 [Vocabulary Question]

When scientists pondered how the moon was formed, they thought about how that had happened.

2 [Negative Factual Question]

There is no mention in the paragraph about which theory is considered the most likely to be right.

3 [Factual Question]

The author declares, "This theory states that Earth was struck by a large celestial body. It was roughly as big as Mars, which is half the size of Earth."

4 [Factual Question]

The author notes, "However, there are some who question the validity of the giant impact theory. They state that a Mars-sized object impacting Earth would have greatly increased the planet's rotation. They claim that Earth's rotation would be around twelve times faster than it is today. So according to them, this theory is incorrect."

5 [Rhetorical Purpose Question]

The author writes, "The fission theory is another one popular with some astronomers. It imagines that a fission event caused the moon to break off from Earth. Some believe that the Pacific Ocean basin was the place on Earth where the moon broke off from."

6 [Vocabulary Question]

An itinerant body in the solar system is a wandering body.

7 [Sentence Simplification Question]

The highlighted sentence notes that scientists might learn about the moon's formation if they get to visit it in person. This is best explained in answer choice Ⓒ.

8 [Inference Question]

The author mentions, "If men ever set foot on the moon again, perhaps they will be able to do enough research to find the answer to the question of how the moon was formed." So the author implies that it may be possible to find out exactly how the moon was formed.

9 [Insert Text Question]

The sentence before the first square reads, "This caused it to get captured by Earth's gravitational field." The sentence to be added provides a result of the moon being captured by Earth's gravitational field. Thus, the two sentences go well together.

10 [Fill in a Table Question]

According to the passage, the giant impact theory claims that Earth was hit by a large object. It also explains why the moon has no iron core. There is a lot of evidence that supports the theory. As for the fission theory, it could have happened if Earth had rotated very quickly, and it stresses the importance of the Pacific Ocean basin.

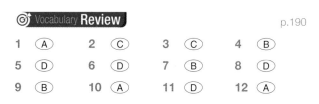

Vocabulary Review   p.190

1	Ⓐ	2	Ⓒ	3	Ⓒ	4	Ⓑ
5	Ⓓ	6	Ⓓ	7	Ⓑ	8	Ⓓ
9	Ⓑ	10	Ⓐ	11	Ⓓ	12	Ⓐ

● Chapter | **08 Environmental Sciences**

Mastering the Question Types A   p.192

1 Ⓒ   2 Ⓑ   3 ②, ⑤, ⑥

1 [Rhetorical Purpose Question]

The author notes, "Most glaciers are located on mountains and in icecaps in the Polar Regions."

2 [Vocabulary Question]

When ice accumulates somewhere, it builds up.

3 [Prose Summary Question]

According to the passage, a large sheet of moving ice is a glacier. For example, some glaciers move several meters a day, glaciers on mountain slopes often move, and it may take years of snowfall for a glacier to be formed.

✎ **Checking Reading Accuracy**

1 F   2 T   3 F   4 F

Mastering the Question Types B   p.194

1 Ⓐ   2 Ⓒ   3 Low Zone: ①, ③, ⑦   High Zone: ④, ⑥

1 [Inference Question]

The author notes, "The intertidal zone is found on ocean coastlines. It is the area between high and low tide." It is also written, "An intertidal zone can be a sandy beach, a rocky shore, a mudflat, or the base of a cliff." These sentences imply that the intertidal zone exists in every coastal area.

2 [Negative Factual Question]

The author does not mention anything about caves in the entire passage.

3 [Fill in a Table Question]

According to the passage, the low intertidal zone has more fish in it, is the deepest part of the intertidal zone, and is exposed to air for a short amount of time. As for the high intertidal zone, it is covered by water for a short time and is the part nearest shore.

✎ **Checking Reading Accuracy**

1 T   2 T   3 F   4 F

Mastering the Question Types C   p.196

1 Ⓒ   2 Ⓓ   3 Ⓐ, Ⓒ   4 **4**

1 [Sentence Simplification Question]

The highlighted sentence notes that getting through swamps was hard or could not be done in the past. This is best explained in answer choice Ⓒ.

2 [Reference Question]

The "They" that can safely reproduce in swamps are many fish, birds, and reptiles.

3 [Factual Question]

The passage reads, "They also remove pollutants from lake and stream water. This purifies the water when it leaves the swamp. Swamps are also breeding grounds for many fish, birds, and reptiles. They can safely reproduce in swamps."

4 [Insert Text Question]

The sentence before the fourth square notes that freshwater swamps are found near lakes and streams. The sentence to be inserted mentions that these bodies of water—lakes and streams—suffer from regular flooding.

✎ **Checking Reading Accuracy**

1 T   2 T   3 F   4 T

Mastering the Subject A   p.198

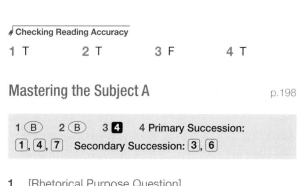

1 Ⓑ   2 Ⓑ   3 **4**   4 Primary Succession: ①, ④, ⑦   Secondary Succession: ③, ⑥

1 [Rhetorical Purpose Question]

The author states, "Sometimes natural disasters take place. For instance, a volcano might erupt. Perhaps the eruption covers the land with lava. This causes the soil to disappear. All of the life forms in the region are killed as well."

2 [Reference Question]

The "them" that are dropped by passing birds and other animals are plant seeds.

3 [Insert Text Question]

The sentence before the fourth square notes that plants and trees both begin to grow. The sentence to be inserted mentions that forests will begin to appear after a while.

4 [Fill in a Table Question]

According to the passage, in primary succession, when it begins, there is no life in the region. It is the first stage of ecological succession, and simple plants start to grow during it. As for secondary succession, it refers to changes in an area that has life forms in it, and the soil becomes more productive during it.

1 d   **2** b   **3** a   **4** c

Mastering the Subject B   p.200

1 Ⓐ   **2** Ⓑ   **3** Ⓓ   **4** ②, ③, ④

1 [Sentence Simplification Question]

The highlighted sentence notes that the climate of a region determines which crops people can grow in it. This is best explained in answer choice Ⓐ.

2 [Factual Question]

It is written, "Rice, for instance, needs a lot of water to grow. Rice requires several centimeters of rain in the paddies where it grows. As a result, areas that get heavy rainfall in a short period of time are ideal for growing rice. That is why rice grows well in places in Asia that have summer monsoon rains."

3 [Rhetorical Purpose Question]

The author writes, "These are warm-weather crops. Some of them are eggplants, beans, corn, peppers, and tomatoes."

4 [Prose Summary Question]

According to the passage, the crops that can grow in various areas are often determined by the climate. For example, cool-weather crops grow in places with cold climates. Warm-weather plants grow in hot places that get lots of sunshine. And some crops need a lot more rainfall than others do.

1 a   **2** d   **3** b   **4** c

Mastering the Subject C   p.202

1 Ⓒ   **2** Ⓐ   **3** Ⓓ   **4** Ⓑ

1 [Negative Factual Question]

The author writes, "A volcano's effects are not just local either. In some cases, they can result in regional or even global changes."

2 [Vocabulary Question]

A barren land is infertile. It has no life and cannot support life.

3 [Factual Question]

The passage reads, "It shot out lava and ash over a wide area. The lava and ash blocked rivers and filled in lakes."

4 [Inference Question]

The entire third paragraph describes the global damage that Krakatoa caused. This implies that the eruption of Krakatoa was much stronger than the eruption of Mount St. Helens.

1 c   **2** a   **3** d   **4** b

TOEFL Practice Test   p.204

1 Ⓑ   **2** Ⓓ   **3** Ⓐ   **4** Ⓑ   **5** Ⓓ
6 Ⓐ   **7** Ⓒ   **8** Ⓒ   **9** ■
10 First Atmosphere: ⑤, ⑧   Second Atmosphere: ②, ⑦
Third Atmosphere: ①, ③, ⑨

1 [Factual Question]

The author notes, "The atmosphere today is much different from how it was in the past. In fact, it has changed a great deal since the Earth was formed."

2 [Vocabulary Question]

Atmosphere that is dense is thick.

3 [Rhetorical Purpose Question]

In paragraph 3, the author focuses on how algae helped put oxygen into the air.

4 [Inference Question]

The author mentions, "The ozone moved high into the

atmosphere. It helped protect the planet from solar radiation. This allowed more life forms to evolve and survive on the Earth." Thus it can be inferred that solar radiation is harmful to life.

5 [Factual Question]

About the third atmosphere, the author writes, "For instance, the first plants began to appear on land."

6 [Vocabulary Question]

When experts theorize about something, they speculate about it.

7 [Negative Factual Question]

The author fails to mention mammals in the entire paragraph.

8 [Factual Question]

It is written, "Scientists further believe that, over millions of years, the planet's oxygen level will change again."

9 [Insert Text Question]

The sentence before the first square notes that vast numbers of oxygen-breathing life forms appeared on the Earth during the Cambrian Explosion. The sentence to be inserted mentions that more animals appeared during that period than at any other time in the Earth's history.

10 [Fill in a Table Question]

According to the passage, the first atmosphere was mostly helium and hydrogen and had almost no oxygen. The second atmosphere was affected by ocean algae and had some carbon dioxide taken out from it. The third atmosphere saw some oxygen become ozone, had its oxygen level increase because of plants on land, and contained enough oxygen to support land animals.

Vocabulary Review   p.210

1	B	2	C	3	C	4	A
5	C	6	C	7	A	8	B
9	D	10	D	11	C	12	A

Part C

Experiencing the TOEFL iBT Actual Tests

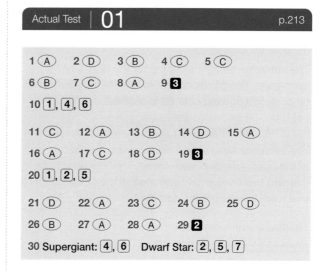

Actual Test | **01**   p.213

1 Ⓐ	2 Ⓓ	3 Ⓑ	4 Ⓒ	5 Ⓒ
6 Ⓑ	7 Ⓒ	8 Ⓐ	9 **3**	
10 **1**, **4**, **6**				
11 Ⓒ	12 Ⓐ	13 Ⓑ	14 Ⓓ	15 Ⓐ
16 Ⓐ	17 Ⓒ	18 Ⓓ	19 **3**	
20 **1**, **2**, **5**				
21 Ⓓ	22 Ⓐ	23 Ⓒ	24 Ⓑ	25 Ⓓ
26 Ⓑ	27 Ⓐ	28 Ⓐ	29 **2**	
30 Supergiant: **4**, **6** Dwarf Star: **2**, **5**, **7**				

1 [Negative Factual Question]

There is no mention of the time when Thebes was founded in the paragraph.

2 [Reference Question]

The "those" who were in the employ of the pharaohs were some people.

3 [Inference Question]

The passage reads, "Most of the city was located along the eastern bank of the Nile River. The western bank was used for the necropolis—the city of the dead. It got that name for the many royal tombs and burial grounds located there. Some people resided on the western bank." It can therefore be inferred that more people lived on the eastern side of Thebes than its western side.

4 [Negative Factual Question]

The author writes, "In 2055 B.C., the Theban leader Mentuhotep defeated the rulers of Herakleopolis." So Mentuhotep was a ruler of Thebes and was not a ruler of the Old Kingdom Period of Egypt.

5 [Vocabulary Question]

When sections of something are converted, they are changed.

6 [Factual Question]

It is written, "Karnak was a complex with many temples. The largest and most important one was the Temple of Amun."

7 [Rhetorical Purpose Question]

The author describes the contents of the Valley of the Queens in writing, "The Valley of the Queens is similar in purpose and design. It serves as a burial place for the queens of Egypt of the nineteenth and twentieth dynasties and their children. More than ninety tombs have been found there."

8 [Factual Question]

The author writes, "Most of the tombs were well concealed. The pharaohs feared that their tombs would be subject to looting after their deaths."

9 [Insert Text Question]

The sentence before the third square notes that some of the Luxor complex was looted. The sentence to be inserted mentions what happened to the priceless relics that were taken from the complex.

10 [Prose Summary Question]

According to the passage, Thebes was an important city in ancient Egypt. For example, it was a trade center and sometimes the capital of Egypt. Many pharaohs and their wives were buried in the area. And the Temple of Amun was a major complex in Thebes.

11 [Negative Factual Question]

The author does not write anything about salt water in the entire paragraph.

12 [Inference Question]

The author writes, "In deserts and other dry lands, most ponds are short lived. They appear only during the rainy season. Then, they vanish quickly because the desert has such a high evaporation rate." It can be inferred that ponds in the desert last for the shortest amount of time.

13 [Factual Question]

The passage reads, "Farmers may use a pond's water to irrigate their crops or to provide water for their animals."

14 [Rhetorical Purpose Question]

The author mentions that there are no fish in temporary ponds. Then, the author spends time writing about how this affects temporary ponds, including the organisms that live in them.

15 [Inference Question]

The author mentions, "But without fish in a temporary pond, these animals not only survive but also thrive." This implies that the insects and amphibians in temporary ponds multiply in great numbers.

16 [Vocabulary Question]

A place that is arid is very dry.

17 [Factual Question]

The author comments, "When heavy rains fall, the toads come to the surface. They mate and find temporary ponds."

18 [Factual Question]

It is written, "This happens due to the unusual mix of acids and salts in the soil caused by the changes in water levels. This creates the conditions necessary for some rare plants to grow. The mesa mint is a rare plant that only grows near temporary ponds around San Diego in the United States."

19 [Insert Text Question]

The sentence before the third square notes that many predators find the frogs' eggs and eat them. The sentence to be inserted mentions some of the predators that do this.

20 [Prose Summary Question]

According to the passage, temporary ponds create unique ecosystems for both plants and animals. For example, both insects and amphibians live in great numbers in the ponds since there are no fish. Many animals lay eggs in the ponds whenever they form. And there are some rare plants that only grow around temporary ponds.

21 [Inference Question]

The author only mentions the Yerkes classification system but notes that there are many ways to classify stars. By mentioning only the Yerkes classification system, the author implies that it is one of the most accepted systems of classification.

22 [Vocabulary Question]

Stars that have relatively short lives have comparatively short lives.

23 [Sentence Simplification Question]

The highlighted sentence notes that giant stars are both larger and brighter than the sun. This is best explained in answer choice Ⓒ.

24 [Vocabulary Question]

When the hydrogen in stars is expended, it has been completely spent.

25 [Inference Question]

The author writes, "They were once stars like the sun. But they changed once they expended all of the hydrogen in their cores. Then, their cores contracted while their surfaces expanded. They became brighter and turned into giant stars." By noting that the sun is a star like these, the author implies that the sun may become a giant star in the future.

26 [Negative Factual Question]

The author notes, "Some dwarf stars are similar to the sun. Yet they can be bigger or smaller than it." There is no mention that most dwarf stars are larger than the sun.

27 [Factual Question]

The author mentions, "The vast majority of stars in the universe are red dwarfs. They have about half the mass of the sun and have low surface temperatures. Their luminosity is always low, which makes them difficult to observe."

28 [Factual Question]

It is written, "Astronomers believe that the white dwarf stage is the final one in a star's life."

29 [Insert Text Question]

The sentence before the third square notes that red dwarfs have low luminosity, which makes them difficult to observe. The sentence to be inserted mentions that a telescope must be used in order to see them from the Earth.

30 [Fill in a Table Question]

According to the passage, supergiants are the second brightest stars in the universe and usually look red or blue. As for dwarf stars, they are the most common stars, they are similar to the sun, and they are some of the universe's youngest stars.

Actual Test | **02**   p.235

1 (B)   2 (C)   3 (D)   4 (A)   5 (A)

6 (D)   7 (B)   8 (B)   9 **2**

10 Principle Photography: **2**, **4**, **7**   Postproduction: **1**, **3**

11 (D)   12 (A)   13 (C)   14 (D)   15 (D)

16 (A)   17 (B)   18 (A)   19 **2**

20 **2**, **3**, **6**

21 (B)   22 (D)   23 (D)   24 (A)   25 (A)

26 (B)   27 (A)   28 (D)   29 **3**

30 **1**, **5**, **6**

---

1 [Negative Factual Question]

The question about which editing stage takes the most time is not answered in the paragraph.

2 [Vocabulary Question]

A tedious process is one that is dull.

3 [Rhetorical Purpose Question]

About computer editing platforms, the author points out, "There are much faster and simpler ways. Computer editing platforms do much of the work."

4 [Factual Question]

It is written, "During principle photography, the director takes many shots of the same scene."

5 [Inference Question]

The passage reads, "As each scene is printed and editor, the editor makes short clips to view. These clips, called dailies, let the director see how the film is coming together." It can therefore be inferred that some parts of dailies appear in the completed film.

6 [Rhetorical Purpose Question]

The author mentions *Star Wars* to point out that it had temporary images in its rough cut.

7 [Factual Question]

The author writes, "A wide group of people see the rough cut. These include the studio heads, the producers, the director, and other trusted people. At this point, the film may be approved or not."

8 [Reference Question]

The "who" that adjusts the color of the final film is the color timer.

9 [Insert Text Question]

The sentence before the second square notes that the orchestra times the music to fit the film. The sentence to be inserted mentions that changes may be made to the film if it does not match the music.

10 [Fill in a Table Question]

According to the passage, principle photography is when scenes in films are recorded, dailies are created, and the rough cut is created, too. As for postproduction, audiences rate the film then, and an orchestra creates the music score.

11 [Negative Factual Question]

The paragraph reads, "Still, plants do not always repel animals. In fact, they often need animals to survive."

12 [Rhetorical Purpose Question]

The author writes, "The primary defense of many plants is their composition. These are physical defenses. For instance, most trees have tough bark."

13 [Factual Question]

The author notes, "A coconut has a tough outer shell that is hard to open."

14 [Negative Factual Question]

The author mentions nothing about jungle plants while describing plant poison.

15 [Vocabulary Question]

Something that repels animals drives them off.

16 [Inference Question]

The author notes that peonies and salvias repel deer. But that is the only animal that is mentioned. So it can be inferred that other animals may eat parts of them.

17 [Factual Question]

The author comments, "The tree also produces sweet nectar, which the ants eat. In return, the ants attack all other insects that try to eat any part of the acacia tree."

18 [Factual Question]

It is written, "Despite having many defenses to protect themselves from animals, plants may need assistance from them. For example, pollination requires insects and other animals to spread pollen inside plants' flowers. This lets the plants reproduce."

19 [Insert Text Question]

The sentence before the second square notes that the ants eat the sweet nectar of the acacia tree. The sentence to be inserted mentions that this nectar gives nourishment to the ants.

20 [Prose Summary Question]

According to the passage, plants have evolved many defenses that protect them from animals. For example, their bark and thorns give them external physical protection. Some plants have relationships with animals that protect them. And some plants use chemical methods of protection such as poisons.

21 [Factual Question]

The author writes, "This division happened for several reasons. First, it was easier to administer the empires since they were smaller."

22 [Inference Question]

The author mentions, "Rome was the largest empire of its time. Its size made managing the empire difficult.

While the Romans had an excellent system of roads, running the empire was still hard." This implies that roads were very important to managing an empire.

23 [Factual Question]

The author remarks, "Provincial governors controlled local areas. They usually did as they pleased. Money was sent to them from Rome. It was for building roads and supporting troops."

24 [Vocabulary Question]

When there is a time of turmoil, it is a period of chaos.

25 [Vocabulary Question]

People who were assassinated were murdered.

26 [Factual Question]

The author notes, "His close friend Maximian became the Western Roman emperor. But they were not equals. Diocletian was the supreme ruler."

27 [Rhetorical Purpose Question]

It is written, "So he moved to the east and built the great city of Constantinople. It became the capital of the Eastern Roman Empire."

28 [Factual Question]

The author writes, "Once he died, the split became permanent. His two sons inherited one empire each."

29 [Insert Text Question]

The sentence before the third square states that Diocletian increased tax collection. The sentence to be inserted gives a result of that: The empire gained access to more money.

30 [Prose Summary Question]

According to the passage, there were several reasons why Diocletian split the Roman Empire. For example, doing that made it easier to defend the empire's borders. Diocletian also hoped to strengthen the empire by reforming it. And the civil wars in the empire had made it unstable, so Diocletian hoped to make the empire stronger once again.

MEMO

MEMO

MEMO

MEMO

MEMO

MEMO

TOEFL®
MAP
New TOEFL® Edition

Reading

Basic